E-BUSINESS AND ERP

E-BUSINESS AND ERP

RAPID IMPLEMENTATION AND
PROJECT PLANNING

MURRELL G. SHIELDS

JOHN WILEY & SONS, INC.
New York · Chichester · Weinheim · Brisbane · Singapore · Toronto

Library of Congress Cataloging-in-Publication Data

Shields, Murrell G.
    E-business and ERP : rapid implementation and project planning / Murrell G. Shields.
        p. cm.
    Includes index.
    ISBN 0-471-40677-5 (cloth : alk. paper)
        1. Electronic commerce. 2. Business enterprises—Computer networks—Management. I. Title.

    HF5548.32 .S524 2001
    658'.05—dc21   00-054563

Printed in the United States of America.

10 9 8 7 6 5 4 3 2 1

To my son, Robert, as he begins his own
career in systems development

PREFACE

Organizations are going to have to change the way they implement packaged applications systems. The old ways have never been successful and are incapable of supporting the needs of a rapidly changing business economy. The e-business phenomenon has only accelerated the rate of these changes and created more severe consequences from failing to implement solutions in a timely manner. Organizations that want to be successful in the future are going to have to develop a core competency in rapid implementation of packaged business applications to solve existing business problems and take advantage of new opportunities in Internet time.

Organizations have been implementing computerized applications to support their business processes for over 30 years. During the early years, most of these systems were custom developed: each organization designed, programmed, tested, and implemented financial, human resource, and operational systems to meet unique (or at least believed to be so) organizational requirements. Most of these systems were developed by the organization's in-house information systems (IS) department—with or without the help of consultants.

During the last 20 years, a whole industry has developed around the construction and marketing of standard application packages: software that a vendor develops and sells to a wide variety of organizations. With standard software, organizations do not have to create their own systems; they can purchase and tailor the standard systems to meet their own needs, often in much less time than it would take to develop these applications from scratch. Several of the packaged software vendors have grown into large, global organizations.

The majority of the projects that have implemented these applications over the last 30 years have been failures. They have taken much longer than planned, have cost many times more than originally estimated, and have not produced the business results that were expected. Many of these projects were aborted after years of effort and millions of dollars of cost. The primary reasons for these failures are well documented and widely known. However, organizations continue to make the same mistakes—and get the same results. This history of failures has created a bad image for business system implementation projects.

In the past, many of these system failures were masked from the view of organization's customers and suppliers. Most of the applications that were implemented were back-office systems that did basic transaction processing. These projects were usually done to reduce transactional costs and mainly affected processing within the four walls of an organization. As such, they did not directly touch an organization's customers and suppliers. Often managers and employees did not rely on information in these systems to make decisions and provide accurate information to business partners. A number of substitute processes and redundant data sources were used instead.

Because of significant changes in the last five years in the functional richness and variety of the applications offered by the software vendors and the use of several new technologies in their development (e.g., Internet protocols and standards, web servers, wireless communication, handheld devices, graphical user interfaces, various middleware products), the potential business returns from implementing these new applications have skyrocketed. The new applications can enable significant changes in the way organizations perform business processes, share information with customers and suppliers, and change business models and relationships.

Organizations are scurrying to take advantage of these new products and capabilities. The software vendors and consulting organizations are all transforming themselves into e-business product and service providers. New applications and uses of technology are surfacing every month.

These new applications go beyond the traditional applications available in the Enterprise Resource Planning (ERP) suite of modules (e.g., financials, distribution, human resources, and manufacturing) and extend to customer relationship management (CRM), supply chain management (SCM), e-procurement, data warehouses, and a multitude of new e-business enabling products (e.g., e-retailing, e-mail management, and electronic marketplaces, exchanges, auctions). Organizations are not willing to wait the normal one to three years it has taken to implement major systems in the past. To meet rapidly changing business needs, organizations need to find ways to implement most or parts of these new applications in a matter of months, not years.

This is where rapid implementation comes in. As with most things, there is good news and bad news here.

The bad news is that projects that used to take years to complete now have to be done in a matter of weeks and months. Not only that, but they have to be done successfully the first time. Solving critical business problems quickly and taking advantage of opportunities resulting from the e-economy makes implementation speed and time to market critical success factors. In this environment, in many situations there is not time to fail and make a second attempt. The market will pass you by.

A second issue is the fact that most of the problems that plagued traditional implementations still apply to rapid projects. So, in addition to figuring out how to do implementations faster, the teams and their managers have to figure out how to avoid the problems that have caused these projects to fail for the last 30 years.

Finally, the solutions that have to be implemented rapidly, avoiding traditional sources of failure, have to be better than those implemented in the past. In today's rapidly changing business environment the solutions that are developed must be flexible and scale well. Business situations are continuously changing. Mergers, acquisitions, changes in supply chain composition, increasingly demanding customers, globalization, the Internet, and a number of other major trends mean that any process design implemented today will probably be obsolete in a year or two. Therefore, these designs (and the software that supports them) must meet current requirements and be able to be adapted to a number of possible scenarios in the future.

Fortunately, there is good news to offset the bad. With the right implementation approach, vendor package, accelerator tools, and management principles, it is possible to implement these products in a third or less of the time that these projects have taken in the past. And this can be done in a way that better manages the risks associated with these products. This is not idle speculation. There have been hundreds of projects that have already proven the validity of this statement. But it does take a different approach and the availability of a particular toolset to make all this happen.

That is what this book is about:

- Chapter 1 presents a case for making rapid implementations the preferred method for approaching these projects.
- Chapter 2 describes the activities that are necessary to perform a rapid implementation.
- Chapter 3 covers three different approaches for selecting application packages that can be implemented rapidly.
- Chapter 4 deals with the challenges of managing these projects.
- Chapter 5 discusses methods to address the people issues that have often been the primary source of failure in the past.
- Chapter 6 describes what needs to be done to ensure that these projects are business driven and deliver the business results that were used in justifying the project in the first place.
- Chapter 7 covers issues around supporting the IT aspects of these projects.
- Chapter 8 deals with tools, called *accelerators,* that must be present to support a rapid implementation approach.
- Chapter 9 covers trends and changes in the business and the packaged software industry that will impact implementations in the future.
- Chapter 10 gives guidance on what factors should be present before an organization is ready to have a successful rapid-implementation project.

This book is based on my 20-plus years of experience implementing custom-developed and standard package systems in various roles: project manager, process team member, programmer and database administrator, steering committee member, functional sponsor, information systems department manager, and end user. I have implemented many of the major packages using traditional and rapid implementation methodologies and tools.

Most of the projects I have been involved with have required solving a multitude of problems that I believe are an inherent part of managing and working on these initiatives. I have fought many hard battles trying to successfully improve business processes through the implementation of enabling technologies. There are a tremendous number of barriers that have to be overcome for that to happen.

My goal has always been to try to do each project better than the last. Therefore, I have continuously experimented with approaches and tools — always looking for ways to make these projects more successful. This book describes the lessons I have learned over the last 20 years and some key insights that I believe will help others on the journey toward successful rapid implementation projects.

ACKNOWLEDGMENTS

There have been many people who have taught me a great deal about business, project management, systems development, and consulting over the last 20 years. Those whom I have considered as mentors on my professional journey have included Bob Anderson, Lee Marston, Dick Cardin, Scott Wilson, Rita Valois, Mike Stipa, Tom Stadler, Bob Ruprecht, and David Edwards.

I want to thank Professor Bob West, of Villanova University, for encouraging me to write about some of the lessons I have learned helping companies implement these systems. I also want to express thanks to Sheck Cho, my editor at John Wiley & Sons, for encouraging and supporting me through the publishing process.

My deepest gratitude goes to my wife Nancy, son Robert, and daughters Rebecca and Amy. They serve as the motivation and inspiration for everything I do.

CONTENTS

E-BUSINESS AND ERP

1

WHY MOST IMPLEMENTATIONS SHOULD BE RAPID BUT ARE NOT

There is a tremendous need for a different approach to implementing business computer applications. Instead of large, full-scope projects, organizations should be doing a lot of smaller, focused projects. Historically it has taken many months, and even years, to complete these implementations. In the future these projects will have to be done in a matter of weeks and months.

There are important business reasons why the old way of doing these projects will have to change. Organizations are now in a business environment where their success will depend on their ability to rapidly respond to changing business requirements. There are no alternatives to becoming better at making quick changes. Business changes require changes in business processes and the systems that support them. Therefore, organizations must learn how to rapidly implement new business application systems.

This chapter lays the groundwork for the material that follows. We begin by making a case for rapid implementations. Then, we establish a foundation for the types of applications that are being implemented by looking at the journey that standard software has taken over the last 40 years and describe an architectural framework for looking at the new applications. The chapter then examines the difference between installing and implementing software. After that, we look at how fast is rapid. The chapter closes by laying out the key success factors for rapid implementations.

NEED FOR SPEED

The way that organizations have traditionally implemented complex business applications has to change. The old approaches are too slow, expensive, and unreliable. In an age of rapid, continuous change brought about by the Internet, reengineering, and

1

globalization, projects that take years before an organization starts receiving benefits are no longer acceptable! Recent changes in business and technology have permanently raised the implementation bar.

As a result, organizations need to find ways to speed up the implementation process to solve their business problems and take advantage of new opportunities. With the availability of new tools and resources for these projects, taking a rapid approach to the implementation of standard business software is possible. For most situations, it is the preferred approach.

Business applications (e.g., accounts payable, order entry, manufacturing, payroll, shipping, inventory management, loan processing, student registration, customer billing) support, and to a certain extent determine, the way work gets done in organizations. In the past, midsize or larger organizations typically took one to three years to implement suites of these applications. In most cases the organization did not receive any benefits until the entire project had been completed and the organization went live with new software and business processes. In the new economy, organizations must figure out how to solve problems and get benefits from these systems in a matter of weeks or months.

To achieve this goal requires a different way of looking at these projects. The desired results should drive the solution. Instead of starting from how long these projects have taken in the past, we must let business requirements determine how long they *can* take in the future. The key question should be: How long can the organization take to change business processes and the systems that support them in order to meet the increasing demands of the marketplace?

Once they know the target, organizations must get serious about figuring out how to get these implementations done quicker—in the required time frames. Increasingly, parts of complex systems will need to be implemented in two to six months in order to meet competitive pressures. Fortunately, there are already many examples that prove that, with a different approach and new tools, meeting these shorter time frames is possible.

The drivers for business change (and faster implementations) are everywhere. There are tremendous changes occurring in the business (and nonbusiness) world as a result of new technologies, business models, global interests, changing customer expectations, and competitive challenges.

As evidence of the magnitude of these changes, you have only to consider the number of new e-businesses that have been created in the last three years. These companies cannot wait years to get financial, operational, and human resource systems up and running. They need to quickly get systems operational to take orders, ship goods, pay employees, and produce financial statements for investors.

In addition, existing organizations are all scrambling to become e-businesses. New technology enablers are forcing most of them to reevaluate their business models and relationships, change organizational structures, and redesign business processes to be more responsive to the increasing demands of customers. Internet technologies are creating many new possibilities.

No company can ignore the availability of new technologies that, perhaps for the first time, truly support the redesign and implementation of new ways of doing business. The only question is how they can take advantage of these new technologies. Most organizations have not been very successful in doing this in the past; many have recently gone through painful implementations of new systems.

The good news is that there are now software packages (standard software) for enterprisewide and external-facing applications that leverage the newer technologies. They support business processes that we would not have dreamed of five years ago. With these packages, organizations will not have to develop their computer applications from scratch in order to create some tremendous capabilities.

The bad news is that we are going to have to implement these new technologies in much shorter timeframes than ever before. Organizations must figure out how to do successful rapid implementations of new processes using these new packaged solutions.

CUSTOM DEVELOPMENT (1960s AND 1970s)

Before we go any further in our discussion of rapid implementation, we need to set the stage by briefly examining how organizations have implemented these packages in the past. To do this right we need to briefly look at the history of ERP, what is meant by ERP and e-business applications, the reason for implementing them, and the distinction between installing and implementing standard applications. We begin in this section with the early use of computer applications.

When computers first started to be widely used in a business setting, in the early 1960s, they were used to automate simple, routine business tasks. Payroll was a natural place to start. The calculation of payroll amounts (multiply hours worked times hourly rate and then subtract for taxes and deductions) was not particularly complicated but had to be done many times every week or so—and very accurately. The next areas to be automated were the financial applications: general ledger, accounts payable, accounts receivable, and fixed assets. Because of these historical roots, many of the IS departments in organizations historically reported to the controller or vice president of finance.

The computer excels at doing things very fast and doing them the same way every time. Those are two things that we humans, no matter how hard we try, generally have problems doing. (That is especially true when we are tired or do not feel particularly motivated.) Therefore, computer systems were widely used to automate back-office functions.

These early business applications had to be programmed by people from the IS department, or by external consultants. When a computer was purchased, it could not do anything of value for the organization until the IS department wrote some programs. So, every company wrote its own general ledger, payroll, order entry, and billing systems. Unfortunately, IS departments generally were not very successful in creating these systems. As a result, they often gained a reputation for delivering systems that did not meet users' needs, cost twice as much as planned, and were delivered late.

Developing business applications (or any other kind of computer program) is a complex task, one that most organizations did poorly. There were reasons for this situation.

The first programmers were usually people from one of the functional departments who had to learn programming on the job, with little training and supervision. It is a very complicated activity to determine business requirements, design and code programs, determine layouts for data records, and test all the things that should go right and could go wrong. These tasks are especially difficult when the programmer is under a lot of pressure to get the application out quickly, which was always the case because of the multiyear backlog of requests in the IS department.

Also, by today's standards, there were not a lot of good tools available to develop the first systems. The first programmers did not have high-level programming languages, relational database management systems, a lot of memory on the computer to work with, or easy ways for a program to interact with the user's terminal. There were no graphical interfaces back then; it was even difficult to program real-time dialogs with terminals using character-based interfaces.

To make matters worse, after only short discussions with several of the users and managers, the programmers often disappeared into their cubicles to develop these new systems. This development was often done at night when programmers could get time on the computer to compile their programs. So, the development was done without a lot of further involvement from the people who would ultimately use the system or its reports.

As a result, the requirements for the applications were often misunderstood by the programmer (who probably did not have a business background and was guessing what the user wanted), the system did not meet users' needs, and it was delivered late and over budget. Some things have not changed a lot over the years.

STANDARD SOFTWARE (1970s AND 1980s)

Around the 1970s, some of the programmers and computer consultants started to wonder if there was not a better way. Why was every company reinventing the wheel when it created business applications? After all, is the general ledger or payroll application of one company that much different from one needed by other companies? So, companies were started to create *standard* (or *packaged*) software. This is software, perhaps developed for a particular company initially, that is then sold to other companies and adapted for their use.

Using this type of software usually shortened the time for developing and implementing new business applications; after all, the software had already been programmed, tested, and debugged at another company. In addition, using this software leveraged the talents of application designers, experienced programmers, database and hardware gurus, training course developers, and others that most companies could not afford to hire or retain.

For example, five IBM employees in Germany left to start a company to create standard financial software in 1972. That company, SAP, grew to have revenues from software sales and services of over $5 billion in 1999. Other companies were started to create standard payroll and human resource (HR) applications, or any number of other business applications where it seemed possible that a standard set of software could be used by a number of organizations. Even some of the computer hardware vendors wrote standard applications that they could sell to their customers.

These software packages were licensed and implemented by the organizations, usually after they had been *modified* (the programs from the vendor were changed) to meet the unique needs of the organization. Unfortunately, these modifications meant that the software vendor could no longer support the package. There was no way for the vendor to know what changes had been made by the customer. This also meant that the IS organization usually had to reapply these modifications each time they implemented a new release of the vendor's system. The only time this was not necessary was when the new release included new functions to handle what had been supported by the modifications.

In spite of the difficulty this caused when applying new releases of the vendor's package, buying and modifying software was still quicker than starting from scratch. So, the organization assumed responsibility for maintaining the applications after they were implemented.

These standard software vendors started out by producing and supporting a limited number of application modules. Some companies sold only financial applications; others concentrated only on manufacturing modules. In its area of focus, each vendor competed to be considered the *best-of-breed*. For example, in the 1980s many people considered Management Science of America (MSA) and McCormick & Dodge as the two best-of-breed financial package vendors.

As a result of this specialization, if you wanted to get a complete set of applications for your organization, you might buy a general ledger module from one vendor, a payroll module from another, and a loan-processing module from a third. You might also have your internal IS staff design, code, and test four other modules that you needed, but could not find a suitable package for on the market. Most of these modules ran on mainframe computers, operated in a batch mode, and were extensively modified (because of missing functions the organization had to have to do business). Each had its own separate database and there were no real-time interfaces between the packages.

Any interfaces for sharing information between the applications had to be programmed by your own IS personnel or consultants you hired to help you implement these applications. When you implemented a new release of the vendor's package, the interfaces often had to be changed for all the other applications the updated one touched.

APPLICATION SUITES (1990s)

Over the years, the vendors added more and more modules to their suites of applications—acquiring some from other vendors or developing new modules in conjunction with customers. In addition, the applications started to get better functionally as the vendors invested large sums of money in their development and responded to current and prospective customers' demands for new functionality in the next release. The standard applications started to represent best practices in how to use automation to support business processes, as the vendors took the best ideas from all their customers and started to incorporate them into the products.

The vendors also started to change the technology architectures for the applications. They started developing their applications so that they would run on a number of hardware platforms, operating systems, and database management systems. They also started to integrate their various applications so they could use common databases and share information in real time—as the transactions occurred.

By the late 1980s, vendors started to offer fully integrated suites of applications that supported many, or most (depending on size, complexity, and industry) of an enterprise's functions. This created some basic choices. An organization could choose to buy modules from different vendors to get best-of-breed applications that they would have to integrate themselves. The other option was to buy a suite of applications from one vendor that was integrated out of the box.

Because of the advantages of integrated applications and the lower training and maintenance costs associated with going with one vendor, many companies started to go the integrated suite route. (This is the same reason that many organizations use Microsoft Office instead of discrete best-of-breed productivity tools from several different vendors.) What we really had by this time were products from a single vendor that supported all the planning, operational, and resource management functions of the entire enterprise. They were not called ERP systems until later, but the vendors were well along the way to realizing that concept.

In the 1990s ERP became hot. Integrated applications were so desirable and the packages had such extensive functionality and technical capabilities that companies started to replace their homegrown legacy systems with ERP packages. The bigger companies, especially manufacturers, started doing this first and ran the new systems on their mainframes or minicomputers (e.g., HP3000, DEC Vax, or IBM AS/400).

However, the buyer still had to be careful to separate hype from fact. Vendors sometimes announced modules as being available before they had completed developing and testing them. In addition, some of the packages did not include all the functions an organization wanted or needed to do business in its industry. Also, all the package vendors started calling themselves ERP vendors, even if they had big holes in the scope of modules they offered (i.e., no payroll/HR modules or no manufacturing modules).

Throughout the 1990s the major ERP vendors—Oracle, SAP, J. D. Edwards, PeopleSoft, Baan, Lawson, and QAD—had tremendous growth. The demand for these products was driven by the high cost of maintaining legacy systems, the desire for new functionality that could not be provided by in-house developers, the need to handle Y2K issues, and the push of globalization and competition. The three years before the end of the century were great years for ERP vendors. Most of the top ERP vendors had initial public offerings (IPOs) in the late 1990s and the owners and employees did very well. The major players were growing at 40 to 60 percent annual rates. However, storm clouds were forming.

ERP AND E-BUSINESS (2000s)

The months leading up to January 2000 produced shock waves throughout the application software industry. By that time, it was too late for their customers to begin implementing new applications to take care of Y2K issues (many companies had done this earlier rather than fix old legacy systems), so customers put the purchase of new ERP modules on hold until they got through the first months of 2000. Then, when the capital funds were released that spring (and Y2K turned out to be a nonevent), the money was allocated instead, at least in the U.S. market, to a new phenomenon that had captured, by storm, the imagination of business leaders and the general public: e-business.

To be fair, the ERP vendors had been preparing for aspects of e-business for several years. By 1999, most had Internet-enabled their applications (i.e., you could use a browser on the Internet to access information in the ERP system and even perform some transactions). And these vendors were rewriting their systems to take advantage of Internet technologies to deliver new functionality powered by the Internet.

In fact, by this time it was difficult to find one of these vendors still calling themselves an ERP vendor. Almost overnight, they all started to call themselves *e-business vendors*. However, most of the attention in the e-business software space was being given to non-ERP and Internet pure-play vendors. Companies like Siebel, i2, Ariba, BroadVision, and Commerce One had best-of-breed, point solutions that were powering e-business and other advanced applications that everyone was excited about.

Companies were spending hundreds of thousands of dollars on this new software and much more on consulting assistance to implement these applications and the technical infrastructures on which they ran. Gartner Group, a research organization, put the average price of putting up a complete commercial web site for a large or midsize organization at $1 million. And this is before organizations added the complex e-business applications.

However, there was a lot of smoke-and-mirrors associated with the use of these new applications. It was not uncommon for a company to have a great e-store site powered by one of these new packages with shopping carts, credit card authorization, and quick checkout functionality. But, behind the scenes, the orders taken on this web site were printed out and either faxed to a distributor or rekeyed into the organization's ERP order entry screen to handle financial and logistics processing.

Most of these point applications were not integrated with the backbone transaction systems of the organization. In the case of the dot-coms, there often were no transactional systems in the background. This situation makes it very difficult for customers to check on the status of their orders from the web site.

Companies had three basic options for their e-business and advanced applications:

1. They could develop them in-house (programming in HTML, C++, or Java) and interface them to the existing ERP or legacy systems.
2. They could buy best-of-breed products with great functionality and then interface them to existing systems.
3. They could wait until the ERP vendors came out with new e-business modules.

A lot of companies started down each of these paths.

Those who started down the third path did not have to wait long. In 2000 most of the major ERP vendors introduced e-business suites of applications that would significantly expand the functionality of their ERP systems. For example, Oracle released its new applications in May, called version 11i, as part of what it calls its *e-business suite*. This suite of products has the new versions of the traditional ERP modules along with new modules for customer relationship management (CRM), supply chain management (SCM), and other functions that are truly state-of-the-art e-business: iStore, iSupport, Exchange, auctions. They even introduced remote access to Palm devices using Internet messaging for entering and receiving ERP information. In addition, all the functions of 11i have been written for and run on the Internet.

These are pretty impressive applications. If you want to see how iStore works go to the Oracle web site and buy something on their store: they use all their own software internally. Or look at mySAP.com. These new applications may not have all the functions and bells and whistles of the best-of-breed products but they have more than enough for many organizations. And they have the added advantage of coming, out of the box, fully integrated with the other ERP modules from the vendor.

Modules in these suites use the same databases and have real-time sharing of information between applications. And if you upgrade to the next version of these modules, you do not have to spend a lot of time and effort reimplementing the interfaces between all the components they touch. Studies show that companies who go with best-of-breed solutions spend a significant portion of their IT budgets maintaining all the versions of these components and the interfaces between these components.

However, it cannot be ignored that the best-of-breed packages like Siebel, Ariba, and i2 are great products. They have functionality that the full-suite e-business vendors will have difficulty duplicating. And, if this additional functionality is important to an organization, they can still be the right solution — even given the headaches of the interfaces. Even this aspect will get better as all the vendors move toward more standard interfacing schemes (using Internet tools like eXtensible Markup Language or XML) and the vendors and third-party software developers build standard interfaces between the major packages. A whole new generation of tools called enterprise application integration (EAI) middleware is being developed to ease the integration issues.

It is clear that the boundary between what we have traditionally referred to as ERP and the new advanced-function packages and e-business applications is blurring. Traditionally, ERP was used to designate the collection of fully integrated modules that provided automated support for most of the functions of an enterprise. But ERP vendors never supported all the business areas well. Most did not have good functionality to support a number of areas needed by organizations; sales force automation, call centers, advanced planning and scheduling, data warehousing, and analytical analysis are a few examples of poorly supported functionality.

The primary focus of ERP vendors initially was on the needs of manufacturers and distributors. Even the term ERP is a successor to the manufacturing term MRP (materials requirements planning) and came into use when vendors started to fill out the suite of applications provided beyond the manufacturing areas. Throughout the 1990s, ERP vendors provided modules in four primary areas: (1) financial, (2) distribution, (3) manufacturing, and (4) human resources. But this left many major functions in other industries that are just starting to be addressed by these vendors with vertical market and industry solutions.

In addition, the Internet has enabled new functions like e-procurement and e-retailing that were never practical on a widespread basis before. Companies have done electronic data interchange (EDI) and electronic funds transfer (EFT) for years. But the use of these technologies was limited to a small number of large organizations and their suppliers. These technologies were too expensive for smaller organizations.

A key business requirement is that all of these applications, old and new, be integrated. Integration requires that the different applications talk to each other in real time—not in periodic batch updates. Also, each of the applications should not have separate databases. All of the data needed for all the systems should be together in one database so that there is no redundant data and only one definition of what each data item means. All of this should be done seamlessly: the modules should have the same look and feel, users should be able to get to any of the information in the system in real time (as soon as a transaction has occurred), and the IS department should not have to do a lot of work to make the integration happen.

APPLICATION FRAMEWORK

As you have noticed, there are significant terminology problems when business application modules are discussed. Applications have already been referred to as ERP, e-business, CRM, e-stores, e-procurement, SCM, and data warehousing. Overlaps in the traditional boundaries associated with these terms have also been discussed. Figure 1-1 is an attempt to show how all these different types of applications fit together. It provides a common framework for use throughout this book.

FIGURE 1-1 eXtended Enterprise System Framework

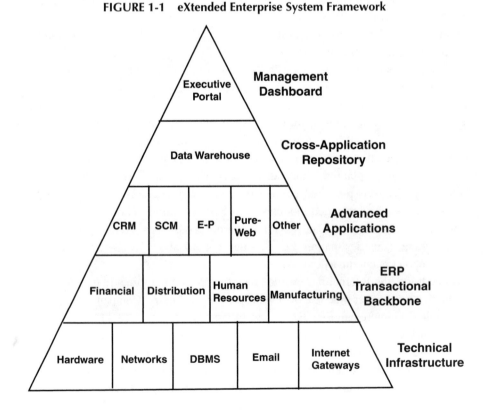

I will use the term *eXtended Enterprise System (XES)* to represent all the applications shown in the figure. Other people have proposed terms like enterprise applications (EA) and enterprise systems (ES) to be used in place of the outdated ERP acronym. But neither of these terms gives proper credit to the role that these systems play in extending business information and processing beyond the four walls of an organization. Enterprise resource planning supported the enterprise, and a lot of organizations still need to successfully implement ERP functionality. eXtended enterprise system include the ERP functions and all the other applications that extend the organization's systems throughout the supply chain—to customers and suppliers. XES represents all the enterprisewide and cross-enterprise applications that have been or soon will be e-enabled as organizations execute their e-business strategies.

TECHNOLOGY INFRASTRUCTURE

Figure 1-1 shows the relationship between the components of a business application architecture and clarifies where the ERP and E-business systems fit into the overall structure. The bottom layer of the architecture is the technology infrastructure that must be in place to support all the other applications. This infrastructure can be developed and maintained in-house or can be outsourced to a number of different companies such as application service providers (ASPs), telecommunication providers, and consulting organizations.

The hardware component refers to the parts of the infrastructure you can touch. It includes, first of all, the computers (mainframes, minicomputers, workstations) installed to function as servers (e.g., database servers, application servers, print servers, mail servers). However, it also includes PCs, workstations, handheld devices, data storage devices, printers, scanners, bar code readers, radio frequency transceivers, and various communication devices (routers, bridges, gateways, and modems).

The networks in the technical infrastructure are of two types. The local area networks (LANs) connect PCs, printers, and servers within a single location. The wide area networks (WANs) connect all the remote locations and LANs together into one corporate network. The WAN includes communication links between the various locations (e.g., public telephone, dedicated telephone services, Internet, virtual proprietary networks, and private networks) that use a combination of copper lines, fiber, microwave, or coaxial cable links. It also includes the network operating systems used to control the hardware and application software.

The operating systems of choice for XES systems are either UNIX (with various proprietary flavors from each of the hardware vendors) or Microsoft NT. Some of the XES vendors have recently announced support for the Linux variant of UNIX; Linux is getting a lot of interest and support, mainly from those who believe that the openness of UNIX has been tainted by hardware vendors who have added their own proprietary features. Other supporters of Linux just want to have a viable alternative to the Microsoft family of products.

The database management system (DBMS) is the software that controls access to the data stored and used by all the applications. For XES systems this database software is usually a relational database system from either Oracle (8i), Microsoft (SQL Server), or IBM (DB2). People called database administrators (DBAs) are responsible for maintaining and tuning the databases, which retain all the information needed to process the XES applications.

Email has become a critical component of the IT architecture. Its use goes far beyond the ability to communicate informally within the organization and with key external partners (i.e., customers, suppliers, regulatory organizations). Email is becoming the means by which workflow functionality in XES applications notifies individuals when they should take action. This transaction approval and exception notification functionality is part of the normal process flow in many of the vendors' applications. It is also used to alert managers of performance metrics that are outside normal tolerance levels.

Email is also becoming an important tool in marketing to customers and providing services. Systems are now available to assist larger organizations in routing the thousands or hundreds of thousands of inbound (and outbound) messages each day to the appropriate individual or department to facilitate the prompt and efficient response to these messages.

The final component of the technical infrastructure layer is the hardware and software used to provide access to the Internet for employees as well as to make it easier for an organization to share information with its customers and suppliers. In the future, this area will also need to address the way that messages and transactional data can be communicated to remote devices such as laptops, Palms and other personal digital assistants (PDA), and other handheld devices using cellular and Internet capabilities.

APPLICATION LAYERS

There are two application layers in the XES framework—the ERP transactional backbone and advanced applications. In the past, different vendors have provided these types of products. Today, the traditional ERP vendors are providing both categories of applications. In addition, the advanced application vendors are partnering with other vendors to provide wider coverage for their products and easier ways to integrate them with other applications.

The ERP transactional backbone layer includes the application modules that have been offered by ERP vendors for the last 20 years. In the financial area the vendors have offered modules for general ledger, accounts payable, accounts receivable, fixed assets, cash and treasury management, and financial consolidations. These modules are available as standalone applications or as part of an integrated suite. The financial products from several of the vendors are good enough to be considered best-of-breed applications.

The distribution modules include order entry, purchasing, inventory management, and shipping. In many cases these products provide multisite functionality to support distribution requirements planning (DRP). With DRP, organizations can check on inventory availability and fill orders from multiple locations. They can also track and account for the transfer of materials between sites.

The order-entry modules are the ones most likely to be modified by an organization during its implementation. Organizations use a wide variety of methods to price their orders. No matter how many options are provided in the standard software, organizations seem to come up with industry practices that are not supported. Therefore, the vendor's code is sometimes modified, or custom code is interfaced to the standard application, to handle requirements in this area.

The distribution area is also one of the first areas to be Internet-enabled. Customers want to be able to check on the status of their orders. Giving them browser access to this information over the Internet was a development priority for most of the vendors.

The human resources area includes personnel, timekeeping, payroll, and benefits modules. Each vendor combines these modules into categories a little differently. Also, once you get away from the top-tier vendors, there are sometimes significant gaps in the completeness of the suite of modules offered by a particular vendor.

One of the topics that will be discussed in Chapter 8 in the hosted applications section is the option of outsourcing the processing of applications. This is not a new option. For many years, small and midsize organizations have outsourced the processing of their payroll and human resource applications. The outsourcing trend is just extending the scope of applications that are hosted by external organizations.

The manufacturing modules include plant scheduling, capacity requirements planning, engineering, bill-of-materials and routing maintenance, dispatching and shop floor reporting, material requirements planning (MRP), and standard costing/variance reporting. These modules were developed to support a number of different types of manufacturers. The requirements to support a company manufacturing chemicals is different from those necessary to support a company assembling airplanes. Therefore, these are often very complex modules to develop and test.

Several of the packaged software vendors called themselves ERP vendors before they had manufacturing modules. They addressed this inconsistency by acquiring the manufacturing modules of other vendors. However, it took several years before these modules were integrated with the original modules in the vendor's suite.

The next layer in the framework includes applications that provide advanced capabilities in specific functional areas. Many of these applications include capabilities that are made better, or perhaps only made possible, by extensive use of the capabilities of the Internet. These modules are the primary arenas for competition between best-of-breed package vendors and full-suite XES vendors.

These advanced applications have been available from best-of-breed vendors for several years. Many of the best-of-breed companies were formed in the 1990s. The products from these vendors have functionality that is not available in the offerings of integrated-suite vendors. In the past, many of these modules were not even available from the traditional ERP vendors. However, that situation is rapidly changing.

Oracle, SAP, J. D. Edwards, and several other major vendors are now offering modules in these advanced function areas as part of a fully integrated suite of e-business applications. Some of the vendors have developed their own modules from scratch; others have acquired the products of niche vendors. There are significant differences with regard to the capabilities of these modules and the level of integration between them and the other modules provided by the vendors. These advanced application modules fall into the areas of customer relationship management, supply chain management, e-procurement, pure-web applications, and a catch-all called other.

Customer relationship management is a particularly hot area of interest from both the business strategy and technology perspectives. Customer relationship management is about supporting all the customer-facing processes in the organization. Its goals are to increase sales and customer loyalty and retention, and to enhance customer service.

The four major types of CRM modules are: (1) sales force automation, (2) marketing, (3) call center management, (4) customer service and support. There are best-of-breed products in all the major areas associated with CRM (e.g., marketing (e.piphany), sales (Siebel, BroadVision), and service (Clarify, Silknet)). However, there are also integrated solutions from the XES vendors that address these same areas and use the Internet to do so. For example, Oracle has (as part of its 11i version) CRM modules such as Marketing Online, iStore, iSupport, Contracts, and E-Mail Center.

Supply chain management includes the processes to manage the relationships among all the entities that are involved in sourcing, manufacturing, and shipping products to the end consumer. These relationships include raw materials and component suppliers, manufacturers, distributors, warehouses, transporters, retailers, and the ultimate consumer. The goals of SCM are to share information in order to drive unnecessary inventory out of the supply chain and to enhance the effectiveness of the supply chain partners in being responsive to the needs of the marketplace.

To achieve these goals, enterprises strive to coordinate the planning between the various supply chain partners and enable collaboration between the various entities. Obviously, this involves a lot more than technology enhancements and giving suppliers access to an organization's master production schedule and orders. There are major organizational, cultural, and policy issues involved with these initiatives.

The major types of applications in SCM are advanced planning and scheduling (APS), warehouse management, and transportation. In APS, the two major best-of-breed packages are from i2 Technologies and Manugistics. However, SAP, J. D. Edwards, Oracle, and several other XES vendors have added APS modules to their product lines.

The goal of e-procurement (e-p) is to use Internet technologies to make the procurement process more efficient and less costly to the participants. There is a lot of room for improvement in this area. It can cost hundreds of dollars to process each requisition and purchase order.

The buyers (and people in accounts payable, receiving, and other areas of the organization) spend a great deal of time tracking down and solving problems with individual transactions (e.g., determining why a supplier has no record of an order, expediting late receipts, investigating unauthorized purchases from unauthorized vendors, reconciling invoicing differences). Often they do not have the time to do the sourcing, vendor analysis, and contract negotiation activities that would really add value to the organization.

The Internet helps in this area by supporting a self-service approach to purchasing. Through web catalogs, exchanges, and workflow technologies much of the requisition, approval, ordering, and payment process can be automated. One of the best-of-breed solutions in the area of nonproduction-item purchases (known as maintenance, repair, and operations (MRO) items) is from Ariba. In addition, a number of Internet-powered exchanges are being set up to handle other types of material purchases.

Auctioning functionality is being extended beyond consumer purchases and is becoming popular in the business-to-business (B2B) purchasing space. The XES vendors are offering this same functionality. These applications sometimes have the same look and feel of the B2C (business-to-consumer) offerings (i.e., some of the vendors are using the shopping cart analogy and checkout process for B2B purchases).

Pure-web includes applications that are only practical because of the maturing of the Internet and its associated technologies. Although it could be argued that some of the things that have already been discussed could fit into this category, what are included are things like e-retailing and Internet remote messaging, applications we never thought were possible, even a few years ago.

Amazon sells an amazing number of books worldwide and records every click made on their site for future use in personalizing the buying experience. Dell allows us to configure our own PCs online and then builds them one at a time using functionality in its backbone systems. Cisco has effectively automated its sales and service functions through self-service functionality on its web site. All these e-retail activities are possible through the use of point solutions like BroadVision—or from the new modules of the XES suite vendors.

What is truly amazing is the potential for remote processing through the use of Internet messaging. At one of the XES vendors' demonstrations, a customer (at the customer site) asked the salesperson whether 20 items could be shipped next Tuesday. To answer this question the salesperson would normally have to telephone someone back at the plant or go back to the office and check things out on the computer. Instead, the salesperson went through a series of screens and data entry fields on a Palm PDA, transmitted the order remotely through the Internet to the XES applications back at headquarters, and received a confirmation, again on the Palm, that the order could be shipped—all in less than a minute.

The final category of applications at the advanced application layer is called Other. It includes a number of different things, including industry-specific applications that are not currently available from the XES vendors.

Each industry has its own unique requirements that often are not adequately addressed by the standard suites of software. Examples include a loan processing system for a bank, a student registration system for a university, a laboratory system in a hospital, and a mutual fund tracking system in an investment company. In the past, many of these systems were developed from scratch in-house by the IS department, often with the assistance of consultants. In some cases these systems were purchased from niche software companies that focused on developing software to meet the unique needs of a particular industry or industry segment. Many of the XES vendors are now beginning to develop these industry-specific modules.

In this category are also the systems that were custom developed by organizations in the past to meet unique needs or provide competitive advantages. Some of these legacy systems may not be replaced by modules in the standard software and, therefore, must be interfaced with the other applications. In certain cases these applications offer real competitive advantages. These advantages might be lost if a company were forced to use the generic functionality of the standard systems in particular areas.

The final type of applications in this Other category are the knowledge management systems that are becoming increasingly important to a wide variety of organizations. These are the repositories of intellectual capital—the knowledge and best practices of the organization. They allow the organization to share knowledge across functions and geographies. This knowledge is maintained in groupware and collaboration products like Lotus Notes, Microsoft Exchange, and other web-based repositories.

INFORMATION PORTALS

At the top two layers of the framework (i.e., cross-application repository and management dashboard) are those components that transform information from the various subsystems into a form for easier analysis and review. Increasingly, this information is being made available over the web in the form of a browser-based portal. There may also be separate portals for the CEO, CFO, and other groups of managers in the organization. Each management role requires different types of information to make decisions and track performance. A portal makes all the various information views available at any time, from any location.

At the layer above the applications is the *data warehouse*. There is a lot of valuable information in the various databases of the ERP and advanced applications, in customer responses to an organization's web site, and in various external databases. This information is at the detailed, transaction level and these databases are optimized to support transaction processing. Because of the potential negative impact on response times the organization would not want to do a lot of ad hoc queries and reporting against combinations of these databases.

Many organizations have found value in extracting information from the various application databases, at either a detailed or summary level, and putting this information into a separate database in a structure and format that facilitates ad-hoc queries, reporting, and analysis. This special database is called a data warehouse and there are special tools from vendors like Hyperion that can be used to analyze this data. The major ERP and E-business vendors also provide data warehousing applications with automated interfaces to their modules to make the extraction easier.

At the top layer of the XES framework is the *executive portal*. This is the radar screen or dashboard for top management. It tracks the key performance metrics of the organization, at a high level, and keeps the pulse on how the organization is doing overall. It also identifies situations that should be brought to the attention of the top managers of the organization. In many cases these applications implement a balanced-scorecard approach to management reporting.

These portal applications are tailored to the unique needs and preferences of the managers who will use them. The output of these applications is often graphical (i.e., pie charts and bar charts and colors to highlight items that are out of tolerance). These top management applications are becoming increasingly valuable in spotting trends and problems early, so they can be addressed in the rapid timeframes required by the new e-business economy.

Now that we have a framework that defines the type of applications that are candidates for rapid implementation, we need to draw some boundaries around these projects. The next section addresses the misconception that the only way to implement these applications in short timeframes is to ignore some of the key tasks in the implementations.

INSTALLATION VERSUS IMPLEMENTATION

Any discussion of rapid implementations must establish an important distinction. That distinction is the difference between merely *installing* software versus *implementing* a new system to support redesigned business processes. When rapid development is described in this book, it is in the context of the implementation option.

However, there are advantages in spending a little time describing the installation option.

An organization can put in new standard software applications very quickly if they are willing to take a number of shortcuts:

- Use a predefined configuration of the software without any modifications to the configuration parameters, source code, or reports.

- Transfer data directly from old systems without a great deal of data cleanup (or do no transfer of data).

- Leave out significant end user or IS personnel training before the new system goes live.

- Have people basically do their work tasks in the same way as they did them before, after going live with the new system.

This approach has often been used when there are excessive budget or time constraints on an implementation. However, this approach basically "paves the cow paths" with new technology while leaving business processes unchanged. It is surprising that any organization would take this approach. After all, if the organization does not change its business processes, how can it get significant business results from the installation?

There are certain situations where using the installation approach may be appropriate. For example, many organizations needed to install new applications rapidly during 1999 because their old systems were not Y2K compatible. In some cases these companies waited so long to start these projects that they had no option other than taking an installation strategy. They often did so with hopes that this approach would at least get them through the first few months of 2000. After that time, many of these organizations planned to go back and do a more complete job of implementing the new systems.

A second scenario could be a company running systems on old hardware and application software that are no longer supported by the vendor. These systems are often very expensive to maintain. In this situation, the company's goal may be to just get up and running on state-of-the-art hardware and applications—and address business process changes, data cleanup, and training at some future date.

A third example could be a startup organization that has no systems, no data, and no existing procedures. Often, the enterprise needs to get some applications in place immediately to handle some basic transactions processing. In this situation, the company must get something up quickly. The systems being implemented may not be strategic at this time and may not even get a lot of attention, support, and visibility in the organization.

The basic problem with each of these examples is that the organizations invested in new systems and technology but got no business return from their investments.

Additionally, these initial projects may have put future projects, and potential returns from these types of investments, in jeopardy.

The companies in all the examples probably are running on applications that people do not understand and with data that is incomplete and inaccurate. People, in this situation, will not trust the new system and will start to do their work with workarounds—using homegrown tools at the local level. As they work around the new system, they will stop feeding all the relevant information into the official system. There is not enough time to enter information into their spreadsheets *and* the new system—and people know which one they are using to support their work.

The organizations that use these short-cut approaches to put in new business applications never get around to doing the follow-on project to finish things like training and process redesign that were out of the scope of the initial efforts. The organizations in the first two examples may end up worse off than before the installation project began.

The end result in the last example depends on what happens after the initial project. A startup does need systems quickly and its people are used to learning fast and working incredible hours to do what has to be done. So, getting something up quickly matches the culture of the organization. And, if the new system does not work exactly as they want it to or does not do all the things that really need to be done, they can live with that. Often that is the least of their concerns. The major concerns are survival in the short term, attracting venture capital, and taking the company public.

However, as these startup organizations grow they soon get to the point where they need robust, full-function systems and need to look at the efficiency and effectiveness of their business processes. Then the challenge is to change the management style and culture around standardized, optimized business processes. Sometimes this transition requires an infusion of new people into the organization with experience from more stable environments.

If an organization goes to all the trouble and expense to purchase and implement a new system, it hopes to get some return from the effort. After all, there will be a lot of headaches and challenges as people are forced to learn a new system with different screens, transaction codes and terminology, and a new look and feel. So, why would any organization go to all this trouble? The answer is to get business benefits.

These business benefits come in a variety of forms. Some are related to cost reductions. Organizations often are looking for ways to reduce operational costs by streamlining business processes and cutting out non-value-adding steps, intermediaries, and jobs. They want to take inventory not only out of their organization, but from the entire supply chain. They want to be able to subcontract or outsource functions that are not core competencies. They want to move toward self-service functions for their customers, suppliers, and employees.

Other benefits are related to increasing customer service and responsiveness. Most organizations are interested in reducing cycle times: how long to take an order, process a claim, take an application for new service, schedule students for the fall term, or produce a patient bill. They want to make it easier and more enjoyable for customers to interact with the organization. And most organizations are interested in increasing sales through better understanding of their customers—what they want, which ones are profitable, how the organization can get more of their business.

To achieve these types of benefits requires changes in three areas: (1) people, (2) processes, and (3) technology. Installing applications focuses on only one of these areas: technology. When an organization implements a new business application it addresses issues and opportunities in all three areas.

The scope of an implementation project includes a number of business objectives:

- It ensures that the new systems are aligned with the business strategies and priorities of the organization.
- It addresses how people are going to be trained and motivated to use the technology to change the way they do their work.
- It looks at alternative ways of doing this work that leverage the capabilities of the standard software.
- It assures that the data in the system is accurate and complete.
- It does all the change management tasks that are required to reinforce the changes that are implemented.

These results will not happen in a project that just installs software. Getting significant business benefits requires a wider scope and a more structured and, unfortunately, longer implementation project. However, as will be seen in the next section, these projects do not have to take as long as they used to.

HOW FAST IS *RAPID*?

One thing that needs to be clarified is what qualifies as a rapid implementation. Is less than a year to implement an ERP package rapid? Would three months to implement a pure-play e-business application be considered slow? The only practical answer is: it depends on a lot of different things.

If you implemented all the modules of SAP in one year at a multinational organization with a great deal of reengineering, some would surely say that is rapid. Other words come to mind, like suicidal or impossible. So, that sort of project would not even qualify for consideration for a rapid approach. However, if you took six months to implement the general leader module of J. D. Edwards in a single location, that would also not meet the definition of rapid. No hard-and-fast rules on this can be given because every organization and situation is different; but some guidelines can be provided.

If an organization is using the implementation approach and tools and techniques that are described in this book, then the following projects would be considered rapid:

- Selection of an ERP or e-business package for the organization in one to two months

- Implementation in a midsize manufacturing company (revenues of $100 million to $1 billion) of the core modules of an ERP package (financial, sales and distribution, materials management, and manufacturing) at the corporate location and one plant, with moderate process redesign in one or two key processes, in three to six months

- Implementation in a services organization of the financial and HR/payroll modules of an ERP package with moderate process redesign in two to four months

- Implementation of a major e-business application (e.g., procurement exchange, auction site, e-retailing, B2B application) in one to three months

- Implementation of a major CRM package in an organization with a large sales force, call center, and customer service function in three to four months

- Implementation of an advanced planning and scheduling system (e.g., i2, Manugistics) in a midsize multinational distributor in two to four months

Now, even with these examples, there is room for a great deal of variation. Factors, such as the project team size, the number of end users to be trained, the quality of the data that must be converted, the speed with which decisions can be made, the politics of the organization, and the strength of the project sponsor, will all impact the time required. Instead of focusing on the actual timeframes given in these examples, think of rapid implementations as being in the two to six months' range—rather than in years. That is the type of acceleration that we are looking for in these projects.

Maybe a better way of looking at the expected speed for rapid implementations is to consider various types of implementations along a time continuum. Our expectations for projects should vary with the types of projects and the goals and objectives that have been established. This is represented in Figure 1-2.

As shown in the figure, the expected time to implement an XES application is a function of the amount of change that will occur as a result of the implementation and the technology solution used. On one end of the spectrum are projects that will result in the transformation of organizations and their processes. Most projects that do significant reengineering of business processes will still take a year or longer. It takes that long to dramatically redesign processes and do all the change management activities required to achieve the desired benefits. On the other end of the spectrum are hosted applications that are preconfigured and ready for the users to enter transactions immediately. Most applications fall between these extremes.

FIGURE 1-2 Implementation Timeframes

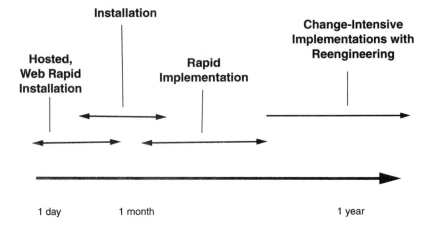

If you go to the web sites for the major package vendors, you will see a lot of remarkable claims. For example, at least one SAP implementation was completed in 21 days. There was also an Oracle implementation of a web-hosted financial system that was done in one day. These claims are probably accurate. However, they most likely have little bearing on how long any other implementation should take.

There are a lot of unknowns with these projects. For example, we do not know from these descriptions what was implemented, whether any historical data was converted, whether a configuration from a sister organization was cloned, or whether training materials and procedure manuals were created or used. Therefore, it is difficult to determine whether such a representation is similar to the situation your organization is facing. The best advice is to contact people who did these implementations and find out what was really done before using these statistics to set expectations for a new project.

However, to their credit, most software vendors are doing things to decrease the time it takes to implement their applications. Many are starting to use less *time to market* as a selling point. The vendors are coming out with preconfigured versions of their packages for the key industries they target. They are also working with the hardware vendors to package their software, preloaded, onto the hardware that an organization purchases to run the new system. They are developing tools and methodologies to speed up implementation tasks. In addition, the software vendors are working with their partners to make a number of application hosting options available.

The point is that there are now available tools and approaches that make rapid implementation not only possible, but proven. There are now ways to accelerate the implementation of the applications. The next section discusses the key requirements for being successful with this approach.

KEYS TO RAPID IMPLEMENTATION

Organizations have a dual challenge with rapid implementation projects: they must overcome the reasons that implementation projects failed in the past, while coming up with ways to do these projects faster. However, they are fortunate in one respect. There is general agreement on the main reasons that these projects have failed in the past. Unfortunately, the track record for most organizations is not very good for taking appropriate action to manage these known risks.

Techniques to address the normal types of project challenges are covered in Chapter 4, which focuses on how to successfully manage rapid implementations. The remainder of this chapter will spotlight challenges and keys to success that are unique, or especially important, to rapid implementations. Many of these keys to rapid implementations can be tailored for use in installation-type projects and projects that cannot be done rapidly—such as those with intensive reengineering and process redesign.

There are several keys to successful rapid implementation:

- Make quick decisions.
- Make technology infrastructure available day 1.
- Have small, cross-functional project teams.
- Do not start the clock until the team is ready.
- Use time boxing and scope management.
- Start with preconfigured versions of the software.
- Select the right package.
- Pick the right consultants.
- Take a process-driven approach.
- Conduct concurrent/parallel activities.
- Manage for speed.

Each of the keys is discussed at a high level below. Later chapters go into more detail on the specific challenges and approaches for each of these items.

Make Quick Decisions

In rapid implementations, you cannot spend the time to review, with all those affected, all the alternatives for every decision. You also cannot always work to develop a consensus for each decision with all the stakeholders before making decisions.

In XES implementations there can be literally thousands of decisions to make. SAP has over 8,000 parameter tables that must be configured for a full implementation of their product. Each of these tables has parameters that define major options for how the system will work. These tables provide the power to tailor the system to the unique needs of an organization, but they also require a lot of choices to be made. The more complex and functionally rich the standard software is, the more choices that are required. Although no organization would use all the functions in SAP, the parts that are normally used still require thousands of decisions.

In addition to configuration options, there will be hundreds of other decisions related to changes to business processes, training approaches, data conversion strategies, testing approaches and detail test plans, standard and special reports, documentation requirements, cutover schedules, and roles and responsibilities for processing with the new system. The necessity to adhere to a formal and detailed review process for a large number of these decisions will bring the project to its knees. Time is the critical resource in a rapid implementation. If the implementation team must review and justify a large number of decisions with a number of managers and end users, the timeline for the implementation will be greatly extended.

Therefore, the implementation team must be empowered to make most of the detail decisions for the implementation and use their judgment to determine when high-level decisions should be brought to the attention of the process sponsors, project sponsor, or steering committee. If the organization staffs the project team with knowledgeable, experienced, respected representatives from the functional departments, they should have the judgment to evaluate the alternatives and make good decisions for the organization. In these types of implementations, a good decision, well executed, will beat a better decision that never gets made or executed.

There will be certain decisions that require the involvement of senior management. Often these decisions center around organizational structure issues, project scope, removing project barriers, policies, capital expenditures, and decisions that will extend the length or cost of projects (other than scope). But they can also involve rollout strategies (which location gets implemented first and what is implemented there), and resolving differences of opinion among various departments that are affected by a cross-functional decision. The project sponsors and the steering committee must make all of these decisions quickly, usually within a few days.

Make Technology Infrastructure Available Day 1

The project team on a three-month implementation cannot wait six weeks to get access to the development system environment that they need to configure. They need a *sand box* environment where they can start to test different configuration options as soon as the project starts. There is a steep learning curve with most XES systems and the team must start climbing that curve immediately. Often, the roadblock is the time required by the organization to purchase and install new hardware, database management systems, and the XES software before testing by the team can begin. Or the roadblock may be that the company is still ironing out the final wording on the contract with the XES vendor, and the vendor will not send the installation CDs until all the details are resolved.

Luckily, there are ways around this problem. If the organization is using an application service provider (ASP) to do the processing for the production system, this outsourcer should be able to provide an instance of the software for use by the project team almost immediately. (As will be discussed in Chapter 3 on package selection and Chapter 7 on the IT support environment, this might be one of the key and unique requirements that will lead an organization to choose one ASP provider over another.)

Access to a development and test system may also be available from the consulting organization that is assisting in the implementation. Most of the larger consulting organizations have labs, centers of excellence, and ASP services where the XES vendor's software is already loaded and operational. One thing to check, however, is whether these organizations have the same version of the software that will be implemented by the organization—and the same operating system and database software.

Have Small, Cross-Functional Project Teams

This issue will be covered in a lot more detail in the chapter on staffing these projects (Chapter 5). However, a few key points can be made at this juncture.

First, it is important to select the right individuals to participate full-time on these implementations. The quality of the individuals assigned to the team—in terms of level, business experience, functional knowledge, talent, team attitude, ability to make decisions quickly, communication skills, and problem-solving skills—can make a significant difference in the success of the project and the ability to do these projects rapidly. These full-time team members should be the best and brightest the organization has to offer. The application cannot just be implemented by the consultants.

People from the organization should make key decisions during implementation because they will have to live with the results. Therefore, the organization's representatives on the team should take the lead in identifying issues, business alternatives, advantages and disadvantages, political factors, and recommended solutions. They provide the internal knowledge that the consultants could not be expected to have.

Second, there is a need to balance the requirement to have full-time organizational representatives from all the major functional areas addressed by the project with the desire to keep the core team small. There will be a lot of other people in the organization who will get involved and provide input during the implementation. But a rapid implementation cannot be done with a massive project team. With large teams it is difficult to have good communications among all the team members and determine and resolve integration issues rapidly. There have been ERP implementations with project teams of 400 to 500 people. However, there have been few implementations with large teams ever completed in short periods of time.

Do Not Start the Clock Until the Team Is Ready

For any implementation to be successful, it must achieve its business benefits. However, the success of a rapid implementation will also be determined, to a great extent, by how long the implementation takes. In order to give the team a fair chance at meeting the organization's expectations, it is, therefore, important for the project team to get a running start on these projects. They must be ready to make progress on project tasks as soon as the clock starts.

For this to happen, there are a number of actions that must be completed before the project officially starts. These items are prerequisites to conducting a project kickoff meeting. Activities that should occur before the kick-off—perhaps while the organization is finishing negotiations with the vendors and consultants and finalizing budget approvals—might include:

- Setting up access to a development environment
- Recruiting personnel for the team (and arranging for others to take over the team members' current jobs and responsibilities)
- Sending project team members to some initial training on the new application
- Arranging for preparation of the team work area
- Arranging for logistical support for the team
- Scheduling initial meetings with key managers and the steering committee members

If these types of tasks are not done before the project starts, the team will spin its wheels waiting for them to be completed before they can really get down to business. Unfortunately, the clock will be ticking while this occurs.

Use Time Boxing and Scope Management

Rapid implementations require *time boxing*: deciding, up front, how long the project will be allowed to take and managing the scope of the project to get it done in that timeframe. Time boxing is one of the most effective management tools to control one of the major problems in application implementation projects—scope creep. Managing scope is perhaps the key to getting the project completed on time—and getting an operational system.

A large number of ERP projects got into trouble, and were terminated, after organizations had spent large amounts of time, effort, and money. A major factor in many of these failed implementations was the inability to agree on and control the scope of the project. An indisputable fact is that an organization cannot implement all the modules of an XES package (or all the functions within complex modules) in the timeframe defined for rapid implementations. So the project's scope has to be limited in a rapid implementation.

Time boxing is also a management strategy and philosophy about application implementation. This strategy supports the position that organizations need to get benefits from their initiatives as quickly as possible—and one way to do this is to break up larger projects into a number of smaller projects. It recognizes that, for long projects, the business conditions and requirements will change before the project can be completed. It also builds on the fact that it is much easier to manage and be successful in a smaller project than in a larger one.

Time boxing is closely linked to Pareto's 80/20 rule. It says that Pareto was right; we can get 80 percent of the benefits from just 20 percent of the functions in most of the XES modules. If this is the case, why not just put in the most valuable 20 percent first? The additional functions can be added as soon as they can be justified in later projects that continuously improve business processes in response to the changing needs of the marketplace.

Start with Preconfigured Versions of the Software

A project team cannot start software configuration from scratch, with empty parameter tables, and still get implementations done in the short times allowed for rapid implementations. There is a great deal of configuration required before testing simple things, like entering an order in the test system. The team needs to start from a version of the standard system that works—and then change that version to meet the needs of the organization.

The quantity of configuration changes that will need to be made depends on how closely the initial configuration matches the needs of the organization. Some vendors only provide one default configuration: the one used for their training courses. This environment is set up to support training on all the modules in the application suite. In order to demonstrate the full range of functionality in the product, most of the training environments are for manufacturing examples. If an organization comes from the public sector, healthcare, or financial services industries, this training environment may not be a good configuration with which to begin the implementation.

Even if you are a manufacturer, there is a lot of difference between the final configurations for a discrete manufacturer (e.g., automotive) versus a company in the process manufacturing vertical (e.g., Monsanto). Therefore, manufacturers need pre-configured versions for their particular industry vertical.

Fortunately, most XES vendors tend to focus on particular industries and the unique requirements of those industries — unless they are as big as SAP and can afford to focus on all industries simultaneously (at least that seems to be the approach). The vendors market different preconfigured versions to meet the needs of specific industries. Therefore, in the selection process for the best vendor and standard package, we need to make the degree of fit with preconfigured versions of the software one of the key requirements. This leads directly to the next key to success.

Select the Right Package

There is no one application package that will meet 100 percent of the requirements of any organization, but there are several packages that will probably meet 80 to 90 percent of the requirements. Therefore, an organization should try to find the package that has the best overall fit with its unique requirements. The key and unique requirements, those things that differ from the standard processes of all organizations, should drive the selection. In general, the closer the fit, the easier it will be to implement the application using a rapid implementation approach.

There are several aspects of the package that impact the time required for implementation. When people think of package fit, they tend to focus on the functionality of the package: how well the package supports the current business processes or the to-be business processes.

A nonfunctional requirement might be the quality of the vendor's code. Buggier software will take longer to implement. It takes a lot of time to find and fix software bugs — even if another customer has previously identified the bug and the vendor has a software patch to fix it. Therefore, the selection process should evaluate the quality of the software and how long the newest version has been in general distribution. An organization does not want to be a test site for a new version of the software and try to do a rapid implementation at the same time.

Other things to assess during the selection process include:

- How preconfigured versions of the software fit and whether the vendor charges extra for these versions
- Whether the vendor has just-in-time, web-based training on the software (sending team members away for weeks of training is difficult during the short duration of a rapid implementation)
- Ease of changing the configuration parameters (i.e., a minimum of "load-bearing walls" that once set up, even in the preconfigured version, are difficult or impossible to change)

- Technology infrastructure required for processing and how quickly it can be acquired
- Availability of ASPs to host the processing
- Availability of accelerators (tools available to be tailored by the team so that many of the deliverables of the implementation will not have to be created from scratch)

Pick the Right Consultants

To succeed with a rapid implementation of an XES package, you need to jump-start the learning process. Without help, it takes a long time to climb the learning curve for these products and the rapid approach for implementing them. Also, the timing of these projects does not allow an implementation team to go down too many false paths or make too many major mistakes. Without experience, that is exactly what will happen in most of these implementations.

The easiest way to bypass these potential problems is to supplement the implementation team with consultants who know the package and are experienced with rapid implementation approaches and tools. Consultants should bring three skill sets to these projects:

1. Project management of rapid implementations
2. Knowledge of best practices and package-enabled process redesign approaches
3. Deep knowledge of the functionality capabilities and configuration requirements for the package that has been selected

By working side by side with the organization's team members, the consultants can keep the project moving forward in the early stages. They can transfer their knowledge to the other team members. And after the consultants leave, the organization will have knowledgeable people who can carry out future projects and enhancements of these systems.

Take a Process-Driven Approach

An XES implementation is a business project—with technical components. The technology is just a means to achieve business goals and support business initiatives. In the case of the Internet, the technology provides a way to do things that were not imaginable or feasible even five years ago. But the technology is still an enabler.

The implementation team must understand the various business processes and how they drive costs and support the strategies of the organization. This understanding is important in determining which processes will be included within the project's scope, which can be deferred to later projects, and which will be candidates for redesign.

There is not enough time in a rapid implementation to analyze in detail and redesign all the processes that are in scope. However, it usually is necessary to change some key processes in order to achieve the business benefits from the investment in the new software. So, process priorities must be established and dependencies determined to focus the work of the project team.

Process modeling will be an important activity during these projects. Process models help the team understand how business processes work and how the functions of the standard software fit into the overall process flow. The process models document the process, support its analysis, facilitate simulation of various changes, provide a means to graphically communicate the team's understanding of the process to end users and management, and serve as a basis for developing procedure and training materials.

Most of the XES vendors provide process models for their applications and tools to tailor these models to the needs of the organization. In certain cases, these process models can be used in configuring the software.

Conduct Concurrent/Parallel Activities

The traditional approach for implementing XES packages takes a serial approach to the various project tasks; some of the tasks are done in the early parts of the project and others get started halfway through or toward the end. In addition, there are major deliverables that are completed and approved, at key milestones, before the team starts any tasks in the next sections of the project.

This approach was acceptable for multiyear projects. On a two-year project you can wait until the second year to start an activity that takes only three months. However, on a three-month project, this same activity may have to be started on day one in order to complete the project on time.

Therefore, on a rapid implementation there will be more parallel and concurrent activities. A lot of activities can find themselves on the critical path. Many of the activities become more iterative in nature. This creates a need for a great deal of communication throughout the team because of the dependencies and interfaces between the activities.

Some of the activities that may go on in parallel are data conversion, training of team members and preparation of training materials for end users, test case development and testing of the configuration, procedure development, and communication and change management.

For example, ensuring the integrity of the data in the new system and getting this data converted is almost always on the critical path of a rapid implementation. Often, a great deal of work is done in data cleanup. Even though the data normally will be transferred to the new system in the month before go-live, the data cleanup must start early in the project for the organization to be prepared for the data conversion.

Manage for Speed

If the company does not have a strong, experienced project manager, the odds of having a successful rapid implementation are diminished. This project manager, usually a key manager and a representative of the user or functional areas of the organization, should have credibility with top management and the respect of the team members and key users. Ideally a skillful planner with the ability to anticipate and manage areas of risk, the project manager must be able to motivate the team members, deal effectively with personnel issues, and ensure that communication among team members and with management and end users starts early and is done often.

The project manager is responsible for managing the risks of the project. This entails anticipating all the things that can go wrong in a rapid implementation and taking action to prevent these things from occurring. Another key role of this manager is to remove barriers that prevent the completion of project activities and keep the project moving forward. A rapid implementation cannot afford to have a lot of stalls and run into a lot of dead ends. The project manager must stay on top of the status of all project activities.

The project manager must minimize major surprises on a rapid implementation because there is no time to respond to these surprises and still finish on time. For example, if one of the team members is getting behind on assigned tasks, the project manager must learn about this early so that person can be helped to get back on schedule or additional resources can be allocated to those tasks.

*   *   *   *

By this time you should understand why it is important to develop the ability to do rapid implementations and some of the advantages of this approach. You have also seen some of the challenges to succeeding with these projects and the keys to successfully doing rapid implementations. The chapters that follow will provide a lot of information about how we actually manage and perform the activities on these projects. We start with a look at the process we use to conduct these projects: the rapid implementation roadmap.

2

RAPID IMPLEMENTATION ROADMAP: WHAT IS THE IMPLEMENTATION PROCESS?

It is important to appreciate all the things that are involved in implementing package systems in order to better understand what is different and important for rapid implementations. These are extremely complex projects at the detail level but are relatively easy to understand at higher levels. This chapter provides a conceptual framework for these projects by walking you through the activities and tasks that occur in the various stages of a rapid implementation.

The implementation process, for a single project, is divided into several stages. At a higher level, the term phases refers to multiple projects or versions that an application or a business process goes through as it evolves to meet the changing needs of business.

For example, in phase 1, an organization may put in the general ledger module from a vendor's suite of packages and in phase 2 (a separate project) it may implement the accounts payable module from the same vendor. In phase 3, the organization may go back and change the general ledger configuration to handle financial processing for a new subsidiary. Under this scenario, the organization's financial systems have gone through three phases of development through the work done on three separate, but related, projects.

Each of the stages of a rapid implementation project produces major deliverables (e.g., reports, plans) for the project and serves as a milestone to show the completion of a significant piece of work. The stages sometimes serve as a decision point to get buy-in for what has been accomplished (e.g., vision, business case) and a decision to proceed with the next segment of the project.

Generally, the same tasks occur in both traditional and rapid implementations. However, as you will see, the ways they are organized and managed are different.

Figure 2-1 depicts the traditional approach to implementation. It consists of five stages. Each of these stages is a major milestone for the project. The major deliver-

FIGURE 2-1   Traditional Approach to Package Implementation

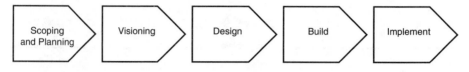

able that is created at the end of each stage is reviewed by management and a decision is made as to whether the project should proceed to the next stage. Each stage is completed and approved before the team begins work on the next stage. Unfortunately, this approach does not produce rapid results.

Every software package vendor and consulting organization has its own methodology for doing these projects. In the methodologies there is a formal *work breakdown structure.* In the work breakdown structure, the stages are broken down into activities, which are a logical grouping of project tasks that result in one or more major deliverables. The activities are then broken down into detail tasks. In some of the commercial implementation methodologies there are hundreds of activities and thousands of tasks.

Even though they may do many of the same tasks that are defined by the traditional methodologies, a rapid implementation team needs to approach these tasks differently. In rapid implementation projects, many things have to happen in parallel. These projects are also more iterative in nature and require more trial-and-error than formal design.

In a rapid implementation there is no time to produce formal deliverables that take weeks or months for management to review and approve before the team begins the next stage of work. Things happen too fast. Management is consulted and involved throughout the implementation but many of the decisions on scope and design are delegated to the project team and key users. Also, the entire project is approved ahead of time — not just one stage at a time.

A rapid implementation is executed more like the diagram in Figure 2-2. This roadmap shows the project's 12 major activities, arranged in three stages. This framework will be used to provide an overview on the work done on these projects. It also serves to highlight some of the differences from a traditional implementation approach.

Even at a high level we can immediately see some differences with a rapid approach. First, Figure 2-2 shows a lot of things going on in parallel throughout these projects. It also implies that there is a lot of iteration and looping back and forth as the project progresses. Finally, it highlights that certain activities must occur before the project is formally kicked off and after it is completed. These pre- and post-implementation activities are necessary for a rapid approach to be successful. They are normally not adequately covered in traditional implementation methodologies.

FIGURE 2-2   Rapid Implementation Roadmap

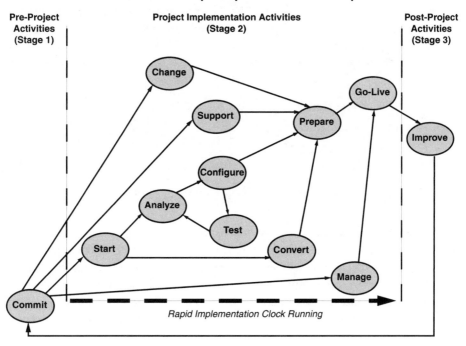

We turn now to what actually occurs in each of the 12 activities on the rapid implementation roadmap.

COMMIT

The Commit activities make up the preproject stage of a rapid implementation. They occur prior to formal project kickoff. Many of the major decisions and actions that ultimately determine whether a project is a success or a failure occur very early in the life of the project. Many of these decisions create expectations for the project, which serve as the standard against which the project will be measured. As a result, handling preproject activities effectively is a key first step toward ensuring that the project will be successful.

One of the primary reasons implementation projects fail is because there is insufficient commitment to the project by top management. However, in order to get this commitment, managers need to know what they are committing to. Therefore, a primary concern of the commit activity is to define the project in terms of its objectives, benefits, and expectations.

There are a number of steps that need to be completed before the implementation project can begin. To start a project without completing these tasks puts the project at risk. Here are some of the things to be accomplished during the commit stage:

- Select the project managers.
- Develop a business case.
- Set up the project team infrastructure.
- Prepare the initial project plans.
- Recruit the project team.

Select the Project Managers

One of the first things that must to be done is to select two project managers. One of the project managers is the lead project manager, and comes from the organization implementing the new system. The other project manager is the person from a consulting organization or the software vendor who will coach the organization's project manager through the implementation process. Once selected, these individuals will do the high-level planning for the project and will be responsible for driving the project to completion.

The lead project manager should be a highly respected individual with broad organizational knowledge and contacts. This person will be ultimately held accountable for the success of the project.

As will be discussed in more detail in the project staffing chapter (Chapter 5), a consulting coach is needed because many key decisions are made early in a rapid implementation that impact the ultimate success of the project. These decisions set the direction and tone for the project and need to be made with the knowledge of someone who has a lot of experience with these types of projects. An experienced consulting manager also helps the organization's project manager avoid mistakes and false starts throughout the project that could be fatal to a rapid implementation.

The coach brings a methodology for doing these projects, experience in managing the risks of these projects, and an independent perspective. The organization's lead project manager cannot be expected to have these tools and traits. However, for important reasons that will be covered later in the book, the organization should *not* have a consultant lead the project. This is a role for someone from the organization.

If the project managers were not involved in the package selection and justification activities, they need to quickly get up to speed on a number of things: What is the project really about? What is the expected scope of the project? What things are specifically excluded from the project scope? What are the expected timeframes? Who are the supporters and who is the opposition? What is the business imperative for the project and how does it fit into the overall strategies of the organization? Much of this information is available from the project sponsor, those who participated in the software selection, and those who worked on the business case for the project.

Develop a Business Case

The business case is the next area to examine. The project managers must ensure that there is a business case or charter for the project. The business case quantifies the benefits and costs associated with the investment in new systems and business processes.

Ideally, a business case was developed as part of the process of selecting the package and justifying the investment to implement parts of that system. If so, this information can be reviewed and updated at this time. If a formal business case was not prepared, then, at a minimum, the high-level goals and objectives for the project need to be put into writing and approved by the project sponsor and steering committee. This may be documented in the form of a project charter. These goals and objectives can be taken to a lower level of detail as required as the project progresses.

This business case will be useful in managing the scope, boundaries, constraints, risks, expectations, and assumptions for the project. The assumptions include things like whether the organization will modify the vendors' code or follow a strategy of going with the vanilla version of the software and change business processes to the methods supported by the package. The constraints might include the budget for the project and a go-live date that must be met for critical business reasons.

Set Up the Project Team Infrastructure

The third step in Commit is to set up the project team infrastructure—before the project starts. This includes constructing the *war room* for the team with PC and phone access for each team member. The team members should be connected to both a local area network and development and test versions of the package software.

The IT support group for the project has a lot of work to do in setting up this environment in time for project kickoff. Since the organization's personnel may not have been to the technical training on the package yet, they may need the assistance of technical support people from either the vendor or the consulting organization in order to get these tasks done on time. In the early stages of the project the organization's IS personnel are often watching, learning, expediting, and making sure things get done to prepare a suitable technical environment for the team. As the project progresses they will be setting up the production environment for the organization, mainly on their own. After go-live, they will be responsible for supporting the new system in actual use.

Other administrative aspects of the team infrastructure also need to be set up in time for the kickoff meeting. The network (LAN) support for the project team (e.g., folder structure, access rights, email, calendaring process) needs to be established. Forms and policies need to be created for issues logging, status tracking and reporting, and expense reimbursement. Many of these items will be covered with the project team members in their team meeting following the formal project kickoff meeting.

Prepare the Initial Project Plans

A number of plans need to be prepared before the project is staffed and started. One of these is a risk management plan. The project managers need to assess all the things that may cause this project to fail and those things that are key to its success. Plans and actions should be identified to mitigate or respond to the risks and to ensure the key success factors will be in place. These responses might include things like adding additional steps and checks to the project workplan or staffing the project with more experienced personnel in certain areas.

All of this should be documented in a risk management plan. If there is not support for actions that are necessary to make the project successful, then the project manager should address this issue with the steering committee. Perhaps the organization is not ready to start this project at this time. After all, there is little use in starting a project that has a high likelihood of failing.

A preliminary workplan should also be developed at this time. It lays out a roadmap for the entire project. It will also be used in determining the proper staffing level for the project. The project managers will not attach names to the various tasks until they have finalized the team organization and evaluated each individual team member's areas of interest, experience, and skills.

The project organizational structure and roles and assignments need to be developed next. The same person may perform several of the roles. If the project is using an application service provider or contract programmers, some of the roles will be outsourced.

For a rapid implementation with a small project team there will be a flat organizational structure. These projects do not need a lot of chiefs; everyone should be doing direct, value-adding work. In addition, all team members will pitch in, wherever required, to get the project complete on time while achieving its business objectives.

Finally, the project managers need to determine the key deliverables that will be created in the project. There will be hundreds of deliverables described in the methodology used by the vendor or the consulting organization. But, in line with the philosophy of doing only value-adding tasks, the project managers need to decide what are the really important, and therefore mandatory, deliverables from a rapid implementation.

These deliverables will guide the activities for each task, control the level of detail that the team members go to, and help the team members know when they are done with a task. The deliverable plan should also address whether the team will require signoff of the deliverables by the end users, the sponsor, or the steering committee.

Recruit the Project Team

The final step in this activity (and stage) identifies those people that will make up the core implementation team. A deliberate effort should be made to recruit the best possible people to be on the team. A lot more will be said on this topic in the chapter on staffing these implementations (Chapter 5). However, it should be noted at this time that the quality of the people who will work on this project is one of the keys to its success.

In a rapid implementation, management is going to have to empower the team to make a lot of the detail decisions that will affect the way future work gets done in the organization. The team members will be required to come up with creative ways to use the package to accomplish what has to be done. They will have to do this under intense time pressures while facing resistance to the changes that will be made from many areas of the organization. This is a lot to ask. Therefore, we need an organization's *A team* for these projects.

If the tasks covered in the Commit activity are not completed before the project kickoff, it will be difficult for the project team to hit the road running. Good planning and preparation *before* project kickoff gets the project off to a good start.

START

The Start activities initiate the project implementation stage of a rapid implementation. This activity officially begins with the project kickoff meeting. This meeting normally takes a full day. In attendance during the morning session should be several top managers of the organization, the steering committee members, key functional managers, the project team, and representatives from the vendor and consulting firms. The afternoon session is just for the project team.

This meeting should be preceded by individual discussions with the project sponsor, the steering committee members, and other key managers. With these meetings, the project managers begin the process of building understanding and commitment for the project throughout the organization. There should be no surprises in the kickoff session.

The organization's project manager should lead the kickoff meeting. However, the most senior executive present should open the meeting with a statement that describes the importance of the project to the organization and the support the team has from top management. It is also useful for this person to lay out some rules of the road for the relationship of the team to the rest of the organization. Some sample rules include:

- Top management expects the departmental managers to make time to be involved with the project.

- The organization is using a rapid implementation approach because management believes it is the best way to accelerate the benefits of the system and respond to quickly changing business requirements. As such, rapid implementation will become a core competency for successful organizations.

- This approach will require the organization to limit the scope of this project. The organization will go live on the new system with all the processes that are ready on the target date. Some good capabilities of the vendor's package will have to be deferred to later phases.

- This approach requires numerous trade-offs. It will only succeed if it has the support of all areas of the organization. Since the future of the organization depends on learning how to do these implementations rapidly to meet critical business requirements, top management expects that the team will get full support from all departments.

- This is not a one-time effort. The organization will do a lot of these rapid implementation projects in the future. Therefore, we need to evaluate the process and capture lessons learned so they can be applied in future projects.

- These projects will be successful only if there is a great deal of user involvement. Therefore, we expect the departments to do whatever is necessary to make their people available for the tasks that require extensive user involvement.

- Top management will not allow individuals and groups to criticize the project and the team behind their backs. If people have a problem with the way the project is going, they should bring it to the attention of the project manager or the sponsor.

- The organization is implementing this new application software in order to have the ability to change business processes in the future and have them supported by the vendor's products. This software has a lot of flexibility in the way it can be implemented. We will not modify the vendor's code to meet the way we do things currently.

- I have instructed the project manager to come to me with any roadblocks to the successful completion of this project that cannot be resolved by the sponsor or the steering committee. I will make whatever decisions and take whatever actions are necessary to support the successful completion of this initiative.

One of the first indicators of the importance of the project is whether the representatives from top management stay for the entire morning session. Another will be the actions top management and the steering committee take to keep this project on track when the inevitable bumps in the road appear. With swift response to resolve the first few project problems, word will get out that something different is going on with these rapid implementation projects.

By this time most of the steps from the Commit activities should have been completed. For example, the workspace is ready, and the team members have been transitioned off their old jobs. It is very disruptive to project progress for the team members to join the project at different times. Those joining the project late miss a lot of the team-building activities and initial training and planning that occur in the first weeks. No matter how hard they try, they often stay behind the others for most of the project.

If all the Commit activities were not done by the project kickoff, they should be completed as quickly as possible at the beginning of this activity. However, it is not a good sign for the project if there are a lot of these activities to complete.

The other main step that occurs in the Start activity is providing initial training for the project team members. This training should be scheduled in the four or five days that follow the kickoff meeting. Initial training should cover the methodology and approach that will be used for the project and provide an overview of the design and capabilities of the software package.

Many of the team members may not have been on the software selection project and therefore may never have seen the vendor's system. It is important to get them into the software quickly. Therefore, these first training sessions should minimize the amount of slide show-based lectures and provide, instead, some hands-on training on things like signing on and navigating through the system, as well as having actual demos of the software by the trainers.

A difficult decision is whether the team should be given the standard training from the vendor at the vendor's training site or receive a tailored version at the organization's location. The problem with the generic training is that it will cover a lot of capabilities in each of the package's modules that are not within the scope of the implementation—and may never be used by the organization. Also, if team members train at the vendor's training locations, they will usually be in classes with people from a lot of different organizations. In these situations a great deal of the class time can be spent answering questions that are relevant only to other organizations.

However, there are benefits from the team members seeing all the capabilities of the system in the vendor's generic training. After this exposure, they may be in a better position to identify functions that could be implemented in the future.

Using tailored in-house training has the advantage of focusing the training on the specific needs of the project. This approach should simplify the training by reducing the number of areas that have to be covered. It also is more in line with the overall philosophy of eliminating non-value-adding or low-value-adding activities from rapid implementation projects.

No matter which training approach is chosen (generic or tailored), the project team usually benefits from receiving the initial training as a group, near the organization's site. This is often easier on the project budget since it minimizes travel expenses for a large number of training attendees.

MANAGE

This activity includes all the things the project managers do to plan and control the project. In a rapid implementation, the managers act a lot like player/coaches. The teams are small and the organizational structure is flat. So, the managers spend a lot of their time doing on-the-job training with team members, offering suggestions, providing examples, guiding the work, reviewing deliverables, and removing barriers in the team's path.

The project workplan is a key tool for the project manager. It lists all the tasks that have to be accomplished before going live with the new system. The project is planned and controlled by means of this document.

The project workplan must be a living document that is used and updated throughout the project. Too often, the plan is prepared at the beginning of the project and then never reviewed, used, or updated. This is unfortunate, because the workplan is the primary tool that helps the project manager determine how things are really going.

The project manager determines project status by reviewing and accepting deliverables from the team members. In this process, there are only two task states that are important: the task is either (1) complete or (2) still in process. The practice of asking people for estimates of the percent of each task that has been completed has never been an effective way for determining project status.

The tasks should be defined at a level where each one should take no more than two days to complete. At the appropriate time, the project manager sits down with each team member and reviews the deliverables from the task. They are either *done* or *in process*—nothing in between. If there is no completed deliverable, the task is not done. Although this may seem simplistic, it is difficult to fall weeks behind schedule and not know about it with this approach.

One of the requirements for rapid implementation is templates or sample deliverables for most of the tasks. They are key accelerators for project activities. It is much easier for team members to tailor documents than create them from scratch. These sample deliverables help define the level of work for each task and provide a consistent format for the documentation. A key project manager task is to select the templates for the project and teach the team members how to use them.

The project manager is responsible for the performance of the team members. If team members cannot carry their assigned part of the load, or have problems that cause them to disrupt project activities, they must be replaced. The project manager must address these problems quickly and decisively. With a flat organizational structure and aggressive schedule, the project managers cannot spend a lot of time counseling and correcting the work of any specific team member. Project manager time is needed in all areas.

Risk management is also a key task for project managers. They must anticipate things that could go wrong in the project and do whatever is necessary to prevent them from occurring. For those risks that are outside the control of the project team, contingency plans should be developed to allow the team to respond quickly to minimize impact on the project. The team must be able to make quick course corrections during the project.

The project managers are responsible for developing the team members. These projects are great opportunities for knowledge transfer and provide team members with a broad understanding of how the organization works. Team members become valuable assets to the organization once the projects are completed. The project managers should look for opportunities to take advantage of the knowledge and experience the team members bring to the project and give them opportunities to develop new skills and knowledge.

The project managers are responsible for keeping the team focused on the goals and objectives for the implementation. Time is valuable in these projects. Every task needs to be challenged to determine the value it provides toward meeting the project goals and objectives. Non-value-adding tasks must be eliminated.

A big part of managing these projects is managing the scope of the implementation. To a certain extent, the detailed scope is not known at the beginning of these projects. The team has project goals and objectives but does not know all the detailed transactions that will be included in this current phase of the package implementation. Therefore, there is a continuous process that defines the scope in more detail. Deciding and documenting all the things that are not included in scope is equally important to the success of these projects.

Finally, issues management will be an ongoing task for the project managers. The issues (e.g., problems, opportunities, decisions) need to be identified by all the team members and then prioritized and resolved. In a rapid implementation, the team cannot take weeks or months to resolve issues. They must be taken care of in a matter of days. Therefore, a useful project metric is how many unresolved issues are in the issues log at any one time and how long is it taking to resolve them.

Chapter 4 covers project management approaches, activities, and responsibilities in more detail.

ANALYZE

In the Commit and Start activities the organization establishes a vision and business imperative for implementing the new system. Also, goals and objectives for the project are documented in the business case or project charter. In this activity the implementation team will determine how to achieve that vision and meet those objectives.

What does the new system have to do to support the desired business process changes? How will the organization use the standard software to achieve these changes? To answer these questions, the team will have to determine how the new subprocesses will work using the capabilities of the package.

This activity is the analysis and design portion of the project. It is where the team puts on its business hat and gets creative about how to improve business processes and solve business problems. It means looking at the as-is processes and determining how they will change going forward. These activities require knowledge of the business and its processes, as well as the capabilities of the software package being implemented. This portion of the project also requires creativity and a focus on finding the simplest, best ways to do things within the capabilities of the vendor's software.

The team analyzes how work is being done now and the problems that people experience with the current process design and technology support. They look for new opportunities and ways to do things that are possible because of the rich capabilities of the package that has been selected. They determine what has to be done within the new system to support the business in the areas that are included in the project's scope. In these activities the team determines the requirements for the new system and begins designing ways to meet these requirements.

Designing new processes addresses how the organization will get information into the system, what processing and decisions will occur (either manually or within the system), and what will be the outputs. These outputs may be in the form of reports, business forms (e.g., checks, invoices), updated databases, and inquiry screens that provide information and help evaluate the results of processing. All these requirements for the new system will be documented in a design specification.

In the past, design specifications were turned over to programmers to code using programming languages, such as COBOL, C++, Visual Basic, or PowerBuilder. Once the programs were written, there was extensive testing to ensure the programs worked as designed. This testing occurred on two levels. First, the programmers tested whether the system worked as they interpreted the requirements in the specifications. Second, the analysts and users tested to determine whether the system worked as they had intended when writing the specifications.

This approach for computer system development has been going on for almost 50 years. It still is used in the development of custom, standalone systems, bolt-on functionality to augment a package's functions, and interface and data conversion programs. However, development gets done differently when using a standard software package and a rapid implementation approach.

The main difference is in the nature of the work that occurs after the team determines the requirements for the new system. Rather than designing a new system in the traditional sense, the team members select from a menu of transactions and package functions and determine how these functions can be configured to fit the needs of the organization.

This difference makes sense when you consider that standard software has already been designed and programmed. The vendor, with the assistance of its customers, has gone through years of requirements definition, data modeling, program design, coding, and various levels of testing. This cycle occurs many times as the vendors provide new releases of their packages.

The vendor's developers have done extensive testing of their own programs and how they integrate with other programs in the application suite. Then, after they believe that the product is relatively stable (and they have completed *alpha testing*), companies are recruited to act as *beta test sites*—to become the first actual users of the software. These beta customers help find additional bugs in the software that can be fixed before the package is made generally available to the public.

In addition to providing tested software, the vendors also have developed system documentation, training programs, implementation templates and accelerators, process diagrams, and data conversion utilities. In some cases, they have developed interfaces to popular packaged software modules offered by other software vendors. These are all resources that the project team does not have to develop from scratch.

Therefore, in a package implementation project, the team starts from a different place than it would for a project to custom-develop a new system from scratch. If the organization has chosen a good package and it supports a preconfigured version for their industry, the project team may have a complete, fully functioning system to work with in the first weeks of the project. However, that still leaves a lot of work to be done.

The standard software usually has several different methods for supporting most processes. So analysis activities focus on selecting which parts of the system will be implemented in this project and determining how to enable these parts of the package and tailor them to meet the needs of the organization.

Lists of all the transactions supported by the system can be annotated to show those in the scope of the project. Process diagrams showing the processes supported by the package can be used for the same purpose. Either method generally shows that most organizations use only a small subset of the total functionality of the top packages. The challenge is to determine what parts of the system must be used to meet the business requirements. Other parts of the system can be implemented in future phases as part of the Improve activities.

For the tasks discussed in this activity it should be obvious that the team needs to understand both the as-is and to-be business processes and the capabilities of the package. The organization's personnel on the team usually understand the organization's current processes very well. However, they usually rely on the knowledge of vendor personnel or consultants on the team who have experience with the package to provide the detailed package knowledge.

As the project progresses, the core team members learn a great deal about the system through additional training, discussions with vendor and consulting personnel, and hands-on experience with the software. There will come a point when all the team members know the package well. After that knowledge transfer has occurred it will be possible for the organization to do these tasks in future implementations of this package with much less consulting support.

The team uses two primary guidelines in making scope decisions during the Analyze activity. First, they need to include enough functions and processes in the scope of the project to address the major problems to be solved and benefits to be achieved. Second, the organization must still be able to carry on its normal work (e.g., manufacture and ship goods; register, teach, and administer student records; bill patients) after it goes live with the new system. These implementations should be transparent to customers — or should delight them with improved service.

Since the team is not implementing all the functions of the package in the first rapid implementation project, they must determine how the other processes in the businesses will continue to get done. This usually means interfacing the packaged software with legacy systems and employing short-term workarounds so the work can still get done while later implementation phases are completed.

The deliverables from of all this analysis work will include documentation, at a high level, that shows how the processes will work in the future to meet the project's business requirements. It will also include a delineation of the parts of the package that will be used to support these processes.

The Analyze activities are shown on the roadmap in Figure 2-2 as part of an iterative loop of analysis, configuration, and testing. The team will not get the analysis and design right the first time they try. They may decide that they can use the system in a certain way only to find out that that approach will not work. During testing they may learn that the package works in a way that is different from what was thought or could be determined from its documentation. On a more positive note, as they learn more about the package and its capabilities, the team may find an easier way to support a process.

During testing and review, key users may surface problems with the design that require the team to find alternative ways to perform processes. The team may also find that some parts of the process are not supported in the current version of the software and, therefore, must be handled with legacy systems, bolt-on functionality, or workarounds. As a worst case, the team may even find that some of the objectives of the project are not supported by the package and cannot be achieved in the initial implementation.

These issues are all part of the challenges and messiness inherent in implementing any new, complex application system. However, after several loops through Analyze, Configure, and Test the team will usually come up with a way to support the business processes with the package capabilities. Then they must configure the system to make it work as designed.

CONFIGURE

Configuration requires detailed knowledge of a vendor's package. Each of these packages has hundreds and thousands of parameter tables that are used to change the way the software works in order to address different business methods and procedures. Changing these parameters is how the team tailors the software to meet the unique needs of the organization. Certain parts of the package need to be turned on and other parts disabled. There are often several different ways the package can be used to support a particular business process. The team must select and enable the alternatives that best meet the organization's needs.

Configuration also maps the organizational structure (e.g., companies, departments, cost centers) to the software database structure. This mapping can have significant implications for reporting and processing of intra- and interorganizational transactions. The system can often be set up to represent one organization with all the related entities as components or it can be set up with each entity as a separate, related organization. These decisions determine how transactions between related entities are handled by the package.

In addition to choosing parameter options and organizational structures, the team defines a financial chart of account and other system codes. These numbers and codes tell the system how to account for and validate the various transactions that occur during processing.

A major risk in configuration is not identifying the "load-bearing walls." These are choices that the team must get right in the initial configuration because they are difficult, or even impossible, to change at a later time. There are many other configuration parameters than can be changed on the fly, at any time, to alter the way the system works. The key is to know how easy it is to switch specific configuration decisions in response to project or business changes.

The nature and number of configuration parameters, and the ease of changing them, varies among the vendors' packages. Some packages have a reputation (e.g., SAP R/3) for great functionality (supporting all the ways an organization could want to perform its processes) but a requirement that the team get configuration decisions right the first time. Other packages seem to be more forgiving of the need to change decisions in the future. In general, the things that are difficult to change are those that affect the way information is organized in the package's databases.

Packaged software needs to be able to be changed continuously to support business strategy and process changes. Making significant changes in some packages can be a difficult and cumbersome process. Other systems are more flexible and can handle certain changes more easily. However, flexibility is a relative term.

There are certain things that are easy or difficult to change in every package. However, the ease of making other changes varies by software product. Some vendors (e.g., J. D. Edwards) market that their product is so easy to change, in response to changing business requirements, that "you can change the tires while going down the road at 60 miles per hour." The truth in all these claims, pro and con, needs to be tested with real-world examples.

Configure is part of the Analyze-Configure-Test loop. The team will find situations where the package cannot be configured to do what has been designed. Also, errors will be made in configuring the package that will be caught and corrected in testing. Additional configuration tasks occur throughout the project as transactions and processes are added and deleted from the project scope. Each of these situations requires the team to cycle through this loop many times.

TEST

The testing that occurs in this activity is primarily at the transaction level. The team is testing whether the individual transactions can be successfully completed with the way the system has been configured. Examples of things to test at this point might be the ability to enter a new customer, take an order, ship goods, receive materials, prepare an invoice, enter a purchase requisition, or print payroll checks.

The tests designed and conducted at this stage require an in-depth knowledge of the business requirements and how the package works. The core implementation team can provide some of the business knowledge based on their experience working in different areas of the company. However, this is one area of the project where the team needs a lot of end-user involvement to define the detail requirements.

The testing activity involves seven steps for each of the transactions included in scope:

1. Create test cases.
2. Prepare test data.
3. Define the expected results.
4. Run the test.
5. Evaluate the test results.
6. Correct problems and retest.
7. Document successful completion of the test.

For each transaction there may be several scenarios or cases to be tested. They usually cover the normal things that occur as well as the exceptions. To get a flavor for the level of testing in this activity, consider some of the things that may need to be tested for a single transaction such as Enter a Sales Order (SO):

- Enter an SO with just one line item.
- Enter an SO with a large number of line items that require multiple entry screens.

- Enter an SO that causes a customer to exceed its credit limit.

- Enter an SO that gives the customer a price discount based on quantity breaks.

- Enter an SO with a manual override on the discount percentage.

- Enter an SO where items are not available in stock and must be back ordered.

- Enter an SO using the customer's item number instead of the organization's number.

- Enter an SO where the customer is exempt from sales tax.

- Enter an SO where freight charges must be calculated.

- Enter an SO where the customer will pick up the item at the shipping dock and should not be charged for freight.

- Enter an SO for an item that is not carried in inventory but can be special ordered.

- Enter an SO where the items must be shipped from several distribution centers.

- Enter an SO that is a release from a blanket order recorded in the system.

Although this list is not complete, even for this one transaction, it gives an idea of the level of detailed testing that needs to take place for each transaction. For each of the cases above there may be one or more tables or switches that need to be set in the system (configured) for these situations to be processed correctly.

The end users who process transactions with the existing systems should be involved in identifying all the different test cases. They know all the variations that occur as a result of business policies and unique customer requirements.

All the test cases should be documented in a testing log. This log can also record the results of each cycle of tests and the actions that were taken to correct errors.

Finding errors is a good thing! The project team does testing to find errors; they should not expect that all the tests would run the first time without error. The idea is to find the errors early, when they are easy to correct. The team also wants to find and correct the bugs before the system is used to train users or process real transactions.

In order to run these tests, it is necessary to set up test data in the system. For our simple sales order tests we need customers, items, multiple distribution centers, and pricing, freight, and sales tax tables. At this stage of the project the team does not want a large numbers of items in the test databases because that would make it more difficult to trace the transactions. Therefore, the team should not dump all the production data from the legacy systems into the test databases. Rather, they should create the minimum amount of test data to run the tests identified.

However, it is helpful to use actual customer names and item numbers in the tests so the end users can relate to the test scenarios. Often a small amount of data can be entered manually using the entry screens in the system. This implies a hierarchy for the tests. We need to test entering a new customer and changing credit limits before entering transactions for our sales order tests.

A key step in the testing process that is sometimes omitted is documenting the expected results before running the tests. Experience has shown that the expected results need to be put in writing to support an effective testing process. Without this step, people evaluating the test results may check only part of the outputs that are produced or accept the results without sufficient thought or challenge.

As examples, the expected results from sales order tests could include:

- As SO 10887 is created, the five items in inventory for this SO should be reserved for the quantities on the SO and the available-to-promise amounts for each item should be reduced accordingly.

- The customer in test case 4 should have its credit status field changed to "COD only."

- The freight charges for test case 12 should be $26.42.

- The sales tax for test case 14 should be $6.45.

- The freight charge on the pickup order in test case 15 should be zero.

Without documenting the expected results, errors can slip through the cracks and not show up until later in the project when they are more difficult to correct. Even worse, they may be discovered first, after go-live, by the organization's customers in the form of incorrect invoices or wrong shipments.

Once the tests are run, the actual results and the expected results are compared. This is not as straightforward a task as might be expected. When there are discrepancies the team will sometimes find, perhaps after trying several changes to the system, that the system results were correct all along and the expected results were wrong. Researching result gaps requires a good eye and an open mind.

If the system does not perform as designed, it may be necessary to change parameters or data tables to correct the problem. Before rerunning the test it may be necessary to refresh the test data—setting it back to what it was at the beginning of the test. Running several test cycles corrupts the initial test data and the expected results for future tests. Therefore, it is advisable to create a standard test bank (set of test data) that can be used for all the tests. Then the IS support personnel need to provide a mechanism to refresh the test data, as required.

A final testing concern is the fact that changing parameters to fix one problem might cause new problems in another area. A test that worked correctly yesterday might fail today. So, there is a need to run through all the tests multiple times until the system passes all the unit tests in a process area.

The actual and expected results should be retained so project managers and others working with the team can review the tests. This documentation can be used to research other test problems later in the project.

Testing should go more rapidly if the team is using a proven, preconfigured version of the software. A lot of simple errors that occur when setting up all the system parameters from scratch can be avoided. The team will also be able to start testing earlier with a stable, operational system as a starting point. So, in the areas of configuration and testing, having a preconfigured version of the system is a key factor to support a rapid implementation approach.

CHANGE

Putting in new computer systems produces significant benefits for the organization only if the implementations improve key business processes. It is hard to cost-justify these projects solely on improvements they make to the technical infrastructure. Also, it is clear that there is little benefit from putting in new systems that are not used. Therefore, to get the maximum return on application system investments, people and processes have to change, and for the good. The organization must be able to do things faster, better, or cheaper than they did before the new system was implemented.

The changes that result from a rapid implementation occur in three areas: (1) technology, (2) processes, and (3) organizational structure. There will be many groups of people who will be impacted by the changes. The responses from the project stakeholders (i.e., those impacted by the project) will vary across the spectrum from denial, active resistance, and a wait-and-see attitude to excitement and support.

It is not just management and the end users of these systems who must change. As a result of these projects, the people in the IS department often must learn new skills and utilize different tools in their work. In some cases the custom-developed systems they created (and for which the organization relies on them for knowledge on how they work) will be replaced by standard software developed by a vendor. For the first time, users may know as much or more about the system as the application analyst in the IS department. The implementation team may even be discussing the possibility of outsourcing support and processing of the new system.

The users of the new system will be anxious because getting new systems usually means they must learn new ways to do their work. It will change the way the work is done as well as the tools that are used. The new system may replace the Excel spreadsheets, Access databases, and three-ring binders they really use to do their job. It may also change job roles and responsibilities. Users may also have concerns about how quickly they can learn to use new technologies and complicated systems with different terminology, screens, and reports.

Most of the users are not on the core implementation team. Therefore, they may also have worries about the project team—off in another building or location—designing new processes without understanding all the problems and challenges users face on a daily basis.

Managers, especially supervisors and middle managers, often are concerned about how the changes brought on by the new system will transform the organizational structure and the roles, responsibilities, and authority of their department or group. This is especially the situation when one of the stated benefits of the project is to cut out a layer of middle managers. New business systems can sometimes be used to substitute for one of the primary roles performed by middle management: acting as a channel for passing information up and down from top management to the users.

In addition, the managers often designed the current processes and have a sense of authorship and ownership for the ways things are done. Any suggestions for changes to process designs may be taken personally.

All these issues, whether real or imagined, must be addressed during a rapid implementation. The project team members must understand that perception is often more important than reality. These concerns and fears are important because it is the people issues, rather than technology issues, that usually cause these projects to fail.

Therefore, during a rapid implementation, the team must be proactive in managing change. Given the shorter duration of these projects, the change will come quicker to those impacted by the deployment of the new system. Positive changes do not happen by accident. To ensure proper focus on these aspects of the project, someone on the implementation team should be assigned primary responsibility for change management.

There are a number of activities that can be done during a rapid implementation to help manage the changes that occur. They fall into the following areas:

- Assessment
- Involvement
- Communication
- Documentation
- Training

At the beginning of the project, the team needs to assess the readiness of the stakeholders for the changes that will occur. They need to determine the various groups impacted by the new system and their views on the project. Who will be the supporters for the project and who will be its enemies? What groups will be the potential winners or losers in resources, power, and responsibilities once the new system is implemented? Who are the leaders and influencers the team needs to win over? What can be done to develop power users and champions for the new system and the changes it produces? What do the stakeholders know about the project? How much of what they know is accurate?

The project team will perform this change readiness assessment sometimes through survey documents but more frequently through discussions with a lot of people throughout the organization.

A key insight on human nature will have a dramatic effect on the success of the project: no involvement, no commitment. The stakeholders need to be, and feel, actively involved in the design, testing, and rollout of the new system. The implementation team has to have a core group of people working full time on the project; but a lot of other people need to participate in project activities. The nonteam members need to provide information and advice on current processes, system requirements, design alternatives, training approaches, test cases, deployment strategies, and organizational changes.

The worst thing that can happen is for the users and managers to feel that their experience and insights are not valued in the design of the new system. They must not believe that someone else is determining their future without asking for their input. One way to ensure that this does not happen is to proactively work on the two-way communications between the team and its stakeholders.

There is no such thing as too much communication in these projects. Communication needs to come from top management, the core team, and the extended team of stakeholders. The themes to be communicated are simple: This is an important project for the organization. It has the support of top management. This is when the new system will go live. This is the status of the project. Several different methods will be used to get the appropriate involvement of the people in the organization. These are the ways the organization will ensure that people are ready for the new system and their changed jobs.

The modes of communication are briefings at meetings, status reports, newsletters, voice-mail, and email messages. And in this new web economy, the team may even create a project web site, on an intranet or extranet, to communicate throughout the organization.

Good documentation on the new system is important. Often there was never very good written documentation for the old legacy systems. As a result users had to learn through trial-and-error and from information passed down by more experienced employees. With the fast pace of a rapid implementation, there is a need for better aids to enable users to get up to speed more quickly.

The primary documentation for standard systems should be available from the vendor in the form of system manuals and online help text. Often that information is available in electronic format and it can be tailored to the needs of the organization. In addition, the vendor or the system integrator should provide user procedures templates and process flow diagrams to support development of customized user procedures. These procedures can include policies and guidance on how the organization will use the system.

The availability of quality documentation should be a requirement in the selection of a package that will be implemented with a rapid approach. There is just not enough time in these projects to develop this documentation from scratch.

The users must be adequately trained for a rapid implementation (or any implementation) project to be successful. The people using the system need to be comfortable in their understanding of how to do their jobs using the new system. Good end-user training requires quality training materials and well-prepared instructors.

The key resources used in developing training materials should be the user procedures developed by the core team and standard training materials available from the package vendor. Increasingly, the vendors provide some of their training courses in the form of CD or web-based just-in-time instructional materials. Most of the training materials come in the form of instructor-led classes. The end-user training is given in the Prepare activities, just before go-live.

Most projects will use a train-the-trainer strategy to deliver the training. Under this approach, the core team members and power users attend vendor training sessions to learn about the package and its capabilities. They also develop knowledge about the system by working side by side with the consultants on the project team. These organizational representatives then prepare and deliver the initial training to the end users.

There are definite advantages in having people from the organization—not the vendor or the consultants—deliver the training. These people can better teach the users the new system because they are family, already have credibility within the organization, and can use organization-specific examples throughout the training.

All these change activities are important in managing the changes that will result from implementing new systems and business processes. Often they are either ignored or short-changed. This happens because much of this work occurs toward the end of the project, as time and budget are running out and the project is usually behind schedule. However, these activities are some of the most important things that must be done well to make a rapid implementation successful.

SUPPORT

Support refers to the IT activities that must go on, often behind the scenes, to ensure that the rest of the implementation teams have a developmental sand-box in which to test various system configurations. The IS personnel also work during the project to prepare a production environment for use to process real transactions after cutover. Although it has been stated several times in this book that a rapid implementation is business-driven, there are still a lot of technical tasks that have to be done properly to make these projects successful.

The IS department must get an early jump on creating a development environment for the project team. Some of the tasks required to set up this environment have long lead times. Since the team technical environment should be ready when the team members return from preliminary training on the new system, most of these activities must occur during the Commit period of the project.

The project war room must be set up with workstations for all the team members. These workstations should be connected to a local area network so there can be common access to all project deliverables and working documents. A phone should also be available for each team member. In addition, printers, copiers, and fax machines should be available in the project work area. The team will also need a display device to project package screen images for meetings, demos, and testing.

The vendor's software must be loaded on a development server. This is often a smaller server than will be used for the production system. If not already available, this hardware and other network devices may have to be purchased for the project. This same hardware can be used after the project is completed as a developmental environment to test package upgrades, vendor code patches, and configuration changes.

This development system supports the project team, users who are assisting in the design and testing of the system, and IS personnel developing data conversion, interface, and reporting programs. In addition to the vendor's standard software, a database management system and preconfigured versions of the system may also have to be installed.

Once the initial development system is operational, representatives from IS must assume the role of package system administrators and perform other technical support tasks during the project. These support tasks include:

- Creating development, test, and production instances of the system and migrating parameter settings and data between the different versions of the system
- Working with system security personnel or internal auditors to set up security (access authorizations) for the project team members and researching, defining, and establishing all the access capabilities for the end users of the production system
- Establishing backup and recovery capabilities for the different instances of the system
- Programming data-conversion programs and creating data files from the legacy system that can be used to import data into the new system
- Tuning the databases so they operate efficiently with the new applications
- Supporting project team members as problems occur that require maintenance on workstations, software, or peripheral devices
- Researching potential system bugs and working with the vendor's technical support personnel to install code patches to resolve system errors
- Developing special reports and forms using the tools available with the software and other common report-writing tools
- Developing program interfaces between the new system and existing legacy systems so data can be passed back and forth between these systems in real time or with periodic updates to system files

These activities require strong technical skills. Many also require knowledge about the current systems used by the organization. Unfortunately, information about legacy systems is usually not well documented and often exists only in the heads of the IS personnel. Since most of these IT activities require significant amounts of detail work, having full-time IS personnel assigned to the core team is critical to the success of the project.

The new system may use technologies (e.g., databases, operating systems, development languages, and tools) that are new to the IS organization. Consequently, IS personnel must receive training on the technical aspects of the package while the other team members learn the functional aspects.

To ensure the timely completion of the technical activities, the project team often leverages the technical resources of the vendor and other organizations. Vendor personnel may even install the software of the development server. In addition to this initial support, it may be necessary to include, as a full-time member of the implementation team, a technical consultant who has implemented this package before, in the same technical environment. Even with these outside resources, there are a lot of technical challenges to implementing these packages. A lot of IT knowledge transfer and learning must occur throughout the project so the organization's IS department can take on technical support of the system once it is put into production.

A new trend is to use an application service provider (ASP) to host the processing of the system and take some of this load off the organization's IS department. If the right ASP is selected and appropriate contract terms negotiated, this approach can help manage some of the IT risks of the project. This option and a more detailed discussion of some of the technical issues of implementation are covered in Chapter 7.

CONVERT

One of the potential hurdles to rapid implementations is the time that it takes to convert data from existing systems into databases for the new system. The data conversion challenges are in five areas:

1. Mapping
2. Cleanup
3. Loading
4. Verification
5. Synchronization

Mapping is the process of examining the information required in the new system and determining where each piece of data will come from. This is complicated by the fact that the new system will have literally thousands of data items in its database but only a subset of these are required fields. Therefore, a first step is to determine which fields will have to be populated before going live on the new system.

The fields that will be required depend on the transactions included in the scope of the implementation phase. If certain processes or transactions are dropped from scope, there may be less data to convert. However, if new transactions are added midway through the project, it may be necessary to plan for additional data requirements.

In a traditional multiyear implementation this is less of a problem. The implementation team would go through a formal design process and produce a system design that would then be frozen as configuration and testing were begun. However, in a rapid implementation a lot of these activities happen in parallel and require close communication and coordination between team members.

Much of the data for the new system will come from existing systems. However, it is common to find certain items of data that are needed that do not even exist in the legacy systems. As a result, some of the data will have to be created for use in the new system. Data creation is a task better delegated to the eventual system users than the project team members. However, it needs to be managed as part of the overall project.

While most of the data to be converted will come from legacy systems, it is not uncommon to find some of this data in manual systems and other ancillary storage areas. Some key organization data is in an Access database or Excel spreadsheet on someone's desktop computer. Just finding out where the information comes from to support the current processes is sometimes a challenge. Often the same data is stored in multiple places, for example, in the legacy system and in an Excel spreadsheet. When this happens, the team needs to determine which source has the most accurate and complete data.

This mapping activity is an ongoing task throughout the implementation project and requires close coordination between the IS personnel who know the record layouts in the legacy systems and the process analysts who are determining which parts of the standard package will be implemented.

Once the data is found, the real work begins. Data integrity is often a big problem that requires a large number of people to be involved in cleanup activities. Data integrity problems are not caused by the implementation project; but they become more visible during a system implementation and must be resolved before the data is loaded into the new system. The old saying "garbage in, garbage out" still applies.

The old systems often have data that is redundant, inaccurate, inconsistent, and incomplete. There are many examples of the symptoms: the same customers or vendors are listed multiple times in the legacy system files with different spellings and numbers. The materials and quantities in bills of materials are often wrong, resulting in invalid inventory valuation and workarounds to produce goods on the shop floor. The balances in subsidiary files do not reconcile with the control totals in the general ledger. Thousands of items appear in the inventory files that have not been produced or sold any time in the last 10 years.

Not all the data in the old system has to be converted to the new system. In a rapid implementation the team often uses various techniques (e.g., ABC analysis, 80/20 rule) to determine what really needs to be converted to be able to run the new system. Some data can be created post-go-live to support specific transactions as they occur. The implementation team should convert only what is really required.

Usually, people using the legacy systems clean up the data in these systems before data conversion programs are run to transfer this information to the new system. In situations where new data is created, this new data can be captured in Access or other databases for automatic conversion at a later time. Consequently, cleanup can be done in parallel with other implementation activities. This also means cleanup activities can start early in the project. There are often surprises in this area. Therefore, the team wants to identify problems as early as possible, while there is still time to resolve them.

Data gets loaded into the new production databases through three primary means. Most of the packages have data-conversion utilities that read external files that have been organized in a prescribed format and load the data into the production databases. In addition, the programmers from the IS department may code custom programs to load the new data directly into the production files. Finally, it is often necessary to load some of the data manually, using the input screens of the new system. In all three methods the data should be subject to the same edit and validation checks that would occur if the data were loaded through regular system processes.

Once the data has been loaded into the system, someone needs to verify that the data was transferred accurately and completely. This task is usually considered standard procedure for financial data but it is just as important for operational data. Various methods are used to verify the validity of the conversion activities.

Integrity checks include looking at the total number of records in each of the tables before and after the conversion runs, calculating control totals for numerical fields, and performing spot checks of all the fields in a sample of the records that were converted. It is best to do some of these specific checks using the screens in the application to make sure that the new system can read the data as stored.

The data-conversion procedures and tools should be tested as early as possible — perhaps as early as transactions testing. Transactions testing uses small quantities of data. Some of this data could be made available using data-conversion routines.

The data-conversion process for the production database should be tested as one of the first steps in integration testing, in the Prepare activity. The team cannot afford to discover a few weeks before going live that they do not have all the data needed for the new system, or any way to get data out of the old system. One of a project manager's responsibilities in rapid implementations is to anticipate and manage the project so there are no surprises. Data integrity and conversion is an area that must be monitored and managed carefully or else it may jeopardize the implementation schedule.

Some of the data may be converted ahead of the go-live date because often there is not enough time or resources to do all the conversions at once. Because some of the data is more static than other data, there are alternative strategies that can be used for doing data conversion, including early conversion and synchronization. For example, the team can convert the customer file and inventory master file weeks before cutover as long as a control process is put in place to ensure that any customers or items added to the legacy systems are also added to the new production databases. In addition, any modifications to records in the legacy systems already converted also have to be done in both systems.

Some files and items with a lot of activity (e.g., open orders) have to be converted right before the go-live date. Therefore, these items are often converted on the weekend before transition to the new system, while processing is frozen on the old system.

PREPARE

By the time the team gets to this activity, they are finally able to see the light at the end of the tunnel. They have done a lot of work throughout the project to get ready for the final push to go-live. How well they prepare for the cutover to the new system in the final weeks of the project will often determine whether the light they see is daylight or an approaching train. A lot of good work can be put at risk by sloppy work right before go-live. The team needs a smooth transition to the new system.

There are several key tasks that take place in the final four to six weeks of a rapid implementation before beginning operation with the new system:

- Integration testing
- End-user training
- Preparing the production environment
- Data conversion
- Establishing ongoing support capabilities

The team did transaction or unit testing in the Analyze-Configure-Test loop. Therefore, they know that the system is set up so that individual transactions work. Now is time to test the business processes end-to-end.

Extending the earlier manufacturing example, for order fulfillment the team tests the entire process from preparing a quote, converting it into an order, reserving inventory, generating a production order, issuing materials to production, recording completed production and scrap, shipping the order, preparing an invoice, recognizing revenue and the corresponding receivable from the customer, and applying the payment received.

Depending on the implementation scope, there may be 2 to 10 processes to test for completeness and integration in this activity. For example, after testing the fulfillment transactions the team may next test the financial close process or payroll processing. Then they may turn to production scheduling or procurement.

Integration testing takes time because of the number of different processes to thoroughly test and the number of steps in each process. It requires a cross-functional team to verify the effects throughout the system. Like transaction testing, it requires preparation of a test plan, test data, and expected results. And, like any testing activity, integration testing will uncover errors that need to be researched, fixed (perhaps by table or parameter changes), and then retested.

Managing the testing process is challenging because of the number of people involved, the complexity of the tests that address integration across the entire system, and the need for strict configuration and version control. Integration testing, as well as the other activities in Prepare, occurs at the end of the project as budgets and time are running out. This is an area of the project where there is a lot of pressure to take shortcuts and not follow a thorough test plan. These pressures must be resisted. No one benefits from having a system go into production that does not work properly.

Some members of the implementation team can complete the preparation of end-user training materials while others conduct the integration tests. However, hands-on training should not occur until the system correctly processes transactions. The team will lose a lot of credibility and create anxiety throughout the organization if the new system does not work properly in the training sessions.

End-user training should leverage the user procedures and system documentation that have been developed by the team. These are the aids the users should refer to as they perform their jobs; so, they should be introduced and used in the training courses. These procedures walk the users through the steps for doing their jobs with the new system. Using this approach, training becomes a simulation of real transaction processing using the job aids and a new system.

Depending on the number of users to be trained and the number of times each training session must be offered, it is not unusual for end-user training to take two to four weeks. Users may receive from several days to a week of training on the details of how to do their work using the new system. All users should begin their training with a system overview that includes practice navigating around the package.

End-user training cannot be scheduled too early in the project or people will forget what they learned before they get to apply it. However, if it is started too late, there will not be enough time to do sufficient training. Since end users still have their regular jobs to do while attending training on the new system, scheduling the training to meet project and job demands is a complicated administrative task.

Providing training of high quality is important to ensure people feel confident that they know how to do their jobs with the new system. It is an investment in the organization's people and a prerequisite to achieving the benefits from the system.

Training also provides an opportunity to sell the new system to the users. Therefore, it is a key change management tool.

While integration testing and end-user training are going on, the IS department is working hard to finish setting up the production environment for the new system. In some cases, this requires purchasing and installing new hardware to handle the large number of users and high volume of transactions that will be processed daily after cutover. In other cases, the new system will run on the existing technical infrastructure. In either case, it is necessary to stress-test the system to ensure that it can handle the production load.

Another time-consuming task for IS team members is setting up security authorizations for all the users of the new system. Users should have access to all the parts of the system required to do their jobs, but only to those for which they are authorized. This task goes quicker if it is possible to create role profiles that define authorizations for a particular job. These profiles can then be cloned to develop access lists for all the users doing the same tasks. The internal audit department should be actively involved in this activity and all others involving internal control considerations.

By the time the team has reached these last weeks of the project, all data-conversion procedures and tools should have been thoroughly tested. As the team approaches go-live, it must run the data-conversion procedures and programs to populate the production databases. Throughout this process, audit trails are produced to provide information to research problems and document the conversion results.

Error reports are produced throughout the conversion process. These reports show what information was not accepted by the new system. There are a number of reasons for posting failures. The file sizes on the new system may have been set too small. In addition, some of the data may not have been of the quality required by the new system. This converted data should be put through the same edits and validations that occur during normal transaction processing on the system. If the legacy data cleanup efforts were not completed in time, follow-up activities will have to be scheduled to clear data exceptions and complete the data-conversion process.

Finally, before go-live, the team needs to activate help desk and systems support functions to help users and managers with problems once they start processing on the new system. The project team members will be around for a short period after go-live to assist in this effort. But a permanent function should be established for the ongoing support and maintenance of the system.

This support function may include a help desk, support resources in the IS department, and power users in functional departments who can answer questions and resolve problems people will have in the production environment. Knowledge transfer to this support group should take place throughout the project. Often, some of the team members take on support roles after the implementation project is finished.

GO-LIVE

Go-live is a hectic and confusing time. People have been trained on the new system but now they have to use it in their daily jobs. Often, they find out that they did not understand how to use the new system as well as they thought. The organization has real customer orders coming in and needs to keep customers happy and ship goods on time—even as it works through the inevitable problems that will occur in the transition to any new system.

The organization should expect problems for a period of time following the cutover. This time period varies from a few days to a few months, depending on the situation. In spite of all the preparation and contingency planning that was done, problems will occur. Systems are developed by and used by human beings who, despite the best of intentions, make errors. So things will happen that were not expected and tasks will be done differently than planned.

The limited scope of a rapid implementation may help to minimize the amount of disruption that occurs. However, the organization has had less time to get ready for the new system with a rapid approach. Experience from a large number of package implementations has shown that all organizations should expect a performance dip immediately following the cutover to the new system.

People need a lot of support in the days immediately after beginning to use a new system. Help desk personnel will be available to provide support. However, during the first weeks after go-live, there need to be additional resources assigned to diagnose and solve problems that surface. The project team members provide a lot of this additional support. They often engage in triage activities to identify the biggest problems and ensure that adequate priorities and resources are available to solve them.

During this time people will be tempted to fall back to their old ways of doing things. Therefore, one of the key post-go-live tasks is to remove the old systems and tools and force the users to rely on the new system. This may mean removing access to legacy systems, Excel spreadsheets, and other applications running on the LAN or individual workstations. Management and the project team need to enforce use of the new system.

Some people may try to sabotage the new system and its processes. They may believe that if the new way fails, management will go back to the old way of doing things. Again, these activities and this attitude should be nipped in the bud. Management should show its support and commitment to the new system. This requires visibility and communication in the key days after processing has begun with the new system.

A key, and often missed, opportunity during the final days of the implementation is to capture the lessons learned from the project. The organization should be trying to develop expertise in making rapid changes to business processes and the technologies that support them. If they want the next rapid implementation project to be better, the organization should learn from the mistakes and successes of its prior projects.

A postmortem should take a realistic looks at the project while the information is fresh in people's minds. What went well and should be reproduced in the next rapid implementation project? What did not and therefore requires a different approach in future projects? Given 20/20 hindsight, what could the project sponsor, project manager, and the team have done differently? These items should be discussed in detail, maybe with the same group that attended the kickoff meeting. This could be considered a project close meeting.

This meeting should be followed by a celebration dinner or event for the project. Participating in a rapid implementation project requires a lot of hard work and places a lot of stress on all the project team members. If the project was successful, you can bet that a lot of people made a lot of sacrifices to make that happen.

What the team has accomplished is important to the organization and should be recognized and rewarded as such. Top management should make its support and appreciation for these efforts visible to the team and the rest of the organization. This is especially important if they want others to sign up for these projects in the future.

After the project is completed, management should make good on any commitments made to the team members before the project began. And immediately following the celebration, planning should begin for the next rapid implementation project. No organization is ever finished adapting its processes and systems to changing business requirements.

IMPROVE

In order to do rapid implementations, trade-offs must be made. The benefits from a rapid implementation approach do not come without costs. The assumption is that before management chose a rapid implementation approach for the system that just went live, they deemed the trade-offs acceptable. These trade-offs result from several characteristics required to make this approach successful:

- Time boxing
- Aggressive scope management
- Package-driven process design
- No customizations

As will be discussed in more detail in Chapter 4, many of the activities in a rapid implementation project are time boxed. This means that the team does the best they can on specific activities—within some pretty strict time and resources constraints. Priority was given to making business process and system changes in a short period of time rather than necessarily dotting all the i's and crossing all the t's. These projects are done rapidly in order to accelerate the benefits and change business processes to respond to significant, often short-term business needs.

However, taking this approach does not mean that there is not a case for going back and enhancing the work that was done, at some later time. Examples of things that may be done in the future include preparing additional procedures for handling exception situations, implementing additional processes, and developing and delivering additional training in areas where people are having problems.

The scope of the rapid implementation project is aggressively managed. The 80/20 rule is the guideline for establishing priorities. The implementation team tries to identify and implement the 20 percent of the business processes and systems functionality that provide 80 percent of the benefits. That is the right thing to do if the organization wants to maximize the return on the implementation investment. But again, there may be merit in implementing some of the remaining 80 percent of functionality in a future project.

What additional functionality should be implemented may not be clear at this point in the system life cycle. Sometimes it is best to require the users to make do with the system they have before deciding what additional functionality is *really* required. A good example is making them use the standard reports from the package for a period of time before deciding that customized reports are needed. The fact is that users will be in a better position to determine priorities for future enhancements to a system once they have experience working with the processes that were implemented.

One of the design guidelines for rapid implementation is that it is better to have the organization change its business processes to conform to the way that is supported by the package than to change the package. It is very expensive (time and money) to make modifications to the vendor's software to support the current way that processes are performed. Even worse, these programming changes will have to be reapplied and tested every time the organization implements newer versions of the vendor's package.

Many organizations have some pretty bad business processes that users want to replicate in any new system. Also, if the organization does the same process three different ways in its three locations, managers and users want all three alternatives supported by the software. So, there are good reasons not to automatically implement the existing practices with the new software.

Many best practices are incorporated in the design of the standard packages. These practices leverage the benefits of real-time, integrated systems with enhanced functionality that was often never available in an organization's legacy systems. Also, there are a lot of benefits from standardizing processes within an organization (i.e., deciding on the best way to do things and having everyone do it that way, without exception). Therefore, in many cases, conforming to the way the package does things is a good strategy.

A rapid implementation strategy generally does not support modification of the vendor's code. The project team uses the plain-vanilla version of the vendor's software and then tailors the package to the needs of the organization through the use of parameter tables and reporting tools.

However, there are going to be situations where there is a good reason to add bolt-on functionality to do things not supported by the package. Bolt-on functionality is interfaced to the vendor's system and usually does not involve modifying the vendor's code.

This new functionality may be provided by another vendor's package or may be custom-developed by the organization's IS department, with or without the assistance of consultants. As long as there is a valid business case for these enhancements, there is nothing in the rapid implementation approach that says that these changes cannot be made in a future implementation phase. However, before jumping into these changes, the organization should give the system, as implemented, a chance. Often, after spending some time using the new system, the users will come up with ways to handle difficult requirements using the existing capabilities of the package.

A key message from the roadmap is that the initial rapid implementation project is the first phase in the life cycle of the new system. The organization and its customers and suppliers will be constantly changing. Business strategies, models, processes, and organizational structure will change. Therefore, the system will have to continuously change to meet these changing requirements.

Consequently, there will be many opportunities to change and improve the system that has been implemented. The organization should establish a process to identify and prioritize these changes and, when appropriate, begin the Commit activity all over again.

3

SELECTING THE RIGHT PACKAGE

Picking the right package to enable business process improvements is an important decision for an organization. There are hundreds of vendors that will tell you their package is the best one for your situation. From their claims, it seems that all packages are e-enabled, proven products that can be implemented in days or weeks.

To sort out these claims, organizations perform projects to evaluate and select package software. Sometimes they select a point solution—a package to provide best-of-breed functionality for one or a few business process. In other situations they select an integrated suite of modules to support a large number of processes. Most organizations end up with application architectures that are a combination of integrated and point solutions. These solutions are connected together through a network of interfaces—some provided by the vendors and some developed as part of implementation projects.

A best-of-breed selection might compare e-procurement packages from a number of vendors (e.g., Ariba, Commerce One)—applications with electronic catalogs, shopping carts, and auctioning functionality. These applications can be integrated with purchasing and inventory management systems to provide an end-to-end procurement solution.

An example of an integrated suite selection could be choosing between version 11i of Oracles' applications suite—which includes back-office, CRM, and e-procurement capabilities—and a proposal from J. D. Edwards that includes the JDE OneWorld Xe application suite used in conjunction with Siebel's CRM tools and Ariba for e-procurement. The Oracle option provides integrated modules from one vendor. J. D. Edwards, however, has chosen to preintegrate its applications with those from certain best-of-breed vendors to provide a total solution.

One of the challenges, in either of these situations, is sorting out fact from marketing pitch. This leads to two questions:

1. How does an organization select the right package—one that meets its immediate and long-term needs, can be continuously changed to meet changing business requirements, and can be rapidly implemented?

2. Since many of the benefits of doing a rapid implementation are lost if the organization takes nine months to a year to do a selection, how does an organization do a rapid selection project?

GENERAL PACKAGE CHARACTERISTICS

This chapter will focus on a process for defining organizationally specific selection criteria and requirements that will be used to drive the selection. However, there are some general characteristics of packages that can be rapidly implemented that also need to be considered.

Package Must Fit the Organization

A rapid implementation often requires the organization to change the way processes are done to fit the way the package does things. This will be much easier if the package design is a close fit with the culture and practices of the organization.

Although it may seem like a stretch to think in these terms, each package has its own personality—its own way of looking at how business processes are conducted. Will the processes be performed in a formal, rigid, disciplined manner or is there a lot of flexibility in how a process can be completed using the system? Is the system forgiving of errors (can they be easily detected and corrected) or does it require users to get things right the first time? Does the language used in the package match the terms common to the organization or its industry? Organizations should look for packages that are a good match with how they want to do things.

Package Must Provide Industry Functionality

A rapid implementation requires a plain-vanilla implementation of the package. This means that the team will use the parameter tables in the package to *tailor* the system to meet the needs of the organization. However, the team will not *modify* the vendor's source code or do custom programming to add functionality to the package. These modifications would require extensive design, coding, and testing, which would add substantial time to the project. In many cases these modifications are really not needed—there are often ways that the same process could be done using the capabilities of the package. But this no-modification constraint can create big problems if there are some basic functions or processes for the organization's industry that are not supported by the package.

Software vendors tend to focus on one or more specific industries and verticals within industries. For example, one vendor may focus on higher-education institutions, a second on hospitals. A third may focus not on manufacturers in general, but on the subset of process (e.g., chemical and pharmaceutical) manufacturers. A fourth may focus on engineer-to-order (e.g., aircraft) manufacturers. While there may be a lot of similarities in how these different industries use certain package modules (e.g., financial and human resource), there are often unique functional requirements for specific industries. Therefore, organizations often need to select from among those packages that support their particular industry.

Flexibility Is Needed To Support a Changing Business Environment

Business requirements will change. The system that gets implemented today may meet current business requirements but will not necessarily meet the requirements for tomorrow. Therefore, the package must support a number of ways to perform different business processes. And it should be easy to change the way the package works after the initial rapid implementation project.

Configuration parameters, code tables, and reports should be easy to modify, with no significant ramifications. Tools should come with the package to change screens and reports without invalidating the maintenance agreement for the software. It should not be difficult to add new cost centers, partner relationships, or intracompany organizational structures. The packages must be able to adapt to new business models and processes.

Interoperability with Other Systems Is Becoming Increasingly Important

It must be relatively easy to integrate the package with other systems. In a rapid implementation, it is often necessary to develop interfaces between the package being implemented and legacy systems or other vendors' packages. Some packages have well-designed application programming interfaces (APIs) that make this task of sharing data and processes between the systems easier. Other systems seemed to be designed to work only as part of the vendor's complete suite of packages. Interfacing these modules to other systems is time-consuming, difficult, and risky.

This need for interoperability is increasing. Despite the obvious advantages of using fully integrated suites of applications, organizations will continue to select best-of-breed packages, especially in the areas of e-business, customer relationship management, advanced planning and scheduling, and business intelligence. Also, organizations may need custom-developed applications in special areas to provide competitive advantages. Even if an organization uses packages from only one vendor, it may still need to share information with customers and suppliers who have packages from other vendors.

In response to these requirements, package vendors are starting to *preintegrate* their packages with those of best-of-breed vendors. In other words, the vendors have already developed the interfaces between the packages. In addition, there is a whole category of software becoming available to help different packages talk to each other. Enterprise application interface (EAI) vendors provide these middleware tools. Finally, the vendors are developing capabilities for various applications to communicate with each other over the Internet using the eXtensible Markup Language (XML) data format.

Hosting Must Be Available for the Package

There are going to be situations where organizations will decide to outsource the processing of their applications so they can focus on their core competencies. In some situations the internal IS organization may not be able to provide a development or production environment in the times required to support a rapid implementation. If the package is available from several proven applications system providers (ASPs), then a number of options will be available to the organization and the implementation team.

Implementation Support Must Be Available

The learning curve is too steep for today's complex packages for an organization to do its first rapid implementation on a new package without help. Whether the help comes from the package vendor, systems integrators, or ASP providers, the organization will need the advice and assistance of people who have implemented the package before. The organization may need to augment the project team with those who have process redesign expertise, configuration experience, technical support skills, or rapid implementation methodologies. A rapid implementation project cannot afford to spin its wheels or go down too many wrong paths if it is to finish on time.

Package Must Be Complete, Stable, and Have Good Support

There are enough challenges in a rapid implementation without having to debug error-prone software at the same time. It should not be a surprise to anyone that vendors sometimes release software that is not ready for commercial use. There are tremendous market pressures to match the announcements and functionality of competitor products. Sometimes all the functions required to perform processes are not available in a release. Or there may be a lot of design and programming bugs that cause the package to not work as documented. The system may even frequently crash while processing basic transactions.

Each of these problems will take a lot of time to research and solve, even with the full support of vendor personnel. There is just not enough time to implement a system and find and fix all the bugs on a rapid implementation schedule.

It would be naïve to assume there are any application packages on the market that are bug-free. They all have things that do not work as designed. But the number of bugs is relative. With proven software that has been in use for six months to a year by similar organizations, the customer should expect that the vendor's support personnel should be able to provide code fixes in a matter of days or weeks. Anything beyond that timeframe puts a rapid implementation at risk.

Industry-Specific Preconfigured Version of the Package Should Exist

The implementation team needs to have a working system that is a relatively good fit with the process requirements of the organization as a starting point for a rapid implementation. Then they can make configuration changes to tailor the system to the unique needs of the organization. There is not time to start configuration from scratch. The team needs to rely on the fact that a workable system will be available as a starting point.

Implementation Accelerators Should Be Available

There are a lot of deliverables produced during an implementation project. These include things like training materials, user procedures, help text, data-conversion utilities, process models, detailed workplans, presentations, and checklists. The vendor or consultant should provide templates or samples of many of these items so the implementation team does not have to produce these from scratch. These templates help the team complete many of the tasks in the timeframes required for a rapid implementation.

VENDOR CRITERIA

In a software selection project the organization is selecting two things: a software package that will be used to enable process changes and improvements, and a business partner the organization can depend on to support and enhance the product in the future. There are a lot of things that must be evaluated during the selection process. Most of the items in the second category are considered under the area of *vendor criteria.*

It is important to understand the product development strategy and performance of the vendor. What is its vision and strategy for enhancing the product over the next two or three years? What new modules are being developed? What new technologies is the vendor using? How many people and how much money does it spend on research and development (R&D) each year to implement these changes? What industry verticals does it focus on? What specific functionality is being developed to meet the unique needs of those industries? How often will the vendor come out with new releases of the product and what has been its history in meeting these developmental schedules? How effective has it been in the past in implementing its strategies and visions?

Of course, none of these other things matter if the vendor will not be around two years from now. Therefore, the selection team needs to also evaluate the financial stability of the vendor. There will be a lot of consolidation in the e-business and ERP software marketplace during the next three years. Many of the vendors in this space will go out of business or be merged with or acquired by other organizations. Organizations want to partner with vendors who will be around for the long run.

Therefore, the team should look at things like revenue growth, profitability, and the number of employees. They should also examine how the vendor's stock price has been doing and the stability of its top management group. They should consider other products supported by the vendor. Some of these other products may be more attractive in the marketplace and, therefore, get major portions of the vendor's development investment. Most of the major software vendors went public in the late 1990s, so a lot of this information is now readily available.

In addition, the organization should be interested in the level of support that the vendor can provide. This support exists in many forms:

- The vendor should provide help desk support to answer questions and respond to system errors. Second- and third-level support personnel should be able to research and fix programming errors accurately and quickly.

- The vendor should have easy-to-understand technical and user documentation. This documentation should be available in hardcopy, CD, and online help text formats. Tools should be available to convert this documentation into end-user procedures.

- The vendor should provide templates and other accelerator tools to facilitate the rapid implementation of its package.

- Tailorable process models should show the processes supported by the package and the flow of screens to process transactions.

- The vendor or its partners should provide application-hosting services.

- The vendor should provide just-in-time computer-based training in addition to the normal off-site and on-site instructor-led sessions.

- The vendor should have good data-conversion tools that include edit, validation, and audit trail capabilities.

- The vendor should provide tools to help manage and document configuration activities, showing what decisions have been made and for what reasons.

- The vendor should also provide implementation assistance in the form of technical, package functionality, quality assurance, and project management services. It should provide this assistance itself or through a network of implementation partners.

There are also some intangibles with regard to the vendor and its personnel that factor into a package selection. During the selection project, how easy has it been to work with vendor personnel? Have they been good to follow the scripts developed by the selection team and did they incorporate organizational data in their demos? Were they prepared? Is there a close fit between the two organizations' cultures and good chemistry between the vendor's representatives and those of the organization? Did the vendor have well-qualified people working with the selection team? How flexible is the vendor in contract negotiations? Did they provide information in a timely manner? Were there a lot of surprises from the vendor (e.g., hidden costs for components necessary to implement the package that were not included in the initial bid) throughout the selection and contract negotiation process?

It may seem like the organization expects a lot from the software vendor. That is true. Organizations often spend millions of dollars to purchase and implement these systems. So they have a right to be demanding. The truth is that most of the vendors in the marketplace are not able to meet these high standards. Therefore, organizations must be careful whom they include on the long and short list of candidates.

SELECTION APPROACHES

Selecting the right vendor and package is an important decision. In effect, an organization is outsourcing application development and picking a business partner, one that will be relied on to continuously provide additional application capabilities and functionality to meet changing business needs. Also, the organization is depending on the vendor to track and take advantage of new technologies as they become viable. The choice of package might even determine whether a rapid implementation approach is even possible.

Purchasing and implementing most application packages is very expensive. It is a significant investment for most organizations and should be treated as such. However, this investment is often justified by the benefits that will result from the implementation. But the organization must choose the right package.

FIGURE 3-1   Package Selection Methodology

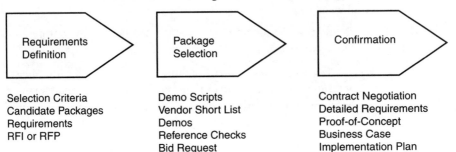

Figure 3-1 shows the major stages in a software selection project and the key deliverables that are produced in each stage. In the past, selection projects have often taken 3 to 4 months to complete. Some organizations have taken as long as a year or more to choose new software. These timeframes are no longer acceptable in a rapidly changing business environment. An objective, in the age of the Internet clock, is to find ways to make selections faster than is possible with traditional approaches, while still making a good choice.

There are three primary approaches for selecting application packages: (1) detailed requirements, (2) key requirements, and (3) proof-of-concept. Each has its advantages and disadvantages and is appropriate in certain situations.

DETAILED REQUIREMENTS APPROACH

The detailed requirements approach is probably the most familiar one. This approach starts by researching the universe of possible packages that may meet the needs of the organization. The objective is to identify a long list (10 to 20) of package vendors to receive a request for information (RFI) document.

The RFI is used to provide the selection team with comparable information on each of the packages and to get information not available from other sources. Some organizations get carried away with the number of vendors to consider. There have been selection projects where the selection team started out by identifying over 50 packages to be evaluated. This creates a large number of vendor responses to be analyzed.

While the team waits for the responses to the RFI (many of the vendors will not respond or will not respond in a timely manner), the selection team does a comprehensive review of the capabilities of the current systems and the as-is process environment. In particular, they are looking for problems that people have with the current systems and gathering information on things that the users and managers would like to see in a new system.

On some selection projects, the team develops detailed process diagrams or flowcharts of the as-is environment. This is done to better understand the existing processes and their strengths, weaknesses, and requirements. Developing these diagrams can take a lot of time. However, this information can be useful in describing the system requirements to the vendors, preparing the demonstration scripts, and communicating within the implementation team.

The next step is to develop a detailed list of functional and technical requirements for the new system. This list will include all the functions and features for the system that surfaced during interviews with users and managers and analysis of the current systems and processes. These detailed requirements are prioritized and put into categories such as mandatory, desirable, and optional. This list of requirements can be extensive. It is not uncommon for the list of requirements to go 50 to 60 pages in length.

The selection team sends this list of requirements to the vendors in the form of a formal request for proposal (RFP). The number receiving the RFP is usually smaller than those receiving the RFI since some of the vendors will not have responded to the RFI or will have been eliminated from further consideration because of information in their responses.

There are two typical responses by vendors upon receiving a detailed RFP. Some of the vendors will not respond to such documents. Either they cannot do so in the timeframe required, or they consider the odds of being selected too low to make it worthwhile to respond, because of the large number of vendors receiving the RFP. If 10 vendors receive the RFP, and each knows their product does not have any specific functionality to improve its chance for selection, then the odds of any specific vendor being selected are considered low.

In other cases, vendors respond to the RFP with "Yes" answers to each of the requirements, whether they have these capabilities or not. The rationale is that surely there is some way to satisfy each of the requirements with their system, at least with some manual workarounds. Or the vendors answer "Yes" because they know that their competitors will also answer "Yes" to each of these questions.

In these situations, the vendors know that none of the packages actually do all the things in the RFP; but they are not going to be the only honest responder who gets eliminated from further consideration for giving a "No" answer to a mandatory requirement. Therefore, they do what is necessary to stay in the game and depend on the demo process to sort out what the packages can and cannot do.

Of course, the willingness of the vendors to respond to an RFP depends on the size of the customer organization (and therefore the potential revenue and commission on the sale), the visibility of the customer (sales to companies like Microsoft, Dell, or Cisco still are valued for their references), and the number of leads that the sales staff is currently chasing. Given the slowdown in sales for ERP software following the

Y2K tidal wave, it may be easier to get the vendors to respond now, especially if the organization is looking for e-business modules.

When using the detailed requirements selection process, the organization will often conduct formal bidders' conferences to answer questions that the vendors have after reading the RFP. These meetings also allow the vendors to better understand the customer organization and ask questions that may affect their bids. These bidder conferences are often mandated in selection projects for public sector institutions.

Another key task for the selection team is to develop the detailed selection criteria and weighting of each item. Sometimes the selection criteria and weightings are documented in the RFP. The high-level selection criteria consists of things like functional fit, cost, technical fit, long-term financial viability of the vendor, vendor training and support capabilities, breadth of other package offerings from the vendor, reliability of the software, references from other organizations using the software, availability of implementers for the package, and the ability of the users group to influence additional functionality in future releases. What varies significantly from project to project is the prioritization and weighting of the various selection criteria and the level of detail in the requirements.

When the RFP responses are received from the vendors, the selection team does a detailed mapping of the responses against the selection criteria and then develops a numerical score to represent the overall fit for each package. This analysis may result in the elimination of some of the vendors from further consideration. However, often the team will find the total scores to be very close after going through this detailed scoring process. Therefore, the team uses product demonstrations to gather additional information and develop support for the various packages.

In the demonstrations the vendors are asked to prove to the selection team that their products meet the requirements that have been identified. However, limits have to be placed on the duration of the demos. Often one to three days is allowed for each package. In this amount of time the vendors are often able to cover just the mandatory requirements and some of the desired ones.

Based on the numerical scoring from the RFP responses, evaluations from the demonstrations, and additional information from reference checks with other organizations using the packages being considered, the selection team then decides which package best meets the requirements of the organization. Usually this recommendation is documented in a selection report that describes the selection process and the results of the selection activities. The recommendation is then turned over to management for approval and contract negotiation with the preferred vendor.

A detailed requirements selection is sometimes required because of internal policies, laws, or regulations that require a formal RFP to be issued. In addition, components of this approach may be needed for selections in new applications areas where the requirements and vendors are not well known. However, generally this approach takes too long when a rapid selection and implementation is required.

KEY REQUIREMENTS APPROACH

The key requirements approach takes a more streamlined path toward making a package recommendation. It falls somewhere between the detailed requirements and the proof-of-concept approaches. The selection team is still trying to decide between several alternative products. But they rapidly get to a short list of vendors. The team also makes a more focused attempt to determine the true discriminators that will drive the selection.

For the traditional modules (e.g., financial, distribution, manufacturing, human resources), proven vendors all have products with a full set of functions and features. Long gone are the days when the selection team would have to determine whether a vendor's general ledger module can handle recurring journal entries, or whether the accounts payable package can do a three-way match among the purchase order, receiving report, and vendor's invoice, or whether the manufacturing system can do a real-time bill-of-materials explosion. In these traditional functional areas, the major vendors all have packages that support most of the detailed functions equally well.

The objective of the key requirements approach is to identify the things that the packages do not all do equally well and the impact that these differences have on the ability to address the key problems and opportunities the organization is facing. These differences should drive the selection of one package over another. And they sometimes get hidden when the selection team spends a lot of time evaluating the detailed functions that all packages do equally well.

The challenge with this approach is that people who have not worked with these packages before have a hard time determining which functions are in the common group and which ones are in the group of items that not all the packages do well. That knowledge comes only with experience and investigation.

There are two ways to determine what functions are normal for these packages and which ones are special. One way is to use experienced consultants to help with the selection. If they have done a number of selections and implemented several of the leading packages, they will have a good feel for what functionality is supported by the various packages.

The other way is to use a software package database that has recorded the "Yes" and "No" responses to the hundreds of detailed questions. The selection team can then focus on a subset of these functions: those that did not have "Yes" answers from all the vendors.

In a key requirements selection, the majority of time is spent developing business scenarios or scripts that must be followed in the package demonstrations. Instead of seeing a little of everything the package can do in the two or three days of demos, the selection team focuses this time on the things the packages do not do equally well and those that are particularly important to the organization.

In this approach, the selection team prioritizes the business processes and determines the problems and opportunities that must be addressed by the package. Then they develop business-oriented scripts to show what functions are needed to solve key business problems or take advantage of opportunities. The number of these scripts must be kept low in order to really see how the software supports these critical business processes. Often there will be no more than 8 to 10 scripts.

The key requirements from the business scripts are included in the selection criteria for the packages. Using information from an RFI, or other sources, it is usually easy to go from a list of 8 to 10 candidate packages down to a short list of two to four packages. The vendors on this short list should be given the demo scripts and time to prepare a demonstration of how their packages can handle the details of these scenarios.

Often, organization-specific data is included in the scripts so that the people viewing the demo can better relate to the processes. The vendors often need two or three weeks to prepare their systems (e.g., adding data, changing configuration parameters) for the demonstrations. The selection team should make every effort to assist the vendors in their preparations—answering questions and providing additional information as requested.

Under this selection approach the team assumes that any of the vendors on the short list have good products that could meet the majority of the organization's needs. The demo scripts are used to differentiate between the vendors in order to select the one that best fits the needs of the organization. The demo scripts focus on the differences that matter.

Care must be taken to manage the demo process. The vendors must follow the scripts and show whether they can support the business scenarios that have been defined as key to the organization. At times it will be necessary to have the vendor slow down or repeat parts of the demo, so the team can be sure they understand what they have seen demonstrated. Also, the demos should be controlled so the vendor does not go off on tangents to show parts of the system that may be attractive but are unrelated to the key selection requirements.

In addition, it must be clear at all times whether the vanilla package is being demonstrated or whether the vendor is using functions in a third-party package to complete the script. Additional costs and issues around the viability of the third-party vendor come into play if a mix of products is being used in the demonstration.

Once the preferred package has been selected, the team can then do the due diligence work to ensure that there are no big surprises in the other parts of the application. The team has made assumptions on the overall functionality of the products in using this selection approach. These assumptions can be confirmed for the chosen product before contracts are signed. However, the advantage of this approach is that these normal features of the packages do not have to be checked for 8 to 10 vendors and have not diluted analysis of the real differences between the packages.

PROOF-OF-CONCEPT APPROACH

The proof-of-concept approach to software selection is often the fastest of the three approaches. That is because this approach is used when an organization believes that it already knows which package is the right choice—it just needs to confirm this selection before signing the contract with the vendor and starting the implementation.

There may be several reasons why the organization already has identified the preferred package. Sometimes the organization knows that the leaders within an industry have all selected and implemented the same package because the package has unique functionality that supports the industry well. An example might be the large number of big chemical and process manufacturing companies that have implemented SAP's R/3 product because of the robust functionality that it provides the process industry. Another example might be the choice of Siebel as a best-of-breed customer relationship management (CRM) package for a large, complex organization.

In these situations, as long as the costs and benefits are in line, the company probably is safe in picking these packages without evaluating other candidates or going through a full selection project. However, these organizations are still not in a position to begin the implementation project. There are benefits from a selection project that are still of value even in these situations. Therefore, it is wise for an organization to go through the proof-of-concept activities before beginning an implementation.

One of the benefits of a selection project is the identification of the requirements for the new system and the gaps between those requirements and what the package supports. The requirements were identified through interviews with top management, supervisors, and users of the current systems; development and analysis of process diagrams; discussions about system scope, selection criteria, and priorities among processes; evaluation of the technical architectures required to support the packages; and a lot of informal discussions between the team members—who represented the major functions within the organization.

Gaps were identified by analyzing the responses to requests for information, in the demos (when the vendor could not meet all the requirements of the demo script), and in reviews of detail requirements checklists after a preliminary selection was made. This gap analysis is useful in planning for the implementation because it may identify the need for third-party products to supplement the package selected or the need to develop interfaces to legacy systems to provide missing functionality.

These gaps may also impact what processes are included in the scope of the initial rapid implementation. In certain situations the vendor may offer the missing functionality in a future release of its product. In these cases, it may be best to defer implementation work in that area until the new release is available.

There are other important benefits from doing a selection project. A selection project provides an opportunity to build excitement and commitment for the selected package. The reference checks and site visits have allowed users to talk to their counterparts who have gone through the implementation process and can offer advice on which parts of the system to use and which parts to avoid. Lessons learned are frequently passed on during these discussions. Often, the business case for the package is developed during the selection project. This document serves as a valuable guide during the implementation and is useful in creating a sense of urgency and support for the project.

Another consideration is the issue of leverage with the vendor during contract negotiations. As long as the vendor knows that two or three packages are in the running, the vendor tends to use a sharp pencil to come in with a competitive bid. What leverage does the organization have negotiating a contract when the vendor knows that the selection has already been made and there is no competition?

Finally, the selection project provides the organization with an opportunity to begin climbing the learning curve for the new package. The team learns a lot about the package during the selection project. They discovered the scope of the various modules, what preconfigured versions are available, what training is provided by the vendor, what is the typical implementation team structure, and what technical environment needs to be supported by the IS department.

The proof-of-concept approach tries to achieve most of these benefits while focusing on only one package. The work is primarily done through a conference room pilot. The vendor provides access to the software application—perhaps to four or five workstations in a conference room—on a preliminary basis while contract negotiations are ongoing. The team develops detailed demo scripts to test how well the package meets the requirements of the organization. Instead of demos of one to three days duration (as was the case during a selection), the team may take four to six weeks to develop and go through these detailed scripts in the conference room pilot.

The team performing the pilot consists of representatives from the organization, the software vendor, and the systems integrator who will assist with the implementation. Obviously, the vendor and consulting personnel must do most of the configuration to test the business scenarios. Key users are brought in to assist in the pilot as their areas are addressed. Management is brought in for key demonstrations of the new system and shown how it will address critical organizational issues.

The end result of such a proof-of-concept approach is a very good understanding of the package, the requirements, the gaps, and the process that will be used to implement the system, and some leverage with the vendor during contract negotiations. Therefore, the team can achieve many of the benefits that they would have received through full-blown selection activities. In addition, the conference room pilot activities are very similar to analysis and design tasks that typically go on during an implementation. As a result, the organization will be in a good position, probably better than it would have been at the end of a normal selection project, to jump-start the implementation.

SELECTING THE RIGHT APPROACH

A number of factors will determine which approach should be used for a particular selection. One is the expectations of the selection team members and management. Some organizations expect to go through a long, formal, detailed process before selecting a package that may cost millions of dollars to implement. Other organizations want to do a quick-and-dirty selection among a small group of good alternatives and then get on to the implementation. Among this second group are those that believe that *how* a package is implemented is more important than spending a lot of time finding the perfect package.

The best approach also depends on the experience and knowledge of the selection team members. One of the reasons to use consultants on these projects is to help the team quickly get to a short list of vendors for detailed evaluation. When an organization performs selections on its own it often has to start with a longer list of candidate packages. Then it may take a lot of time and effort to get to the same short list of vendors that the consultant could have helped the company get to in a fraction of the time.

The complexity of the requirements also dictates the approach. If an organization is picking a package to support an e-marketplace, the functional and technical requirements are more complex than those for picking an accounts payable package.

A final factor to consider in choosing an approach is the availability of documentation, references, and implementation experience with the packages being considered. This is not a big concern with financial, human resource, or ERP packages. However, it may be an issue with many of the newer CRM, advanced planning and scheduling, and e-business applications. Many of these packages have only recently become available. Therefore, there are a lot of unknowns about their capabilities and implementation challenges.

In the past, organizations primarily conducted detailed requirements selections. In an environment with a lot of unknowns, that was probably the right approach. There are now situations where all three approaches are appropriate.

The key requirements approach works well when selecting an integrated suite of modules. Implicit in the key requirements approach are several assumptions:

- There are several packages that will meet 80 to 90 percent of the organization's requirements but no package that will meet more than 95 percent of these requirements.

- There are no more than six to eight leaders in any package market and it is easy to determine who they are.

- An organization should go with one of the leading packages. There are good reasons why they are the leaders.

- There will be a great deal of consolidation in the package software industry in the next few years. Going with the leaders gives the organization the best chance of picking a business partner who will be around in five years.

- The leading vendors leapfrog each other in functions and capabilities as they come out with new releases.

These assumptions hold true in the ERP space where the modules (e.g., financial, distribution, manufacturing, human resources) and functions are relatively consistent across the vendors. Also, in this space most of the vendors have been developing packaged software for 20 years or more. Not all of the assumptions hold true in the CRM, SCM, e-procurement, and e-business package markets.

For example, if an organization were looking today for integrated modules to cover the traditional package areas or a best-of-breed package for finance or human resources, there is a high probability that it could find a proven package to meet its needs by looking no further than J. D. Edwards, Oracle, SAP, PeopleSoft, Lawson, and QAD. However, if the same organization were looking for a CRM system, it might be extremely difficult to come up with a list of six proven packages that the organization could be confident would meet its needs and be supported five years from now.

There are lots of risks and potential surprises with the newer package modules (e.g., CRM, e-procurement, e-business). Therefore, if an organization is selecting a point solution in one of these areas it may be best to use a detailed requirement or proof-of-concept selection approach. The choice between these two approaches depends on the urgency of the selection and implementation projects. If there are no time constraints, the detailed selection approach provides advantages in these selections.

In areas like web-based exchanges, e-storefronts, and e-procurement, the selection team might not even know all the required functions. There are usually no legacy systems that can be used as a reference for these applications. In addition, the vendors are often new companies and most of the implementations of these packages are relatively recent. The organization will not be dealing with established software vendors and a mature software market.

In these situations, the selection team will not have the same sense of confidence that all the packages do the same things well. Therefore, the selection team may be forced to go back to detail function lists and RFIs to find out what the market has to offer and which vendors are good short-list candidates.

If time is of the essence, the selection team should go with one of the acknowledged market leaders in the category and conduct a proof-of-concept selection. The advantage is that the organization may quickly become comfortable that the package will meet its needs. In addition, the information gained and deliverables produced from the conference room pilot can be used during implementation.

GETTING TO A SHORT LIST OF PACKAGES

There are a lot of packages that could be considered and evaluated during an application selection. In fact there are literally hundreds of packages for most of the process and functional areas. However, there is not enough time to look at all these packages in detail before making a decision. (Some organizations seem to take this approach under the guise of completeness and thoroughness.) Somehow the selection team must do enough preliminary research to get down to a reasonably short list of packages and vendors to be evaluated in detail. In most cases, the short list should include no more than two to four packages.

There are a number of ways to gather information on the group of vendors under initial consideration. These methods include reviewing the results of selection projects from other organizations, using package selection databases, reviewing literature on various packages, reviewing reports from research organizations such as Gartner and Meta, visiting vendor web sites, issuing RFPs or RFIs, finding out what packages are used by similar organizations, and getting input from consultants who will assist in the selection project. Information gathered from all these sources must be summarized in a format arranged around the selection criteria. Then the team can start eliminating some of the vendors from further consideration and get to a short list of packages.

In some cases vendors will not respond to inquiries for information and may eliminate themselves from further consideration. This can be a good or bad thing. It is a good thing if the vendor did not respond because it knew that its product did not have required functionality or was weak in several selection criteria areas. It is a bad thing if the vendor did not respond because it did not have time and was busy chasing other opportunities.

A vendor will be eliminated at this stage for a number of reasons:

- It may not have integrated modules in all the required areas.
- Its future viability as an organization may be questionable (e.g., it is losing money and has little revenue growth in the last two years).
- The package may not run on the operating system and database that have been selected by the organization.
- The vendor may not have a focus in the organization's industry, and some of the basic, unique functionality needed is not available.
- The vendor's software may not be Internet-enabled or use state-of-the-art technologies.
- The vendor may have a reputation for buggy software and lousy support.
- The CEO might have heard horror stories of implementation failures with a par-

ticular package from his or her cronies and, therefore, would never have that package in the organization.

- The vendor cannot provide references to prove that the software can be implemented rapidly.
- The vendor's representatives were unresponsive or rude to selection team members.
- There are already a number of candidates that seem much better suited for the organization.

The weight placed on each of these factors varies significantly from selection to selection. But experience has shown that after a reasonable amount of data gathering and analysis, the selection team starts to clearly see two or three leading candidates. If the team has done enough due diligence to feel relatively comfortable that any of these packages could meet most of the organization's requirements, then it is time to go on to the more detailed activities to determine the package that best meets the organization's needs.

It is a good idea for the team to document the short-list development approach and rationale. This can be used to get the appropriate buy-in and approval from the steering committee to move on to the next selection steps.

This documentation is also valuable when one of the functional managers goes to the steering committee to complain that the one package that perfectly meets the needs of that department has been unjustly dropped from further consideration. Or when a vendor contacts top management to tell them that the selection team was incompetent, did not understand the capabilities of its package, and has made a terrible decision in not including it in the short list. No one ever said that participating in these selections was without its little nuisances and political risks.

A key insight is that in-depth information on all the packages under consideration is often not required in order to get to a short list of vendors. The selection team can usually make a good decision on the short-list candidates from the information at the selection-criteria level. Therefore, it is often a waste of time to try to gather detailed information on all the vendors on the long list. The process for developing the short list of candidates and the final recommended solution is illustrated in Figure 3-2.

These comments are not meant to imply that the selection team is not concerned with the detail capabilities of the packages under consideration. Once they get to the short list, the selection team will look at capabilities in much more detail to determine the recommended package and to confirm that it is a good choice for the organization.

Where the selection criteria is to be quantitatively evaluated the selection team uses a four-step process:

FIGURE 3-2   Getting to the Short List and Recommended Package

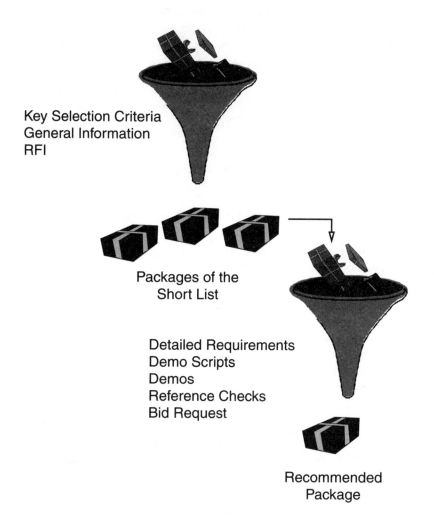

1. Decide on the various criteria that will be used in the selection. Place these criteria into categories.

2. Determine whether each of the selection items should be considered mandatory, desirable, or optional. Determine whether not having a satisfactory rating in a mandatory item should disqualify the package from further consideration.

3. Identify priorities by assigning weights to each of the selection categories.

4. Based on the vendor responses, assign points to each of the detailed selection areas and calculate the score for each candidate package.

The short list of vendors should include those that seem best suited to meet key requirements. It is a good idea to decide early how many vendors will make the short list. Too many on the list will result in a lot of wasted effort reviewing, in detail, packages that have little chance of being selected. Too few on the short list might mean that the organization will not give adequate consideration to a package that may ultimately be the best choice. As stated earlier, two to four vendors seems like a good number to be included on the short list.

DUE DILIGENCE

One of the keys to evaluating a package, using any of the three selection approaches, is to separate truth from fiction. The team needs to discover facts about the package that differ from the image the vendor portrays. Doing this work is part of the due diligence activities of a selection project.

The team should get a list of other organizations that have already implemented the package and contact them to gather additional information. Sometimes this step is done only for the preferred package. In other situations this reference checking is done for all the packages on the short list. If there was no clear winner after the demonstrations, these checks may provide information that sways the team toward or away from one of the packages.

The vendor should provide the selection team with a list of all companies in a similar situation (e.g., same industry, same size, same modules) who have already implemented the package. These customers can be called or visited to verify the vendor claims and serve as an additional source of product information. These reference checks also provide insights into implementation problems, challenges, and lessons learned.

This is an area that is often short-changed in the selection process—to the chagrin of organizations once they start implementing the selected package. Reference checking is a risk management requirement.

From its site visits and phone conversations, the selection team needs to determine what parts of the package the company implemented. How is the other organization using the system? What sort of team was required for the implementation? How long did the implementation take? What were some areas where the functionality of the system was less than anticipated? How flexible is the system and how easy is it to change configuration parameters? What were the technical requirements to get adequate response times from the system (in terms of hardware sizing and network bandwidths)?

The selection team also needs to find out what the other organization would have done differently if they could start their implementation over. What things were surprises? How do the users of the new system like it and how much training was required to get them up and going? How extensive were the software bugs and how responsive was the vendor in acknowledging that there were bugs and then providing software patches to fix them?

In most cases the vendor will provide references only for projects that went well. The selection team needs to find other customers whose implementations did not go as well. Information on failed implementations will not necessarily cause the package to be eliminated from further consideration. There are a lot of reasons for a failed implementation, many of which have little to do with package capabilities. The team searches for good and bad implementations to gather information so they can adequately understand the capabilities of the package and plan for the implementation.

Another activity in the due diligence stage of the project is to go back and review the detailed list of functions and responses that are available from commercial selection databases or from the consultants that are helping with the selection. Reviewing the list of all the detailed things that the package can and cannot do may not be required to get to a short list or determine the preferred vendor, but it is a task that can prevent some embarrassing surprises down the road.

Remember, the basic assumption was that all the good packages do most of the common things equally well. Based on that assumption, the team selects a package based on the most important and unique requirements of the organization. However, it is prudent to confirm that the selected package does do all the normal things that the team assumed it did. Going down the detailed list of vendor responses will give assurances that the assumption was valid. It could also point out routine functions that the package does not support. Then the question becomes one of deciding the importance of the missing pieces and possible workarounds to overcome these deficiencies.

A second due diligence approach is to send some of the key people on the selection and implementation team to vendor training. This training should be hands-on rather than presentation oriented. This training will let team members learn more about the recommended package and provides an opportunity to look at the vendor's training materials and documentation. Questions addressed to the instructors in the training can often clarify how the product performs certain functions that are required by the organization.

A review of training materials will also help in developing training plans for each of the implementation team members. Evaluating the coverage and ease of use of system documentation will provide some indication of how easy or difficult it will be to research package capabilities and options. Since these materials will be valuable in creating the procedure manuals and end-user training during the implementation, it is important to make sure the team knows what is available.

The final due diligence activity might be a mini- or full-blown conference room pilot. The need for this activity will be determined, to a large extent, by the uncertainty that still exists about the ability of the package to meet the organization's needs without modification. The results from this proof-of-concept work will either be confidence that the package meets the requirements or a better understanding of the issues that will have to be addressed in the implementation. In some cases the findings may cause the selection team to reevaluate the initial selection and choose one of the other packages on the short list.

SELECTION TEAM MEMBERS

One of the first decisions in planning the selection project will be deciding on the organization of the selection team. Who should participate and what should their roles be during the selection? What time requirements will be imposed on them during the selection?

Selection of a package for rapid implementation is best done as a project with formal objectives and a defined timetable, not as an ad-hoc activity. Using a focused project approach, selections with dedicated project teams can be done in one or two months. Selections done more informally may take much longer to complete.

The project team is usually composed of a mix of full-time core team members and other part-time participants. The overall team needs to include people with a variety of skills, representing the major parts of the organization: management, key business functions, the IS organization, and key users of the system that will eventually be implemented.

There are several roles that an individual could play on the selection project. Some people play more than one of these roles. The key roles are project sponsor, steering committee member, project manager, consultants, functional representative, key users, and information technology specialist.

The project sponsor is a member from top management who is the champion for the selection project. The sponsor will often act as the chair of the selection steering committee. This person should not be from the IT function. Selection is primarily a business project, with technical implications. The sponsor needs to take an enterprise view of the selection, ensuring that the best interests of the organization overall are addressed. In this role the person must sometimes guide the project around potential conflicts that result from power struggles between areas represented on the selection team.

The project sponsor must help remove barriers and resolve problems during the selection process. This person must be empowered to make quick decisions to keep the project on a rapid course. However, the organization must remember that rapid does not mean of lower quality. Depending on what modules are eventually included within the scope, this sponsor may or may not become the sponsor of the initial implementation project.

The steering committee is usually composed of key managers in each of the functional areas impacted by the system being selected. For an enterprise system selection an organization may have vice presidents from finance, marketing, manufacturing, engineering, human resources, information technology, and distribution on the steering committee. This committee usually meets two or three times during the selection process and will ultimately approve the recommendations of the selection team.

The project manager manages the selection project. This responsibility includes ensuring that there is adequate involvement from the people designated as selection team members. The project manager makes sure that project tasks get completed on time and in a quality manner. The project manager acts as the primary liaison with consultants assisting in the selection and vendors demonstrating their products. This person should be a well-respected manager in the organization and is often a prime candidate to continue as the project manager of the first rapid implementation project. Having the same person manage both projects provides continuity between the selection and implementation projects and facilitates rapid transition between these two projects. The project manager is usually assigned full time to the selection project.

Consultants are often used in the selection project because they have three things that often are not available from the organization's own resources:

1. They have a methodology for doing selections (along with associated task descriptions and deliverable examples) and experience doing these projects.

2. They have knowledge of the key vendors and their products and can help an organization quickly get to a short list of potential vendors.

3. They often have people in their organization who have hands-on experience implementing all the major packages and can provide insights on the strengths and weaknesses of the packages—information that will not be freely offered by the vendors.

This implementation experience will also be useful in planning the implementation of the package and estimating the implementation costs. In most cases, it will be difficult to do a rapid selection without consulting assistance.

Each of the key departments or functions affected by the new system will usually provide a person to participate as a core selection team member. These are the working representatives of each of the executives on the steering committee. These people should be very familiar with the business processes of the organization and will represent their areas in developing high-level process models, identifying system requirements and selection criteria, developing demo scenarios and scripts, evaluating the packages from the various vendors, and selling the team recommendations throughout the organization.

These people must be team players who take care of their constituencies while considering the best interests of the overall organization. Some of these representatives may become full-time project members on the initial implementation team.

Although not part of the core selection team, there is a role for other people in the organization. The functional representatives will not know everything about how work is done throughout the organization. The key users in the various functional areas will fill in many of the holes by providing information to the selection team, helping to develop some of the project deliverables, and even observing the demos of the short-listed packages. Their involvement is important because they have knowledge, insights, ideas, and experiences that will be important to the selection.

Adequate involvement of the key users of the new system is also important in beginning the change management process and selling the benefits of the new system to the real users of these systems. They need to be and feel part of the selection process.

Finally, we need to include representatives from the IS organization on the team. They will assist in identifying the technical selection requirements and evaluating the technical capabilities of the various vendor products. Ultimately, they will be responsible for installing the software on the organization's systems. As such, they may have to acquire and implement new hardware, systems software, and communication capabilities to support the production environment of the new system. In some cases the package selected will require the IS organization to learn new technologies that are used in the vendor's technical architecture.

During a selection, most of the team members will not be assigned full time to the project. Often they will spend two or three days a week on selection activities. The project manager and several of the core team members may be assigned full time. In addition, all of the team members may be involved full time during the vendor demo process that may take one or two weeks depending on the number of vendors on the short list and the number of detailed demo scripts that need to be followed.

Overall, a rapid selection for an enterprisewide solution for a midsize organization can usually be completed in 8 to 10 weeks. If the organization is looking for a more limited-function package (e.g., a general ledger system, online storefront packages, e-procurement software), then the selection can often be accomplished in two to six weeks.

FAST SELECTION PROJECT REQUIREMENTS

This chapter has covered a number of approaches to package selection and various issues involved with running these projects. This last section provides a final look at what is required to perform these selection projects rapidly.

What does it take to speed up the selection process in order to select a package in 2 to 10 weeks rather than 2 to 10 months? The following things not only make the selection project go quicker, but will result in the selection of a better package for the organization:

- *A core selection team representing the major functions of the organization focusing significant time on the selection.* This cross-functional team will have the information to quickly prioritize the business processes, identify the major problems and opportunities facing the organization, and see the advantages and disadvantages of the capabilities of each package.
- *A process to quickly get to a short list* of the two to four vendors who will be around for the long term and whose products meet the needs of the organization.
- *Empowerment of the selection team to make quick decisions.* There is no time in a rapid selection to get the review and approval of top management for each decision that is made.
- *No requirement to do a formal business case.* It can take 4 to 6 weeks to prepare a formal business case.
- *A key requirements or proof-of-concept approach to the selection.* A detailed requirements approach takes longer to do.
- *Vendors that commit to be responsive to the needs of the selection process* and are working with the selection team during the entire selection process.
- *The development of focused demo scripts.* These scripts provide the team with information on things that should differentiate the offerings of the various vendors.
- *Performing selection tasks in parallel.* There are a lot of activities that can go on simultaneously in a selection, such as doing reference checks and site visits while waiting on the vendors to prepare for the demos.
- *Commitment to a team decision process.* Each selection team member must agree to discuss (and challenge) the pros and cons of the various alternatives during the project and, once a decision is made, to support the decision as if the entire team made it unanimously.
- *Goals and objectives for the new system.* The team needs a clear vision of what the new system is going to accomplish for the organization once it is implemented. What is the business imperative that created the need for package selection and implementation?
- *Use of process modeling.* The use of high-level process models helps the team quickly identify priority processes and those that are in and out of scope. They also facilitate communication within the team and with the vendors.
- *Selection accelerators.* There are a number of things that can accelerate the selection process. These include things like research reports on the various packages, predefined process models for the organization's industry, functional

checklists, and templates for demo scripts. Included in this category would be anything that can jump-start project activities so the team does not have to start from scratch.

- *Consulting assistance.* If the organization is using consultants to assist in the selection process, the team should leverage the knowledge and experience of the consulting organization to quickly get to a short list of vendors, manage the selection process, challenge information from the vendors, and better estimate the total implementation costs of the packages. However, the selection must be made by the organization and not by the consultants.

Selecting the right software package is a prerequisite for rapid implementation. The wrong package takes longer to implement and may not meet the business needs of the organization in the short or long term. Taking a long time to select a package negates some of the benefits of the rapid implementation approach. An organization needs rapid selection and implementation of the right package to respond quickly to business changes.

4

MANAGING A RAPID IMPLEMENTATION

It takes outstanding project management skills to be able to rapidly implement a complex system. Therefore, this is not a good project for a first-time project manager. Managing projects is different from managing a workgroup or a department. Consequently, project management takes skills, tools, and approaches that are new or unfamiliar to many managers.

Since people often get assigned responsibility for managing these projects without the requisite experience or training, they frequently need help. This help can come from someone within the organization who has prior experience managing this type of project. Or, if this is the first such project for the organization, help can come from a manager from the package vendor or systems integrator assisting with the project.

Usually several people have project management roles on these implementations. For example, in addition to the project managers, there can be several process team leaders and someone who leads the technical team. Ultimately, one person must have the responsibility for managing the overall project. Who this individual is should be clear to the steering committee and the team.

The job of the project manager is to plan, manage, and control the resources of the project in an effective and efficient way so that the objectives of the project are achieved. On a rapid implementation that is a big task.

This chapter will discuss the following tools and techniques that are important in managing a rapid implementation:

- Business case

- Project workplan

- Status reports

- Scope management
- Time boxing
- 80/20 management
- Templates and deliverables
- Risk management
- Issues tracking and resolution
- Knowledge management

Many of these tools and techniques are useful in managing other types of projects, including traditional package implementation projects. However, they take on increased importance and a somewhat different spin when used to manage a rapid implementation.

Many managers know about these techniques but very few use them consistently and effectively. A project manager might be able to get away with not doing all these things well on a long project, but not on a rapid implementation. Excellent project management execution is a key requirement for rapid implementation.

Now we take a look at each of the components of successful project management.

BUSINESS CASE

Organizations have a variety of reasons for implementing new business applications and investing in information technology. They also have expectations about the benefits that will be achieved and the returns they will get on these investments. Unfortunately, these reasons and expectations are often not well defined or understood. Different people often have dissimilar viewpoints on what will be accomplished. This is especially problematic when the key managers affected by a new system have different expectations.

Some of the typical goals and objectives of these projects include: reducing operational costs, improving productivity, standardizing business processes, providing better information for decision making, reducing cycle times, providing better customer service, reducing headcount, transforming the organization into an e-business, adding functionality to better manage the supply chain and business relationships, adopting the same system as the parent organization, and taking advantage of new technologies. Achieving these goals requires a combination of business process, organizational, and technology changes.

The dilemma is that no implementation project can achieve all of these objectives. There are trade-offs between some of the objectives; several are in direct conflict with others. Therefore, the project needs to focus on those objectives that provide the highest ratio of benefits to costs. This is especially important for a rapid implementation where the scope must be limited. Given the challenges of these projects, the goals and objectives should be examined to determine whether they are feasible with a rapid implementation approach.

Some organizations have policies that require the preparation of detailed business cases to justify all capital investments. In these organizations, IT investments are treated like any other investment. There must be quantifiable benefits associated with the investment. The benefits not only must be identified and quantified, but the timing of the benefits stream is factored into the calculation of internal rates of return (IRR) and payback periods.

In the most demanding situations, individual managers must sign up to achieve each of the benefits. In these cases, achievement of these benefits is often tied to the person's annual goals, performance assessment, and compensation.

A detailed business case also carefully calculates investment costs. In the case of a package implementation, the total costs might include: additional hardware and network costs; the purchase price of the packaged software; annual maintenance fees for the software; the salaries for organizational members on the project team; vendor training costs for the project team members; systems integrator and consulting costs; the cost to set up and equip the project war room; and the cost of using the services of an application service provider (ASP).

Once the benefits have been quantified and the costs itemized, it is relatively easy to calculate the payback periods and IRR. Some organizations also consider intangible benefits and project risks in the investment decision; others make decisions only on quantifiable factors.

Many of the benefits from an investment in packaged software are intangible, and therefore, difficult to quantify. Even if they are not factored into the financial analysis of the investment, they should be at least documented. These intangible factors include: better information to make decisions; systems that are flexible and will be easier to modify to meet changing business requirements; automation of routine tasks to give knowledge workers more time for analysis and the higher-level tasks; access to future functionality and capabilities from the vendor, especially in the area of e-business; better system documentation; and capabilities to provide improved customer service.

In contrast to those organizations that require a formal business case for investments, some organizations make these decisions for a number of other, sometimes arbitrary, reasons. For example, the organization's legacy systems may be getting old and difficult to maintain. The organization may have Y2K and other event-based problems that can only be addressed in time by installing packaged software (a big justification in 1999). The organization may respond to the fact that all its competitors are migrating to SAP or PeopleSoft applications and they are stuck with less functionally rich systems. Management may decide that all the organization's systems need to be Internet-enabled. Sometimes, in these situations, the expectations for the new system are not even put in writing.

In addition to the capital allocation reasons for developing business cases, experience has shown that those organizations that develop a detailed business case in advance have a higher percentage of successful implementations. Therefore, having a business case seems advantageous to the project manager and the implementation team. It is not hard to figure out why this is true.

A business case provides focus and direction for the project. It is much easier to manage a project if you know where you are going. The business case tells what the organization is trying to achieve with the project and defines the benefits that should result from its completion. A clear understanding of the goals and objectives of the project helps team members make the hundreds and thousands of decisions on these projects. All decisions and alternatives can be evaluated based on whether they support, prevent, or are neutral in achieving the project's objectives.

The decision on which tasks to include in the project workplan can also be made using the business case as a sounding board. It has been previously stated that there is little time for non-value-adding tasks in a rapid implementation project. However, how can the team tell if a task adds value? One approach is to ask the following question for each task: Does doing this activity help the organization achieve the goals and objectives established in the business case? If the answer is no, why is the team doing it?

The business case provides other benefits for the project. It demonstrates to management that there are valid business reasons or imperatives for doing the project. This helps get their attention and support. It helps project leaders manage scope. Those processes and transactions that support the business case are in—all others are out.

The business case guides team members to those processes where they should focus the limited time available in a rapid implementation for process redesign. It also provides a standard and metric for determining whether the project was successful. Finally, it gets the attention, involvement, and support of those managers who have signed up (or been signed up) to achieve the specific cost savings or revenue enhancements that should result from the project.

In the past, it was often difficult to cost justify implementation projects. This hurdle often resulted from the fact that these projects tended to deal with back-office processes that never affected the customer. Today, the e-business and CRM applications provide much greater opportunities to impact the revenue line of the organization and customer satisfaction. This makes them easier to defend from a value-added perspective.

If the project manager does not have a business case to work with, a proxy needs to be created. At a minimum, through discussions with the sponsor, steering committee, and participants in the software selection process, the project manager can gather information to document the high-level goals and objectives for the project in the form of a project charter. Once these goals and objectives have been reviewed and approved, the team has a high-level business case to guide the project.

The project charter may, in some cases, be different from the business case. It may take several rapid implementation projects to achieve all the benefits defined in the business case for the overall investment in a new application system. In this situation, a project charter needs to be established for each project to define its specific goals and objectives.

PROJECT WORKPLAN

The project workplan is a key tool for planning and managing a rapid implementation project. It is used to determine all the tasks that must occur during the project, estimate how long they will take, allocate the project resources, assign responsibilities to individuals, identify the deliverables to be produced during the project, determine the status of the project, and estimate the effects of changes to any of the project variables.

The workplan is a living document. It loses its effectiveness if it is not revised to reflect the realities of the project. It also is used at different levels of detail during the project. The workplan is developed at a greater level of detail for activities that will occur in the next month. It is kept at a higher level for activities that occur later in the project. There is little value in doing a lot of detailed planning for tasks that occur further in the project since, in all probability, the plans for those tasks will have changed by the time the team gets to them.

One use of the workplan is to list all of the tasks that occur in the implementation. What are all the things that have to be done to implement the packaged software and achieve the benefits defined for the project? A lot of the tasks are common sense: the vendor's software should be installed on a server; the team should determine the business requirements for the system and configure the package to meet these requirements; the system should be tested; users need to be trained; and data needs to be converted.

However, at a detail level there are literally thousands of tasks that have to take place during an implementation. Some of these tasks can occur only after another task is completed; many can occur in parallel. The challenge to the project manager is threefold. First, ensure that nothing falls through the cracks, that all the tasks that need to be done are completed and in a quality manner. Second, the project manager should eliminate all non-value-adding tasks from the workplan. Third, the team needs to do as many things as possible in parallel and minimize the number of tasks on the critical path.

This second responsibility is critical to a rapid implementation. Every hour and day worked on the project is valuable. The mantra for the project team should be: *Our time is valuable and cannot be wasted!* The project manager and the team members should challenge the value of each task to see whether it moves the project toward achieving the benefits defined in the project charter.

Project planning occurs at two levels. The high-level, *overall* plan is developed during the Commit and Start activities of the project. *Detail* plans are developed as each of the project activities is begun. For example, although a testing strategy and a training strategy are developed in the Start stage, the detail plans for user training and integration testing will not be created until the beginning of Prepare activities.

The next step, after identifying all the required and value-adding tasks, is to assign responsibility for completion of the tasks to members of the core implementation team. Individual responsibility should be established for each task. There is not time during a rapid implementation for several people to watch another person complete a task. This often happens when groups of people are assigned to jointly accomplish a task.

Having individual task responsibility does not mean that several people will not provide input and assistance on the task (as long as they are getting their own tasks completed on time). It also does not mean that the team will not jump in and help any team member that falls behind schedule. It does mean that ultimately one person should be held accountable for each task; and this person should know that the project manager would be coming to him or her to check on the task status.

Individual accountability for tasks will also help the project manager quickly determine who is pulling his or her weight on the project and who is not. Team members who cannot pull their weight on a rapid implementation should receive coaching and guidance. However, if that does not turn the situation around quickly, they must be replaced.

Ideally, people should be assigned tasks they have the experience and skills to complete in a timely and high-quality manner. However, on a rapid implementation many team members will be doing some tasks for the first time. People will also be pulled into new areas as the project manager reallocates resources to keep those tasks that are on the critical path on schedule. Being assigned tasks outside a team member's comfort zone is not necessarily a bad thing. After all, being stretched—doing new and challenging things—is how team members grow and develop on these projects.

Some project managers assign time estimates to the tasks early in the planning process. Others wait until they assign resources to the tasks before developing the estimates. This second approach takes into account the fact that some people, especially with experience in a certain area, may be able to perform the task in half the time it would take someone else.

Once the time estimates have been established, along with a staffing schedule (showing vacations, holidays, and training sessions), the project manager can forecast when different activities of the project will be completed. However, this projection requires estimates of such variables as the number of processes that will be configured and tested and the number of training sessions that will be developed and delivered. If the results of these forecasts do not match the timeframe allowed for the project, the project manager needs to take appropriate action (e.g., reducing scope, adding resources, extending the timeline).

The tasks on the workplan should be defined so that each task should take no more than two days to complete. (We will discuss this in greater detail in the section on time boxing.) Assigning two-day-or-less tasks is a key factor in controlling these projects. These short deadlines provide focus and a sense of urgency for the project team members.

Associated with each task is a definition of the deliverable that must be completed to prove that the task is done. The task is done when the deliverable is finished and found acceptable. With short task durations and predefined deliverable templates, the task of keeping up with project status becomes relatively straightforward.

Using this task-sizing approach, and the rule that a task is either 0 percent or 100 percent complete, there should be no way for the project to get significantly off schedule without the project manager knowing. This is not the case for most traditional implementations where all tasks seem to be 90 percent complete (for weeks and months) and right before go-live management discovers that the project will be three months late.

When the team gets behind schedule, the workplan projections and resource allocations should be changed. Keeping the workplan up to date takes a lot of time and effort; but it is an essential task in tightly controlling these projects. A rapid implementation project must be well managed to have any chance for success.

The project manager must have an automated project management system, like Microsoft Project, to keep up with the project details. There is a learning curve with such a tool that must be quickly surmounted. However, the benefits of having such a tool outweigh the effort required to learn and maintain the planning system.

The project manager's responsibility for maintaining the project plan and databases should not be viewed as a non-value-adding administrative task. Obviously, if there are purely administrative aspects of this task, they should be leveraged wherever possible. However, in maintaining the project workplan, the project manager is not performing a clerical job. The project manager is doing the work necessary to gather and analyze information to measure the pulse of the project. The project manager is spending time with team members and reviewing deliverables before updating the system. Accurate and current information helps the project manager evaluate the project status and take actions early in order to keep the project on schedule.

The project manager will have close contact with the individual team members. This allows the project manager to personally evaluate their progress and the quality of the deliverables being produced. These reviews also provide coaching and teaching opportunities throughout the project.

STATUS REPORTS

The project team members and project managers prepare status reports periodically. These are communication tools. The team members' reports focus on the activities of each individual. They show what tasks have been completed or started since the last report and what problems are being encountered in completing the tasks.

The status reports prepared by the project manager are for the benefit of the executive sponsor and the steering committee. These reports focus on whether the project is on schedule, the activities completed in the last period, things that will be started in the next period, and issues that need to be brought to the attention of the project steering committee.

Some of the status reports are in writing; others are verbally presented. The ones put into writing are usually better thought out and reflect the true status of the project. The informal, verbal status reports often reflect the optimism of the participants rather than the true situation.

In a rapid implementation, the team should not spend a lot of time preparing status reports. They do not have to be fancy. They just need to communicate the true status of the project.

Measuring actual performance and comparing it with the standard that has been established for the project is the true way of determining project status. This standard is the project workplan. One benefit of this comparison is to identify where tasks have been skipped.

In some cases tasks fall through the cracks because different people or groups think someone else is doing the task. In other cases, especially when people get behind schedule, it is easy to rationalize that a task really does not have to be done. This is especially true at the end of a project when time and budgets are gone. In these situations it is common for teams to decide that all the testing and training that were originally planned are overkill and not really required.

The status reports also indicate where things are taking longer than expected. With this information, the project manager can determine the cause and take appropriate action.

Several things can cause a task to take longer than estimated:

- The original estimate may be bad.
- The person doing the task is just slow or fooling around instead of getting the work done.
- The person doing the task did not understand what really needed to be done and therefore took longer than planned.
- The team is waiting for a decision from someone outside the core group.
- The person did not spend as much time on project activities as was originally scheduled.

The project manager is responsible for keeping the project on track and removing barriers that get in the way of project success. Whenever the project manager reports a problem to the steering committee, it should always be accompanied by an analysis of the various alternatives that were considered and the plan to get the project back on track. In some cases the plan to get things back on track will require quick decisions by the steering committee or actions they must take to support the project.

The standard solution when the project begins to slip should not be just to have the team members work harder and longer to get back on schedule. Such an approach rarely solves the problems; it just mitigates the immediate symptoms. In cases where an individual or the team is getting behind schedule, there are several actions that can be taken to get things back on track:

- Assign additional resources to tasks that are behind schedule.

- Give additional training on how to perform more difficult tasks.

- Provide examples of completed deliverables or templates to communicate the work requirements and level of detail for the task. (Sometimes people get behind schedule because they spend too much time going to unnecessary levels of detail.)

- Reassign a task to someone who is faster or more experienced, and has better knowledge about how to do the task.

- Coach team members through their tasks, explaining what is done and why.

- Modify the project scope so the task is not required. (This may sound like heresy, but it is a valid approach when using a rapid implementation strategy. Remember, with this strategy, another rapid project will be starting soon after this one is completed. The missing tasks can often be added to the next project.)

- Bring in a specialist to augment the team and perform some of the tasks that are extremely complicated and require too steep a learning curve for the core team members.

- Allow team members who are ahead of schedule on the tasks they were assigned to help others complete their tasks.

- Have individuals or the team work a little overtime or some time on weekends until they get caught up. (This is only a short-term solution and should not be used longer than is required.)

- Reestimate the project because the project manager realizes that the original estimates were not good.

The climate on the project should be such that team members do not feel they have to hide the fact that they are behind schedule. The sooner schedule slippages are known, the more options are available for the individual and the project team. A key objective of status reporting is to prevent surprises. Teams do status checks to discover problems early so they can be addressed.

On many traditional implementations, a lot of time was spent calculating an estimate-to-complete for each task being worked on. This was the team member's best guess of how much time it would take to complete the task. These estimates usually proved to be unreliable.

People are just too optimistic in predicting how quickly tasks can be completed and reluctant to admit how far they are behind schedule. Besides, in more cases than not, the estimate-to-complete turned in was the original budget minus the time already spent on the task. These estimates did not reflect the true status. The use of shorter tasks and only three task states (i.e., not begun, in process, and 100 percent complete) is a better way of determining task status.

There are six questions that the steering committee wants answered in periodic status meetings:

1. Is the project on schedule?

2. Will it be completed on time and on budget?

3. What are the problems that may get in the way of completing things on time?

4. What is the team doing to get back on schedule?

5. How large are the risks that the corrective actions will not fix the problem?

6. What does the steering committee have to do to solve the problem or help get things back on schedule?

Status reporting is intended to provide comfort to management that things are going well, or, if not, to make problems visible so they can be addressed. Preparing these reports also helps the project manager. The work done to prepare status reports and answers to the predictable questions of the steering committee helps the project manager keep up with the project's progress and problems. For a rapid implementation, the project cannot be allowed to get significantly off course. Frequent checks of progress and small course corrections are therefore desirable.

In all this discussion of status and corrective action, we must not forget the importance of quality in these projects. It is extremely important that team members do quality work and produce quality deliverables. Tasks are in the workplan because they are required for project success and their completion adds value to the project. The quality standards for the project should never be lowered just because the project is behind schedule. Skimping on quality is no way to get the project back on schedule.

SCOPE MANAGEMENT

Managing scope is important for any project. Scope creep is one of the primary reasons that projects go over budget and do not get completed on time. However, scope management takes on critical importance for the success of a rapid implementation project. Rapid implementations are by nature limited-scope projects. They are projects where speed of implementation is more important than trying to implement all the valuable functions of the package. These projects will fail miserably without aggressive scope management.

In a rapid implementation, the organization is trying to implement the minimum set of processes required to solve critical problems or take advantage of business opportunities. Driven by the business case and the project goals and objectives established in the project charter, the team determines what parts of a package are required to achieve the goals and objectives and leaves other parts of the package to be implemented in future rapid implementation projects.

Scope expands naturally in a package implementation project for a number of reasons:

- The difficulty in defining detailed scope in the early stages of the project
- The kid-in-the-candy-store effect
- A lack of good communication within the project team
- Related process requirements
- Misunderstandings about the basic trade-offs in package implementation

Scope is usually not well defined at the start of a package implementation project. It is defined at the 30,000-foot level, while the implementation team must operate throughout the project at the 1-inch level.

After a package is selected, the organization may define the scope of the first implementation project as implementing the order-entry and financial modules. But each of these modules has hundreds of components. The order-entry module may be able to take orders over the Internet, through EDI transactions, from remote devices (e.g., PDAs, laptops, cellular phones), at a call center, or from workstations located throughout the organization. The financial modules include functions such as general ledger, budgeting, accounts payable, accounts receivable, cost accounting, fixed assets accounting, treasury management, and financial consolidation. Which of these capabilities must be implemented in the first rapid implementation project for these modules? And at what locations or organizational entities are they to be implemented?

There often are no specific answers to questions like these at the start of the project. However, that does not mean that people within the organization do not believe they know the answers. Often, their interpretation is based on strong opinion on the parts of the package that must be implemented to help their departments solve known problems.

Decisions on the detailed package functions to be implemented are therefore made during the project. Depending on the things that are included in or excluded from the project scope, one implementation project may implement twice the functions or business processes of another. However, they both might have started with the same budgets and timeframes.

In this scenario, one of the projects may be completed on time and deemed a success, while the other (where the people worked just as hard and smart) might be deemed a failure. Or both projects might be considered failures in the minds of sponsors and key users who expected more, or different, processes to be included in the scope of the implementation. Therefore, managing scope expectations is important in producing successful projects.

The kid-in-the-candy-store effect is understandable. The packages available today have capabilities to support ways of doing business that were unimaginable even a couple of years ago. For managers who have had to depend on old technologies and limited functionality in custom-developed legacy systems, the range of menu items and options available from the new packages can be mindboggling. Predictably, the reactions on seeing the capabilities of these packages can be: "I would like one process from module A and two from module B" or "We *have* to implement that function if my group is to meet budget next year" or "Getting that new feature is a mandatory requirement."

Each transaction and process included in the project scope requires time from the project team for analysis, documentation, configuration, testing, end-user training, and data conversion. Therefore, there is a significant cost to the organization, in terms of time and money, for each addition to scope.

There may be a valid case for including all the requested functions and features. However, if the scope is not limited in these projects, the organization will not get a rapid implementation. If all requested functions are included in the initial project, it may take two or three years before any parts of the system are in production. These large-scope projects will also require large project teams that are more difficult to manage. Suddenly we are back to the typical problems with the traditional implementation approach.

Communication problems also create scope issues. As stated earlier, the implementation team members will be making decisions that affect the scope of the system throughout the project. They do this as they define the transactions that will be supported in the current project. If the detailed scope decisions and issues are not communicated throughout the team, then individual team members may make decisions and commitments to user groups that affect the ability to finish the project on time.

There must be awareness throughout the organization of the importance of scope management. Everyone involved should understand that scope additions will be challenged and that all scope changes will be analyzed to determine their impact on the project. Scope issues, decisions, and impacts should be covered in team meetings, status reports, and project newsletters. A large part of scope management is communicating and managing expectations. Ultimately, all high-level scope decisions will be made by the steering committee.

The integrated nature of new systems provides great benefits to the organization and produces tremendous challenges for the implementation team. Transactions in one part of these systems have touch points throughout the other modules and processes. Entering an order can affect the inventory, manufacturing, distribution, and financial modules of a package.

Therefore, another source of scope creep is the requirement to implement other parts of the package, which were not planned for the initial implementation, in order to support a process that is in scope. An alternative to implementing more parts of the package is to develop additional interfaces to legacy and other systems. That is often not an attractive alternative.

Often these module interdependencies are surprises. They are not well understood until the team has received the vendor training and learns more about how the package works. Frequently they are not discovered until testing. How they are addressed will have dramatic effects on the schedule for the project.

The final problem for scope management is the fact that management and the key users of the system do not understand the basic trade-offs in implementing these systems. There are fundamental and unalterable relationships between the scope, resources, and time for a project. (In many cases the timetable and cost for the project are directly related.) These are shown in Figure 4-1. Varying any one of the components of this relationship requires changes in the other two.

As a result of these relationships, if the organization wants to increase the scope of a project then it will increase either the time required to complete the implementation or the resources (people) assigned to the project. Saying that the team will just have to work a little harder and longer each day is not an acceptable answer to this dilemma.

FIGURE 4-1   Fundamental Project Trade-Offs

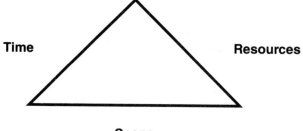

Time   Resources

Scope

In spite of these fundamental relationships, the shape of this triangle does change with another variable: project management (PM). Most implementation projects are not managed very well. As a result of not doing the things that are covered in this chapter very well, organizations get less (scope) for their time and resource investments.

This situation is depicted in Figure 4-2. This figure shows that, for the same time and resource investment, more will be accomplished in a well-managed project. Therefore, the level of project management determines the basic shape of the relationship triangle. However, after the shape of the triangle is determined, the same relationships and trade-offs among scope, time, and resources apply. The point is that outstanding project management can get more out of a project with the same time and resource constraints.

There are several tools that can be used to help manage scope creep. These include process models depicting subprocesses in and out of scope, detailed transaction lists of those transactions in scope, and lists of transactions or subprocesses that will need to be addressed in future rapid implementation projects or phases. However, the most effective tool for managing scope is the eternal vigilance of the team. The team must challenge all transactions to determine whether they are required to meet the project objectives. They should also carefully analyze the impact on the project of accepting scope that does not meet this standard.

In a rapid implementation, the final scope will be fixed right before the team begins the Prepare activity. In the activities up to that point, scope and expectations are managed as the team determines what can actually be delivered within the timeframe and staffing defined for the project. Keeping the detail scope flexible until later in the project is a major difference between rapid and other implementation approaches.

This scope flexibility has its benefits. As a result of this approach, the organization gets parts of the system live more quickly, starts receiving benefits and solving business problems earlier, and has a process in place to immediately begin other rapid implementation projects to add additional functionality and processes. This approach also results in implementing only those functions and features that are necessary to

FIGURE 4-2   Project Management Effect

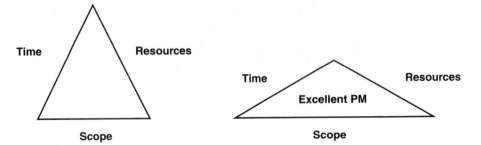

meet the goals and objectives of the project. It is the most efficient and effective way to get returns on the investment in new technologies and applications.

TIME BOXING

Time boxing is an extremely important management technique in rapid implementations. Essentially, team members are given a certain number of hours or days to finish a task, and that is all the time they are expected to spend on it. They do the best job they can within those time constraints and then move on to the next task. This concept can be applied at the task, activity, or project level in a rapid implementation. There are many places in these projects where it is an excellent technique; there are some where it should not be used.

There are several things that make time boxing effective. Time boxing creates a sense of urgency for each task and focuses the attention of the team on quickly completing each one. It is consistent with the 80/20 rule that will be discussed in the next section. It counters the attitude that "we know we are behind schedule but we can make the time up later in the project." And, finally, it counters the common attitude in these projects that, no matter what the estimates may be, things will take as long as they take to complete.

The truth is that a lot of time is wasted in the early and middle parts of package implementation projects. The cause is often the lack of a sense of urgency to get things done as quickly as possible and within the project estimates. People do not work as efficiently as they could. This is a killer situation for a rapid implementation where "everyone's time is valuable" and there is no slack in the schedule.

A project manager must face the fact that most people are, by nature, procrastinators. If something is due by a certain date, they will usually wait to the last minute to start it and then race to complete it on time. If they believe that completing things on time is not really important, then the last-minute push may not even occur.

In addition, people are generally overly generous in the assessment of their progress on tasks and how long it will take to finish what they have been working on. That is why tasks stay 95 percent complete for weeks at a time and a common response is "I only need a few more hours (or days) to wrap up the loose ends." Team members often believe these statements or make them without actually analyzing the amount of work that is left.

The longer the timeframe and the further apart the milestones in a project, the harder it is to create a sense of urgency. If a team is on a three-year project, there is a natural tendency for team members to feel the need to pace themselves. Why push hard early in the project (working overtime or weekends) to complete each task on time when there is still six months before the deliverable for the phase is due?

If team members have six weeks to finish a task, it is normal to find that their level of effort will not be even throughout that time period. Inevitably, people work at a comfortable pace for the first five weeks, and then at a frantic pace for the last week to finish the task on time.

Time boxing helps create a sense of urgency every day someone works on a task. A team member may be given a week to design, develop, and review a training module, or two days to configure a certain part of the system, or two weeks to define the security authorization for the production system (broken down into six segments of work, each of two days or less duration). That is all the time that will be allocated to these tasks because the next week the person will be assigned something else, also with a finite timeframe.

Each team member will be *done* with a task, by definition, when the time runs out. These frequent, short-term, finite task deadlines will create a strong sense of urgency and focus on the assigned tasks. Team members know they must complete individual tasks and deliverables that are final and subject to review by others on the team each week.

The sense of urgency is maintained only if the team members know that exceptions will not be made and that they should not expect to have their time extended if they are not done. If the deliverable for a task is incomplete or unacceptable, someone else on the project team should be assigned to finish it or clean it up. This should not be viewed as a good thing by the team since there will be limited resources available to finish other people's tasks. The more experienced team members will do this cleanup work. But they also have their own tasks to complete.

Fortunately, the deliverables from a time-boxed task are usually acceptable. The 80/20 rule applies here as in most other aspects of life. If there is a sense of urgency and focus on the task at hand, most of the value from a task will be produced in the first 20 percent of the time allocated. Therefore, whether we give a person two days or four days to complete a task, the end result is often nearly the same. Of course, with an additional two days the deliverable can be cleaned up, made to look prettier, and some additional content added. But for a rapid implementation these are often luxuries that cannot be afforded. Rapid implementation is lean and mean and focused on content rather than form.

The role of the project manager in monitoring project status was covered earlier. However, what historically happens if the project falls behind schedule? Regrettably, often nothing special happens. This is because the team falsely assumes that although they are behind schedule by two weeks at this time, they can make that time up later by completing integration testing or end-user training in less time than was budgeted. This almost always proves to be a bad assumption.

Experience shows that a project that goes over budget on early tasks will also go over budget on later tasks. When this does not happen it is usually because the team took short cuts, eliminated required tasks, or spent less time than necessary on the tasks scheduled at the end of the project. That is why there usually is insufficient testing and training on new systems. In many cases, the implementation teams just ran out of time and took unacceptable short cuts to finish the projects.

Time boxing will keep the project on schedule and ensure that adequate time is available for the important tasks that occur at the end of a project. Using this approach, a project will not be allowed to get two or three weeks behind schedule by the end of the second month.

Finally, time boxing helps curtail the attitude that tasks will take whatever time they take. Forget the estimates, just work on the task until it is done. This attitude is one reason why one-year implementation projects often take two years to finish.

Sometimes, bad project estimates contribute to this attitude. If the estimates for initial tasks and milestones are unrealistic and the project gets behind schedule early, the team members may before long ignore the estimates and just plod along working on their tasks. No matter what the estimate says, the team members just continue working on the task until they believe it is complete.

In this situation, there is no sense of urgency or responsibility for completing the tasks more quickly. Under these conditions, tasks take many times longer to complete than they should and deliverables are sometimes polished to levels that are not required. Value-adding activities become a smaller and smaller percentage of the time spent on the project.

So, time boxing addresses many of the issues that cause tasks to take longer than necessary and helps keep the project on schedule. However, there are tasks and activities in the project where time boxing should not be employed. For example, although the project manager may set a goal for how long integration testing will take, testing should not be cut off if the team knows that there are parts of the system that still do not work. Accordingly, judgment must be used to determine what tasks can be time boxed and which ones should be managed by other techniques.

Time boxing is basically a more effective way of using the valuable time of the team members. It helps produce higher-quality implementations since time boxing early tasks creates more time at the end of the project to complete those activities essential to the success of the project. Team members will get a sense of accomplishment for tasks completed, project managers will get deliverables that can be analyzed and reviewed earlier, and there will be a feeling of momentum and progress throughout the project.

80/20 MANAGEMENT

The 80/20 rule applies throughout a rapid implementation project: 80 percent of the business benefits from the new system will come from 20 percent of the transactions in the package; 80 percent of the system errors will originate in 20 percent of the test scenarios; 80 percent of the resistance to the project and the new system will come from 20 percent of the end users and managers; 80 percent of the time spent on the project will be spent on 20 percent of the tasks; 80 percent of the team's personnel issues will come from 20 percent of the team members.

The list could go on. Obviously, the numbers will not always be 80/20. Sometimes they will be 90/10 or 70/30 or 95/5. The point is that a few elements in the population of most project variables will have a disproportionate effect on the activities and outcome of the project. The project manager must find ways to spend more time on those opportunities and problems that have the greatest effects and less on those things that have little real impact.

The 80/20 principle is one of the keys to rapid implementation. In a rapid project there is often only time to do the 20 percent. These projects cannot attempt to do everything. Given time and resource constraints, project scope must be limited.

The focus must be on a few key goals and objectives and not all the things that could be accomplished from such a project. The team cannot implement all the modules in the package or all the transactions in any module. They may not be able to clean up and convert all the historical data. They may not be able to produce publishable quality procedures manuals and system documentation.

But there is enough time in a rapid implementation to do the 20 percent of project tasks and implement the 20 percent of the package that creates 80 percent or more of the value. Therefore, done well, these can be extremely high-leverage projects.

The problem is that most project teams do not prioritize among the large list of things they could work on and focus on those with the highest priorities. As a result, the team spends equal time and resources across all project activities.

The team implements all the transactions in a module, regardless of the value they add. They do all the tasks in the standard workplan even though some of the tasks are not necessary for their particular project. If they are going to redesign processes as part of the project, they redesign all the processes. Unfortunately, there is not time for all these things in a rapid implementation. Trying to do all these things results in a lot of activities that are done badly and a project that goes way over budget and schedule.

Driven by the 80/20 rule, the project management principles for rapid implementation are as follows:

- Projects should not try to do everything. Focus on the few key things that have the greatest benefits for the organization, and do them well.

- Identifying things not to do on a project is just as important as identifying things to do.

- Quick and dirty often produces the same benefits as slow and complete—with much less cost.

- Do not spend a lot of time defining and implementing the perfect solution because the business problem will change next year and make this solution obsolete.

- Detailed analysis and pretty reports get trumped by learning fast through trial-and-error.

- Project managers should identify and spend their time on the critical 20 percent.

There are several actions the project manager can take to apply the 80/20 rule. Perhaps the most important is to use this principle in defining project scope.

One technique for documenting project scope is to list the transactions that will be implemented during the rapid implementation. A spreadsheet is often prepared showing all the transactions supported by the various package modules. Each transaction is a different row and is denoted by its transaction ID, screen number, or name. An "in scope" column can be used to indicate those transactions that will be implemented in the current project. An adjacent column should give the rationale for including the transaction in this particular project.

In order to identify the 20 percent of transactions that will provide 80 percent of the benefits, the team should take the viewpoint that there are only two reasons for including transactions in the project scope: the transaction is *required* to achieve one of the goals and objectives of the project (the specific benefit it produces should be noted) or the transaction is necessary to *support* a required transaction. An example of a required transaction might be one that applies advanced pricing functionality to determine an item price based on a number of customer parameters. A supporting transaction could be the transaction that allows the organization to set up a customer record in the system and maintain these parameters.

This is a lot like zero-based budgeting. The project starts with no transactions in scope and only adds those that are required to produce the benefits specified in the project charter. The result should be that only 20 to 30 percent of the transactions would be deemed in scope.

The transactions not included in the scope of the initial project may still be important to the organization. They are just included in the next phase of the package implementation. Under the rapid implementation approach the organization will be continuously adding new functionality and improving the system in response to changing business needs. So the next project may be kicked off soon after the current one is completed, or even with some overlap.

To help the next team, it is useful for the first team to identify those transactions that they believe are good candidates for phase two or three projects. However, the decision on whether they will be included in scope on the next project should depend on the goals and objectives for that project.

There are many other areas where the project manager can apply the 80/20 principle:

- Coaching and teaching time should be focused on the few project team members that are struggling.
- The project manager can eliminate many tasks from the standard project workplan because they are not required or do not add significant value to this project.

- Project deliverables are defined at the level that produces the greatest value with minimal effort. Often this means that the deliverable will be specified as a one- or two-page document. Without this guidance the team members may attempt to produce 10- to 15-page documents where most of the value is in the first two pages.
- Specialists should be brought in to handle the parts of system configuration that are the most complex and will produce the most errors.
- Change management activities and resources (e.g., communication, involvement, selling) should be focused on the key users of the new system and those managers who need to support the new system and processes.

Applying the 80/20 rule throughout the project will help make a rapid implementation successful. This requires the project manager to continuously examine the value of all project activities. Spreading project resources thinly across all the possible aspects of a project will prevent these projects from being completed on time and achieving the desired benefits.

TEMPLATES AND DELIVERABLES

Effectively managed implementations are deliverable driven. A deliverable is something created as a result of the completion of a task: a data file is converted, end users are trained, procedure manuals are prepared, a deployment strategy is defined, an issue is logged. In each of these cases, some sort of documentation is produced as proof that a task has been completed. This documentation also describes the results from doing the task.

In a rapid implementation, if the project manager cannot clearly define a deliverable for a task—one that moves the project closer to a successful go-live—then the task probably is not necessary. And if it is not necessary, it should not be done.

It is possible to waste a lot of time on activities that are not required to achieve the goals and objectives of the project. People are prone to go off on tangents. They can spend time on things that may be interesting but that do not move the project toward its goals. When time is spent on tangential activities, resources (mainly the time and energy of the project team members) are consumed but nothing results that has any effect on the ability of the team to meet the go-live date. A rapid implementation cannot afford such diversions.

The organization's managers and project team members sometimes do not see the value in creating a great deal of documentation during these projects. What they fail to understand is that often the process of creating the documentation is as important as the document that results.

Team members learn while creating task deliverables. The documentation activity causes the team members to think about what has been done: Have they met the task objectives? Is the task complete? Does the rationale for the conclusions reached make sense? Have all the relevant issues and alternatives been considered and reflected in the final result? Does the documentation adequately reflect the conclusions and decisions made? If the team members are unsure of the answers to these questions, then additional work may need to be done.

Reviewing the deliverables produced by team members is one of the major responsibilities of the project manager. The project manager needs to review deliverables to determine project status, identify training and coaching needs, evaluate decisions that are being made by individual team members, and integrate the activities across the entire team.

The project manager reviews deliverables to determine whether a task has been completed successfully. This review also provides an opportunity for the project manager to evaluate the quality of the work. If the work has not been done in a timely and high-quality manner, this may indicate a need for additional training and coaching for team members. This review also helps identify situations where additional resources need to be assigned to the task to keep the project on schedule.

Implementation tasks are assigned to individual team members. In performing these tasks the team members are empowered to make decisions that are appropriate for their project role. In making these decisions, each individual makes assumptions and considers a number of alternatives.

However, team members sometimes make decisions without knowing all the other things that are going on in the project and having an understanding of all the potential integration issues. In addition, many of the team members may be making these kinds of decisions for the first time. A key role for the project manager is to challenge the assumptions and decisions, and provide guidance and insights so team members can make better decisions in the future.

Many of the vendors and system integrators have their own methodologies for implementing packages. Unless the organization believes it has something better, these methodologies should be used on the implementation project. Some of these methodologies, such as SAP's ASAP methodology and FastForward from Oracle, are specifically designed for rapid implementation projects. But even in these rapid methodologies, there are more tasks and deliverables defined than would normally be used on any particular rapid implementation project.

During the early planning activities, the project manager should go through all the deliverables identified in the methodology and decide which subset of these is mandatory for this project. Only those high-value-adding deliverables that are required to meet the project objectives should make the cut. The project manager should challenge each item on this list for its contribution to project success. This list also drives definition of the tasks included on the project workplan. Again, if the task does not produce a key deliverable, why is the team doing it?

A key success factor for rapid implementations will be the availability and quality of sample deliverables, or templates, for each task. These are effective project accelerators for a number of reasons.

First, they save a lot of time because each team member does not have to design the deliverable from scratch. It can take a lot of time for someone who has never worked on these types of projects to decide on the format, content, and length of documentation that must be produced. Some team members will spend days on this activity and have nothing to show for their ponderings. If several people are working on the same types of tasks, there may be little consistency between the deliverables that each produces. A template provides quick answers to these design questions and promotes better consistency throughout the project.

Second, the templates help the team members understand what they are trying to achieve in the task. Having a good idea of what must be produced at the end of a task guides the person through the task activities. If the deliverable is well defined, it focuses the work on the things that are important for task completion. It also provides direction on the level of detail that is expected in the task.

For example, the deliverable from the task, Design a Data Conversion Strategy, could be a one-page high-level document or a 50-page detailed plan. If a one-page strategy is all that is needed at a particular point in the project, development of the more detailed document may be a waste of valuable project time. The details may change as a result of other things that happen before the detail plan is needed. Having a one-page template for the task should steer the team member to the right level of detail.

Some of the templates provided by the vendors and integrators are particular to the package that is being implemented. This provides a jump-start in ensuring that package-specific issues and characteristics are being addressed in the task. For example, the AcceleratedSAP (ASAP) methodology and toolkit provides hundreds of user procedure templates for processing transactions using SAP's R/3 product. These templates show the transaction and screen flow to accomplish certain business processes and even include screen-shots of the SAP screens used in each step of the procedure. Tailoring these samples to the needs of the organization and the system design takes a lot less time than starting from a generic user procedure template.

Having good deliverable examples and templates, especially those that have been tailored to the package being implemented, provides tremendous benefits to the implementation project. These types of project accelerators help make rapid implementation of these complex packages possible.

RISK MANAGEMENT

Another primary responsibility for the project manager is risk management. There is no time in a rapid implementation for the project to get bogged down or off track.

Therefore, the project manager must anticipate and plan appropriate responses to quickly remove barriers that could potentially get in the way of these projects. Typical barriers to rapid implementation include:

- Slow decisions
- Bad technical support
- Buggy software
- Complex project tasks
- Resistance and sabotage
- Personnel problems

Some of these risks are under the control of the project manager. The executive sponsor or the project steering committee must quickly address others. We will now take a look at each of these areas in more detail.

Slow Decisions

In a rapid implementation there is no room for slow decision making. The team cannot wait for days or weeks while someone does a detailed analysis of the pros and cons of all the alternatives before making and implementing a decision. Also, there is no time to build consensus throughout the organization for every decision before it is finalized.

There are literally thousands of decisions that must be made on these projects. The project team must be empowered to make most of them. That is one reason organizations must put their best people on these teams.

The team members will make decisions that impact the way the organization performs its business processes in the future. Of course, team members must seek information and input from those who will be affected by the decisions. But, after gathering this information and examining the alternatives, they must quickly decide based on their detailed knowledge of the business processes and the capabilities of the packaged software. If management is not willing to empower the team to make this level of decisions (and not second-guess them), then the organization may not be a good candidate for a rapid implementation strategy.

It is equally important for the team to recognize those decisions that should be made by the executive sponsor and the steering committee. There are some decisions that are so important that they must be made by top management. Included in this category are things like changes in organizational structure and responsibilities, major scope modifications, deployment strategies, replacement of team personnel, and changes to budgets and schedules. These issues should be quickly brought to the attention of management; and, in most cases, these decisions should be made in a two-to three-day timeframe.

The project manager must stay on top of all the decisions that are being made by the team and others in the project hierarchy. The need for key decisions should be logged and tracked in the issues management system. The project manager should be proactive and aggressive in ensuring that there are no delays in decisions that could hold up the project.

Bad Technical Support

There are a number of technical support issues that can hinder project progress. One is not having the project's development environment ready on time. When the team members get back from their initial training on the package, they need a sand box so they can start analysis and configuration activities. If this environment is not available, it becomes extremely difficult to proceed with many of the project activities.

The systems used by the team members need to be available at all times. The team will be challenged to get any work accomplished, for example, if they are not able to access project deliverables because the LAN is down for a day or two. Even worse would be a situation where the network goes down in the middle of the project and the project deliverables cannot be recovered because the system cannot be restored from the backup files. During integration testing the team depends on the technical support personnel to migrate parameter files from development to test instances quickly and to restore test databases before each test cycle is rerun. The team could lose hours or days of critical project time if they do not have a competent, responsive group supporting the technical aspects of the project.

Buggy Software

All software packages have bugs—things that do not work as they should. There is no way that any vendor could possibly test every possible scenario for how a package may be used by its customers. However, if the organization has selected a proven software package (where the current release has been out in widespread use for 4 to 6 months, by similar organizations) then the number of bugs, and their severity, should be lessened.

In spite of these precautions, there will still be a need for the IS organization to work closely with the vendor's support organization to resolve system and programming problems that are detected during the project. In a rapid implementation these activities should be given high priority and visibility. In the middle of final testing, and with go-live in sight, the team cannot afford to wait for weeks for the vendor to provide a fix for errors that are occurring with the software. The project manager must stay on top of these situations and escalate the priority with the vendor account manager, as required.

Complex Project Tasks

In any implementation there are some activities that are more complex and challenging than others. In some cases these activities may require enhanced knowledge of how the package operates (perhaps at the database level) to configure the system to solve certain business problems. In others, the issue might be a technical one or one dealing with complex business processes or regulatory requirements. The learning curve may be extremely steep in these areas and the team can get stuck spending days and weeks on the task without coming up with a solution. In a rapid implementation such delays can have dramatic impacts on an already-tight schedule.

The project manager should carefully monitor these situations. It requires a great deal of judgment to know when to turn to outside specialists. If the project manager brings in a specialist too early, this will unnecessarily impact the project budget and not give the team a reasonable opportunity to solve its own problems. However, bringing in the specialist too late may jeopardize the project schedule.

Resistance and Sabotage

Organizational politics play a role in all major projects. Each project produces winners and losers. Responsibilities, access to and control over information, and perceived power can change as a result of any major initiative. This includes rapid implementation projects. People who do not want the project to be successful will often do anything within their power to delay the go-live. In extreme situations they may even sabotage the project in hopes that something will change in the business or management structure to cause the project to be abandoned.

The project manager must be alert to these situations. In many cases, the person doing the sabotage will use subtle means to slow the project down. This may include constantly second guessing or challenging decisions made by the team, preventing users from participating in testing and training activities, creating doubt and concern about the validity of the rapid implementation approach, or not making a reasonable effort to support data cleanup or other project activities.

In some cases the person creating these types of barriers has a powerful position in the organization. Therefore, these situations should be handled carefully but directly. The project manager needs to have reasonable evidence that the individual is working to prevent the project from being successful. This information should be brought first to the executive sponsor. If the sponsor is not able to resolve the issue, then it should be taken to the steering committee.

If top management is serious about the importance of the new applications and the benefits of a rapid implementation approach, they will take swift and visible action to remove barriers to these projects. Such action can make two strong statements to the rest of the organization. The first is that these projects are important! The second is that the organization's managers and employees must support these critical initiatives or others will be found who are more supportive.

Personnel Problems

The final barrier deals with problems associated with people on the core and extended project team. Human resource problems can have a tremendous impact on the success or failure of these projects. The project manager first needs to monitor whether the project is getting all of people's time that has been committed to the project. Are the full-time team members working full time on project activities? Are the key users available to work with the team a day or two each week?

The project manager also needs to take actions to retain team members until the project is completed. In addition, there is a whole category of problems around poor performance by team members and the need to replace those that cannot meet expectations for a full-time core team member. These personnel problems are covered in more detail in Chapter 5 on the people issues associated with rapid implementation projects.

As can be seen by these examples, there are many potential barriers to completing these rapid implementation projects on time. The project manager must take a proactive role in quickly removing these barriers. In some cases, the appropriate action will not be obvious or may require the support of others. All of these potential barriers will be logged and tracked in an issues management system as they surface. They stay on the outstanding issues log until they are resolved.

ISSUES TRACKING AND RESOLUTION

A key tool used by the project manager is an issues tracking system. This tool captures potential issues that should be brought to the attention of project management. Anyone on the team can add an issue to the issues log. The project manager is responsible for ensuring that the issues are appropriately defined, analyzed, and resolved in a timely manner.

A number of things can be included in the issues log. If any project team member believes that something is a potential issue, it should be captured. Whether it really is an issue can be sorted out later by the project manager.

To denote its nature, each issue is assigned a category. Some typical categories include decision, scope, technical, people, reporting, integration, and data.

Decision issues record key design decisions made during the project that *may* require management review and approval. The issues log is not designed to be a repository of all decisions made during the project. As noted earlier, there are literally thousands of decisions made by the team; most do not require any special visibility and attention. However, certain key decisions are of significant importance to the organization and warrant the attention of project management, the executive sponsor, or the steering committee.

Examples of these types of issues might include: Should the manufacturing system use discrete work orders or repetitive schedules to track product costs? Will suppliers and customers be given access, perhaps through an extranet, to the organization's systems and information? Will the same system configuration be used at all the locations or will variations be allowed to tailor the system to the unique needs, real or perceived, of each site? Will organizational policies be changed so the system can be used, without modifications and enhancements, to support a particular business process? Will the organization go-live using only standard reports from the system and defer design and coding of special reports until the next implementation phase, after the standard reports are given adequate consideration?

These examples show decisions best left to management. Still, the project team should be expected to take the issue to the point of a decision. They should carefully define and craft a description of the problem or issue, document the pros and cons of each alternative, describe how the system supports the various alternatives, and provide a recommendation to management. This preliminary analysis is required for management to make quick decisions on each issue.

Scope issues surface throughout a rapid implementation project. The project team is continuously learning about the organization's business processes, capabilities of the package, how long it takes the team to complete project tasks, and the ability of the organization to absorb change. The team members also have a list of goals and objectives for the project and a target go-live date.

On a weekly, and sometime daily, basis the team will make decisions on what will be included in the scope of the initial implementation and what can be left to future implementation projects. The steering committee should be briefed on key scope decisions. They should be involved in making these major decisions.

Scope issue discussions help to manage the expectations of the organization. Management and key users need to understand the impacts of changing scope and the trade-offs among project scope, time, and resources (including cost). These are basic business decisions that affect how quickly the organization can respond to business changes and begin to receive the benefits from the new application.

In many situations, decisions will be made to defer some functions and processes to the next phase or project in order to complete the current project on schedule. In some cases, however, the steering committee may choose to extend the go-live a month or two to include additional processes in the initial implementation. This second course should be used sparingly, since a basic objective of rapid implementations is to get the system up and operating quickly. With the rapid approach other functions and processes can be added later as the organization follows a continuous enhancement and improvement process.

Technical issues primarily deal with the availability of the development system and with response times and the capacity of the production system to handle a large volume of transactions. If the development system is frequently down, the ability of the team to get its work done will be impacted. If the team discovers bugs in the package, they must be fixed quickly. If the testing databases need to be refreshed, the next test cycle cannot start until that is completed. If shipments of new hardware are delayed, this may affect the ability of the team to go live on the target date. If the training room is not equipped with workstations on time, then the training schedule will be impacted. All these technical issues need to be identified early so an appropriate response can be taken and these issues can be taken off the critical path.

People issues address problems with team members, management, or the users of the new system. These issues include full-time team members being pulled to work on their old jobs; lack of participation by key users in testing or training activities; or situations where managers are doing things that threaten the success of the project.

Sensitive personnel issues are often not recorded in the issues log. Not everyone on the team needs to see them. Instead, the project manager and the steering committee handle them discretely but vigorously.

Reporting issues often center on the differences between the reports that are being produced by legacy systems (and that people have come to expect) and the standard reports provided by the package. A design strategy for many of the new packages is to reduce the number of printed reports. Since most of the data is available online, there are other ways to get at the same information.

Where the packages provide standard reports, they are often in a different format or contain different combinations of information than exist in current reports. In a rapid implementation there will be little time to code custom reports or change the format of standard reports to mirror the current reports. Therefore, requests for additional and special reports need to be carefully scrutinized.

Decisions made in one part of a project sometimes unexpectedly impact other areas. Integration issues identify points where configuration decisions in different modules within a package need to be coordinated. This category also captures issues associated with integrating the package with third-party products or legacy systems. Through good project team communications, the project manager attempts to reduce the number of integration issues. However, many of these issues will only surface during the integration testing that occurs toward the end of the project.

A final issue category deals with data problems. These may concern mapping mismatches between data available in legacy systems and those data elements required for processing with the new package. There may be integrity problems with existing data. There is also the question of who should be the *owner* of certain types of data in the new system. These issues may force decisions to be made in situations where there is not sufficient time to convert all the historical data in time for the go-live. Each of these issues and the impact of each alternative approach for addressing them should be analyzed and resolved by the team.

Logging issues and tracking their resolution helps ensure that problems and opportunities for the project are captured and addressed. With this process in place, issues should not slip through the cracks. In a rapid implementation, most issues should be addressed in a matter of days. There are others, however, that require more time to resolve. That is why it is important to identify all issues early and begin the resolution process.

KNOWLEDGE MANAGEMENT

Frequent communication and knowledge sharing are critical activities for a rapid implementation. A lot of the knowledge transfer and sharing takes place during informal discussions between team members. Other information (e.g., project plans, status, and integration issues) is addressed in project team meetings, either for the entire team or subgroups. Information for key users and managers is often disseminated through presentations and project newsletters. However, the primary source of information for the project is the *project repository.*

The project repository is an electronic storage area for project plans, deliverables, tools, and information. This repository often resides on the organization's local area network (LAN). Folders are established for materials in various project areas: project administration, vision and strategy, planning, business process redesign, configuration, testing, training, data conversion, technical support, issues tracking, and change management. As deliverables are drafted, reviewed, and approved, they are stored in these folders. This technology makes these items accessible for all the project team members.

The use of a LAN for the project repository is a great improvement over the old paper-based filing cabinet or three-ring binder approach to project documentation. The material in the repository can be periodically backed up so it could be recovered in the event of a computer malfunction or fire in the building. In addition, several people can review the same documents simultaneously (although they might have read-only access to documents that are being updated by others). The project manager can review deliverables for quality and completeness from any of the workstations, or even remotely.

A key advantage of the electronic repository approach is that materials can be easily archived at the end of the project for use by future project teams. Making a good set of deliverables from the initial rapid implementation project available to future projects helps provide continuity and knowledge transfer between projects. These materials provide an effective jump-start for subsequent projects.

Recently, Internet technologies have been used to support and enhance the project repository concept. Commercial web vendors provide tools and space to store and access project deliverables. These vendors also provide collaborative tools like discussion databases, electronic calendaring, and e-mail to facilitate communication between team members and other project stakeholders. Each team can develop its own project web site. This site can be hosted on the Internet or on the organization's intranet.

The advantage of the Internet approach is that it provides greater access to project knowledge and deliverables. Ultimately, anyone with access to the Internet or the corporate intranet and a browser can get to all the project information. Assuming that security issues are handled appropriately, the team can use technology to better support communication and knowledge sharing for rapid implementation projects.

5

PEOPLE ISSUES IN IMPLEMENTATION

The main cause of failure in package implementation projects is not technical problems or vendor package problems. These projects usually fail as a result of people problems. Picking the right people for the project team and closely managing the soft issues associated with these projects are key factors for a successful rapid implementation.

The soft issues for these projects impact a number of different groups. These include the core team, executive sponsor, steering committee, key users, and all those who have a stake in the changes that result from implementing new systems and business processes.

The core team, and especially the project manager, will have to deal directly with the soft issues on almost a daily basis. This will be an ongoing and difficult challenge for the group. Having the wrong people on the team creates its own set of problems. Others problems result from the inability of the team to identify and resolve change management issues in a timely manner.

It is important to pull together a core implementation team with the experience and skills required to handle all the challenges of a rapid implementation. This group needs to be recruited, trained, coached, motivated, and supported throughout the project.

Around the periphery of this core team are a number of people who work with and support the team. This group includes the executive sponsor, steering committee members, people in the IS department, specialists, and key users of the new system. These are generally supporters of the project who can help resolve issues as they surface. However, the team needs to be aware of potential issues that could come from this group

Finally, there are others in the organization that will benefit from, or be adversely affected by, the new system. This includes the ultimate users of the new system, as well as their supervisors and managers. Many of the core team's change management activities are targeted toward these groups. These groups must understand and support the changes that result from these projects or else the changes will not take hold.

The potential human resource issues of these projects are extensive. Given the shorter timeframes and constant pressures of a rapid implementation, many of these issues are heightened. However, if proper attention is focused on the people aspects of these projects and the soft issues of these projects are well managed, then the organization is on its way to developing a rapid change competence that truly provides a competitive advantage.

IMPORTANCE OF PEOPLE ISSUES

People often have the wrong idea about why implementation projects fail. Many people believe that these projects fail because of the challenges of putting in new technologies (e.g., distributed databases, client/server architectures, Internet technologies). Sometimes this perception is a direct result of the highly publicized inability of IS departments, in the past, to deliver business applications on time and on budget. Since IT professionals were often leading these projects, the assumption is naturally that the problems were technical ones. Nothing could be further from the truth.

Although there are significant technical challenges in these implementations, and technical challenges only increase in e-business implementations, the primary reasons these projects fail have more to do with the nontechnical aspects of the projects. Most people that have been through these projects know this to be true. As evidence of this phenomenon we can look at the results from an annual CIO survey performed by Deloitte & Touche that appear in Figure 5-1.

In this survey, one of the questions the organizations were asked was what were key barriers to having successful implementations. The top ten reasons for unsuccessful projects are listed in this figure. Only the tenth item listed, IT perspective not integrated, deals with technology. (And you might speculate that even this issue resulted from communication difficulties between the IT department and the other members of the team.) All the other issues are people and change management issues. So the soft aspects of these projects truly are the things that the project manager and the team must concentrate on to ensure the success of these implementations. These problems only become more difficult to manage in a rapid implementation because the timeline is so compressed.

The other interesting thing to note from the survey is that the barriers to success generally fall into two categories:

1. Those that result from bad planning
2. Those that are caused by bad execution

Some of the items, it could be argued, fall into both categories.

FIGURE 5-1 People Issues in Unsuccessful Projects
Source: Deloitte & Touche 1998 CIO survey.

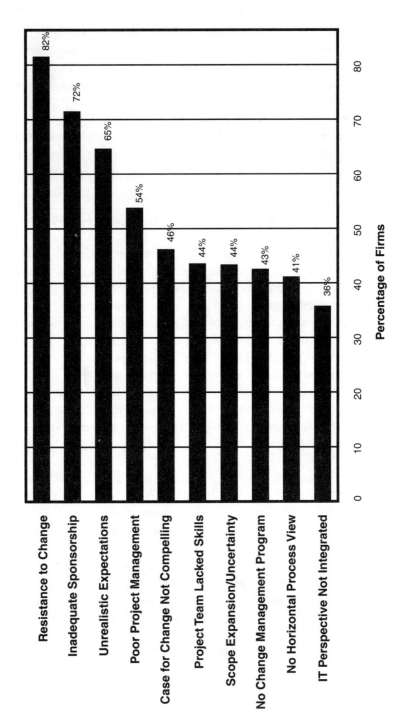

Top Ten Barriers to Success

Resistance to Change — 82%
Inadequate Sponsorship — 72%
Unrealistic Expectations — 65%
Poor Project Management — 54%
Case for Change Not Compelling — 46%
Project Team Lacked Skills — 44%
Scope Expansion/Uncertainty — 44%
No Change Management Program — 43%
No Horizontal Process View — 41%
IT Perspective Not Integrated — 36%

Percentage of Firms

Inadequate sponsorship, unrealistic expectations, no compelling case for change, and problems caused by a team lacking skills are things that often result from bad planning and organization for the project. These are things that need to be addressed before project kickoff occurs. Other things like resistance to change, poor project management, scope expansion, and the absence of an effective change management program are usually caused by bad execution.

The inference is that the people and change management issues need to be addressed both before the project begins and continuously during these projects. Failure to do so in either case may result in an unsuccessful project.

RECRUITING THE CORE TEAM

Most organizations do not pay sufficient attention to the task of staffing an implementation project. Staffing decisions impact two of the key requirements for success: (1) having a team with the right skills and experience, and (2) selecting a project manager who can effectively manage a rapid implementation.

Much of a project's chances for success are predetermined in its early stages when the organization chooses the project team. Pick the right people and the project has a good chance of success; pick the wrong project manager and team members and the organization might as well not even begin the project.

The core team includes those who will work full-time on the project until it is completed. This team usually includes people from the organization implementing the new system, as well as consultants and vendor representatives. Many others in the organization will contribute to the success of the project, but the core team has to do the heavy lifting.

The core team will make the day-to-day decisions and provide continuity throughout the project. They will play the major role in determining how the new system will support new or improved business processes. They will be the ones who will be given primary credit for a successful implementation, and blame if the project fails.

This core team must be a cross-functional team. It should have respected representatives from all the major functions impacted by the new system. In many cases there will be financial, IT, sales and marketing, and operational personnel working side by side on these projects. Each brings different knowledge, experiences, insights, and perspectives to the project.

The team becomes stronger as a result of taking advantage of the collective knowledge from such a diverse group. And, with the right representatives, the various organizational units will be more willing to empower the team to make key decisions.

A universal dilemma is that the best people to work on these projects are the ones the departments can least afford to give up. The team needs people who are highly motivated, intelligent, creative, hard working, team-oriented, and understand the organization's business and strategies. Guess what? These are the same people each department depends on for its day-to-day success. There are many others the departments would be glad to give up for the benefit of the organization's new initiative, but not their stars.

Ultimately, core team staffing comes down to organizational priorities and hard decisions by top management. This is often a key test of top management's commitment to the success of a rapid implementation project. It is also a highly visible test.

How important is it for the organization to quickly adapt its business processes to meet changing business requirements? How important is it to develop a competency for changing organizational processes and systems rapidly? If these are important, then management must ensure the project has a good chance of success by dedicating some of its best people to the core project team. The choice of team members sends an important message to the rest of the organization. It says that this must be an important project if management is putting its A players on the team.

The shorter duration of a rapid implementation makes this decision a little easier but also more critical. In the past, the organization was frequently committing core team members to long-term implementations. Often these projects ran two or three years. It should be easier to get commitment to use people for three to six month projects than for those lasting two to three years.

However, there is also a downside to the shorter timeframes. There is not as much time on a rapid implementation to identify and replace people who are not able to pull their part of the load. By the time the underperformer is identified and coached, the project will probably be behind schedule on the tasks assigned to that individual. Also, before a suitable replacement has been found and brought up to speed, most of the project may be over.

Staffing these projects should be handled using a headhunter mindset. With the blessing of top management, the executive sponsor and project manager should look around the organization and decide who would be the best people for the core team. If they could get anyone in the organization, whom would they want? Then they should go after them!

If they do not know many of the people in each department or remote location, the sponsor and project manager can meet with the steering committee members to develop a list of candidates from each area. Multiple candidates should be identified to represent each area or role in the project. It is helpful to have a senior executive at this meeting to show top management's support for finding the best people for the project. This person can also reinforce the expectation that each area must contribute only its top performers.

Each of the core team candidates should be interviewed. This is not always done—to the detriment of the project. Sometimes the first time the project manager meets the members of the core team, including the consultants, is at the project kickoff meeting. It is difficult to make personnel changes at this late stage.

The requests for the interviews should come from top management and the steering committee members, through the department managers, to the individuals. The department managers should be involved in the selection process since they will be directly affected by the staffing decisions. Having the request come from top management is a good strategy for getting the department managers' support. Sometimes this support comes easier if the managers are reminded that the decisions of the project will impact the departments' processes and that it is important that the department be well represented on the team.

The project manager and sponsor should feel comfortable that each core team member has what it takes to meet the demands of the project. Each should have skills and experience that is valuable to the team. Each should be a hard worker who is willing to jump in and help other team members to keep the project on schedule. The team members should not expect to just manage the activities of others; each person will have detailed tasks to perform. The team members should all have good people skills and be team players.

The candidates should be excited about the project and want to participate. Given the high demands and visibility of these projects, and potential uncertainty about what the team members will do once the project has been completed, this may take some selling on the part of the sponsor and project manager.

Once the potential team members have been identified, this list should be discussed with the project steering committee. Since this group includes high-level managers from each of the areas where there may be candidates, getting the support of this group will help in the next steps. At this point, the steering committee should be in agreement on the need for and benefits from investing in top-notch people for the project.

POST-RECRUITMENT ACTIVITIES

Management should consider assignments on these projects as developmental opportunities for their star employees. The members of these teams will have an opportunity to develop something that few others in the organization have: a holistic view of the business processes of the organization and an understanding of effective methods for changing them.

They will have a good understanding of how technology can be used effectively to enable and support business process changes. They will also have an intimate knowledge of the time, effort, and activities required to implement changes in the organization. In addition, they will understand the benefits of doing many smaller projects rather than a few large, complex projects. All this knowledge makes these individuals valuable assets of the organization.

Once the organization's team members have been identified and approved, it will be necessary for their supervisors to provide career development, backfill, and transition plans for the people on the team. These plans are important for the individuals and the departments from which they come.

Following these short-duration projects, some of the team members will return to their former jobs or to other jobs in the same function. Others, as a career-broadening move, may move to another area of the organization. A third option is for some of the team members to become part of the support organization for the system once the implementation project has been completed or to participate on another project phase. Completion of these projects provides a convenient opportunity to make any of these personnel changes.

A project start date is often established before the core team is recruited. This date needs to be far enough in the future to give all team members time to wrap up activities they have been working on and transition their responsibilities to their replacements.

The steering committee should require a written backfill plan from the supervisors of each of the team members. This should describe how the work formerly done by the team members would be accomplished while they are gone. It may include approaches such as hiring temporary employees for the duration of the project, hiring new employees to permanently take on the former jobs of team members, or realigning job responsibilities in the department. These backfill plans are important because the core team members need to be available to work full-time on the project once it has started and the departments need to get their work done in the absence of the team members.

As a final point, while the sponsor and project manager are finalizing the organization's team assignments, they are also arranging how they will fulfill the need for outside support for the project. In doing this, they usually go through a proposal and contract negotiation process with representatives from the package vendor and systems integrators to identify the remaining team resources.

These outside representatives are required in order to help the team get up the steep learning curve with a new package or a rapid implementation methodology. For these projects to be successful, there is usually a requirement for participation by people who have implemented the selected package before and managed these types of rapid implementation projects.

These people can come from consulting organizations or from the vendor. Several of these people may be full-time team members for the duration of the project. However, there may also be a need in some areas for specialists on a part-time basis. These team members should also be interviewed and evaluated for how they will fit in with the rest of the team.

All these steps are necessary so that a high-quality, cross-functional team will be ready to begin work on the project following the kickoff meeting. The core team typically would include from 5 to 20 people, depending on the number of business processes that are being addressed by the project. The next section describes the different roles these individuals may play.

PROJECT TEAM ORGANIZATION

There are a number of different roles that need to be played on a rapid implementation. Each has its own skill requirements and is important to the success of the project. Some of the roles are full-time and others require the participants to support the team on a part-time basis.

Figure 5-2 shows a typical organizational chart for a rapid implementation. The roles in the solid lines represent full-time project team members. In this diagram there are three different groups defined.

The first group includes those individuals that make up the leadership team for the project. This group includes the steering committee, executive sponsor, project manager, consulting advisor, and vendor representative. These people are responsible for guiding the project and ensuring that it meets the business objectives. They are also responsible for supporting the rest of the team.

The second group is made up of the process and technical teams that do most of the day-to-day work on the project. This group also includes the key and power users who participate on the team on a part-time basis.

The final group are those specialists that are brought in to help the project team in complex areas or to solve problems that will take too long for the project team to re-

FIGURE 5-2   Rapid Implementation Team Organization

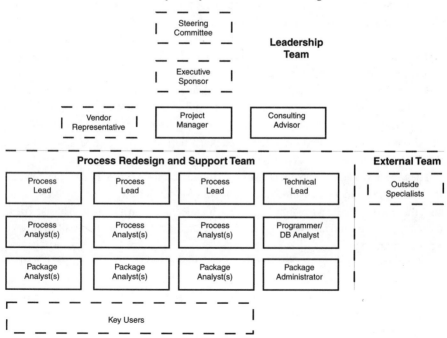

solve. The specialists usually come from the vendor and consulting firms that are supporting the implementation. However, they can also come from other parts of the organization or from third-party companies. Each of these groups is discussed in the sections that follow.

TEAM LEADERSHIP ROLES

Arguably, the most critical role to the success of the project is that of *project manager*. The CIO survey indicated that over half the implementations had problems because of poor project management. In addition, outstanding performance by the project manager is key to addressing all the other barriers to project success. Unfortunately, most organizations do not recognize the importance of this position and the skills required for effective project management. These skills are crucial for successful rapid implementations.

There are several other management roles in a rapid implementation: process team lead, technical lead, steering committee member, executive sponsor, and consulting advisor. Each is involved in managing various aspects of the project. However, one person must have overall responsibility for the project. There must be a final arbitrator and decision maker for the project team. The buck stops with the project manager.

The project manager should come from the business side of the organization. This person should not be from the IT department or the consulting organization. There must be no perception that the project is primarily an IT initiative or that the system that gets implemented is the *consultant's system*. This project must be, and must be seen as, a business-driven project, managed by the business side of the organization.

The project manager must be a responsible, experienced manager, well known and respected throughout the organization. When people hear who has been selected as the project manager, they should immediately assume that this must be an important project. The organization must put one of its stars and future leaders in this important role.

The project manager should have outstanding people skills and a good understanding of the organization's business and strategies. This person will be the primary liaison between the project and the various stakeholder groups. In particular, the person will work closely with the project sponsor and the steering committee.

If this person has been involved in an implementation project before, then the transition to rapid implementation project manager will be much easier. If this individual has prior experience with the package being implemented, then he or she will already have taken a step up the learning curve. However, this is not often the case. That is why there is a requirement to supplement the organization's project manager with a consulting advisor and package analysts.

The project manager is responsible for ensuring that the project meets the goals and objectives that have been established and gets completed on time and within budget. This means the project manager, with the help of the executive sponsor and the steering committee, is responsible for removing barriers to project success. This person also has primary responsibility for managing and coaching the other team members. Much of the project manager's time will be spent evaluating the work of the team members and ensuring their development while on the team.

The *consulting advisor* should supplement the skills and experience of the organization's project manager. There are many key areas of these projects in which the organization's project manager probably has little experience:

- Being a business manager, the organization's project manager should not be expected to have experience with all the tools, techniques, and methodologies used in rapid implementations.

- The person selected as project manager may have managed a department or function within the organization, but may have little experience managing large-scale projects.

- The project manager probably has no experience with the package that is being implemented.

- This person also may not have prior experience in process redesign, change management, or IT infrastructure development.

All of these areas need to be well managed in a successful rapid implementation.

There are also a lot of judgment calls in these projects: How many processes can be implemented in the available timeframe? What are the mandatory deliverables for this project? Are the deliverables of sufficient quality? When should specialists be brought in? Which process redesigns can be supported by the package? How much training and testing are enough? Is the project on track? If the project schedule is slipping, what should be done to get it back on track?

In all of these areas it is good to have an experienced project manager to help identify and analyze the problems and issues and suggest solutions. In the role of a coach, the consulting advisor guides the project manager through a number of potential minefields.

The consulting advisor can also be assigned responsibility for certain parts of the project. For example, this person can be given responsibility for supervising the IT support activities, managing integration testing, or developing end-user training materials. Having someone else take responsibility for supervising some of these activities helps take some of the load off the organization's project manager. That allows the project manager to focus on other priorities such as benefit realization, process redesign activities, and the many change management aspects of the project.

The consulting advisor, along with the vendor representative, can also help identify specialists that can be brought in to supplement the knowledge and skills of the project team. These specialists can address troublesome and complex areas of the implementation. They can also augment the knowledge and skills of the core team.

Each project needs a champion. The *executive sponsor* fills this role. This person is usually a top-level manager in the organization who has overall responsibility for many of the areas impacted by the new system. The executive sponsor should be passionate about the importance of the project and the need to develop a rapid implementation capability within the organization. In some cases this person becomes the owner of the new system or process.

The sponsor often acts as chair of the project steering committee. In this role the sponsor supports the project manager and removes any roadblocks that are beyond the control of the project team. These roadblocks often are associated with getting resources for the project, resolving differences of opinions between steering committee members and key user groups, and quickly making decisions that go beyond the authority of the project team.

The sponsor should be highly visible to the project team. This person should attend key project team meetings and visit the team work area several times each week. The more actively involved this person is with the project, the more top-management perspective will get communicated to the team. In addition, active involvement by the sponsor will allow that person to better understand the issues affecting the project and the positions taken by the team.

The project *steering committee* includes managers representing all the major functional areas affected by the new system. For example, the key leaders of the finance and IT functions are usually members of the steering committee for key implementation projects. The steering committee's responsibilities include monitoring the status of the project, seeing that key business issues are being addressed, reviewing and approving the major decisions and actions of the project team, and ensuring that there is adequate involvement of key users in project activities. They may also be empowered to make organizational structure and policy decisions on behalf of the organization.

Some of the steering committee members may be designated as process owners. If this occurs, these individuals should closely work with subgroups of the team on specific business processes and become involved in significant design decisions for those processes. Some of the steering committee members may also have responsibility for achieving the benefits identified in the business case for the new system.

The steering committee should meet regularly, every week or two, during a rapid implementation. There should be a standard agenda to cover items like project status, issues and what is being done to address them, key decisions made by the core team, and items that need steering committee decisions or involvement to resolve.

The final member of the leadership team is the *vendor representative*. This is often an account manager from the vendor's organization and not the sales representative who made the original software sale. The role of this person is to make sure the customer is happy with the software that has been purchased. (And that the customer continues to pay 15 to 20 percent of the original software price annually to get ongoing support and access to future releases of the package.)

Since the customer's happiness is often a function of how well the implementation is going, the vendor representative does several things to help ensure a successful implementation. One of the roles of this person is to periodically perform quality assurance reviews for the project. From the perspective of someone not involved in the day-to-day activities of the project, this person can come in and, in a short time, evaluate how things are really going. Sometimes the project manager and the team get too caught up in the details of the project to see the true picture of the progress that is being achieved. The vendor account manager can provide this independent viewpoint.

In addition, the vendor representative can help escalate the level of assistance provided by the vendor's support organization when software errors are discovered. The vendor's help desk can respond to many of the questions the team will have. In many cases, what might first be diagnosed as a software problem turns out to be a misunderstanding of how the software works or a data problem.

However, if the team discovers a bug in the software, which must be fixed by the vendor, then it may be necessary to get the help of the account manager to escalate resolution. This is especially important for a rapid implementation where waiting two or three weeks to get a bug fixed can have significant impact on the project schedule.

The vendor's representative can also be helpful in identifying specialists who may be brought in at key points in the project to help the team handle complex problems or get the project back on schedule. The vendor organization should have true experts in various aspects of their package. Often, these individuals are not available to work full-time on an individual project (or might be too expensive to work full-time) but are available to support projects on an ad-hoc or part-time basis.

When the team needs this type of help, it needs it quickly. The account manager can help identify the right resources in the vendor organization and handle the internal politics to make these people available to the team.

PROCESS REDESIGN AND SUPPORT ROLES

The number of process teams in a rapid implementation depends on the scope of the project. If the scope is just one process (e.g., implement a financial reporting system or implement e-procurement), then there may only be one process team. If the scope is to implement financials, manufacturing, and sales/distribution processes, then there may be three process teams for the project.

The role of *process lead* is an additional role for some of the team members; it is not a full-time manager role. All the members of the process team do detailed tasks and help out in any area to keep the implementation project on schedule. However, there are advantages in designating one person to coordinate the activities of the process team and represent them in projectwide discussions and integration meetings.

One role of the process lead is to facilitate the flow of information on the project. This flow goes in several directions.

Frequent internal communication within the implementation team is essential to the success of the project. At times the project manager will get the entire implementation team together to talk about project progress or key issues that have surfaced. But in the majority of situations, the project manager may just meet with the team leads.

Taking this approach minimizes the requirement for all the process team members to attend every meeting. This is a good thing. It is nice to know that some project work will still get done, in spite of the large number of meetings that happen during these projects.

Another role of the process lead is to represent the process team in project integration meetings. The project manager will periodically get representatives from each of the process areas together to discuss things that are done in one process area that impact other areas. With highly integrated business applications, transactions in one process often share information with and affect processing in other areas. Decisions made by one of the process teams may conflict with decisions made by other teams. Or decisions in one area may create new requirements and the need for action in other areas. These integration issues need to be identified and communicated early in the project.

The process lead is also the primary liaison with the process owner and the key users in areas impacted by process changes. As such, the lead has responsibility for many of the change management activities in a particular process area. Of special importance is ensuring that process owners and steering committee members from the function area impacted are aware of, and support, key decisions being made by the process team.

Finally, the process lead works with the project manager to assess the progress of the team, identify issues, and determine actions to take when parts of the project get off course.

The *process analysts* have primary responsibility for analyzing the existing business processes and redesigning these processes to meet the project goals and objectives, while taking advantage of the capabilities of the package. They are specialists both in particular business processes and in methods to create innovative solutions to tricky business problems.

The process analysts are the model builders. They start with industry models and then adapt them to the to-be processes for the organization. They simulate different process designs and determine their strengths and weaknesses. They understand business requirements and the people issues associated with process changes and try to determine the best way to meet project objectives while minimizing the impacts on the organization and its people. They understand how to determine which processes must be significantly changed to meet project objectives and which require minimal redesign.

The process analysts are also heavily involved in data conversion, testing, user procedure development, and end-user training. They work with the IT staff to identify data-conversion requirements and sources of data in the legacy systems. They create test scenarios and data for transaction and integration tests. They use the process models as a base for creating user procedures. They identify policy changes that make processes simpler and more flexible. And they create the training materials and are involved in delivering the training to the eventual users of the new system.

All these tasks require creativity, strong people skills, knowledge of business processes, and an understanding of design principles for improving these processes. The process analysts may or may not have worked with the package that is being implemented. Although they will have to learn the capabilities of the package to determine what process designs are possible and practical, their role on the project is to focus on the business and process design aspects of the new system.

The *package analysts* bring to the team detailed knowledge of the specific package that is being implemented. They understand its capabilities and limitations. They understand the different options that are supported by the package and how to configure the software to support the options selected by the team.

The people filling these positions should have prior experience implementing this package. An important role for the package analysts is to transfer knowledge to the other team members so they can rapidly climb the steep learning curve for any new, complex business application. They cannot perform this role if they are learning the package along with the rest of the team.

The package analysts should have implementation experience. Therefore, they already understand the tasks that the process team will perform during the project. They can help guide the process team through complex tasks such as process prototyping and integration testing.

For an organization's first rapid implementation project for a new package, the package specialists usually come from outside the organization. Often, they are provided by the consulting or vendor organizations. In some cases, organizations hire people with specific package experience to participate on a rapid implementation project and support these systems after the go-live. In either scenario, one of the goals of the first implementation should be to transfer knowledge and train several of the organization's core team members to perform this role on subsequent projects.

Package analysts generally focus on one area of a vendor's software. For the less complex packages, they may focus on the financial, distribution, manufacturing, or human resource modules. For the more complex packages, they focus on submodules within an application area. For example, instead of being a financial module specialist, the package analyst may focus on one of the financial submodules: general ledger, cost accounting, accounts payable, accounts receivable, fixed assets, treasury management, or consolidations.

Realistically, the organization should not expect any one person to know the details of all the areas of even a moderately complex standard packaged application. For complex applications, it is not even fair to expect any one person to know all the aspects of any one area like finance or manufacturing. These systems are just too large and complicated. It requires a team of package specialists to configure all the components of these systems.

The *key users,* or *power users* as they are sometimes called, are part-time members of the team. They are an important source of information for the core team. After go-live, they are also a source of information and guidance to the other users of the system.

Key users are involved throughout the implementation, but their level of involvement varies depending on the tasks being performed. Given the iterative nature of a rapid implementation, their involvement is more continuous than is often the case for traditional, longer-timeframe implementations.

The time of the key users must be leveraged as much as possible. Unlike the core team members, the key users have their regular jobs to perform. Their department managers and supervisors sometimes need to make special arrangements to free up time for them to work with the implementation team. However, it usually is not too difficult to convince the department managers, and the key users, that involvement with the project team is a high priority. Since the decisions being made by the core team will determine how many things will get done in their departments in the future, both the managers and users have a vested interest in ensuring that the right decisions are made.

A prerequisite for assuming a key user role on the team is to be a project supporter. There is no time to waste on people whose primary job in life seems to be to point out all the reasons the new system will fail and why the old way of doing things is better. The key users need to be part of the solution, not part of the problem.

The key users play important roles in requirements definition, prototyping solutions in a conference room pilot setting, data cleansing, reviewing training materials, presenting training sessions to other users, and performing a users acceptance test of the system. Once the new system is live, they are often a source for other users to go to for suggestions on ways to solve problems with the new system.

The last group in this area of the core team organization is the *technical support team.* There is a full-time role for several IT professionals to support each implementation. On a rapid implementation team of 12 to 15 people, it is not uncommon for two or three of these individuals to be programmers, systems analysts, or database administrators. These core team members are also backed up by other individuals in the IS department who have responsibility for the technical infrastructure and legacy applications. There are a number of roles that these people perform.

The *technical lead* is the team leader for the technical team. This person is responsible for planning and reviewing the work of all the technical people supporting the project and coordinates the technical activities with those of the rest of the core team. The technical lead attends the project manager's integration meetings and brings technical knowledge and perspective to the discussions. This person is the primary liaison between the team and the IS organization and between the team and the vendor's technical support group. Like the other team leads, this person also performs detail tasks on the project.

The *programmers and database analysts* (sometimes this is a dual role) are responsible for performing many of the technical tasks for the project. They write and test interface programs and data-conversion utilities. They download bug patches from the vendor and install and test these changes to the system's programs. They use tools provided with the package to create forms and special reports for the team. These individuals also help support the other technology requirements of the team including access to the local area network, email, and project data repositories.

Another key obligation for these individuals is to ensure there is adequate backup and recovery of the technical resources of the project. The project team cannot afford to lose months of work because a system problem or disaster destroys the development version of the system and there is no way to recover the work done to date. This situation could cause the team to start configuration all over again. Or imagine losing the training materials a week before end-user training begins because the hard drive on the server crashes.

Good risk management on these projects means looking for all the things that could go wrong, evaluating the impact if they occurred, and then taking appropriate action to prevent or mitigate those risks that could significantly affect the success of the project. Disaster recovery planning is just one of the areas where this is important.

Each of the new, complex packages requires a *package administrator* to support the implementation and ongoing use of the package. This person installs the software as delivered, often on multiple CDs, from the vendor. This installation includes establishing all the operating system and database linkages for the package. Then the administrator creates and maintains all the different instances of the system: development, test, quality assurance, and production.

Throughout the project, the administrator works to maintain different versions of the application and control access rights to the different versions. This control is necessary so no team member can inadvertently change parts of the system that have already been tested and approved. The administrator also sets up end users in the system and, based on input from the process leaders, implements the access rights for each user or category of user.

Given the small number of people on the process and technical teams, it will be necessary for all the team members to pitch in and help each other out during the implementation. This is especially true when one area on the critical path gets behind schedule. An added advantage of this approach is that there will be a lot of cross training for team members. Because of this, the impact of losing a team member in any of the areas will be to some extent minimized.

USE OF SPECIALISTS

The external team is made up of people who support the project with special skills and knowledge, but are not part of the core team and are not employees of the organization. *Outside specialists* include those brought in for complex tasks or to solve particular problems that are being faced by the team. Effective use of these individuals is critical to the success of rapid implementation projects.

In order to meet a fixed implementation schedule, a rapid implementation cannot lose momentum and have anything slow down progress. It cannot get bogged down solving any of the problems that inevitably will crop up during an implementation. Each problem must be quickly diagnosed and its solution identified and executed.

Given the complexity of the issues faced in these implementations (organizational, technical, package, and process), there will always be things that come up that are beyond the knowledge and experience of the implementation team. There are other things that are just plain difficult and time consuming to do, especially if it is the first time the team members are facing the problem. This will be true even if the project has been staffed with people that have implemented these systems before. No matter how many implementations a person does, there will always be new issues and problems in the next one because every organization is different and uses systems differently.

When faced with these situations on a longer project, the normal approach is for the team members to do their research and homework, and then begin a trial-and-error process to discover a solution to the problem. The learning curve in these situation is often very steep and the solution development process long. The result is that the team can often take weeks or months to come up with a solution. Unfortunately, such a delay will cripple a rapid implementation. All problems need to be quickly addressed.

On a rapid implementation, the project manager must know two things:

1. When to bring in a specialist because it will take too long for the team to figure out a solution to the problem on their own
2. How to find the right person to bring in

In most cases, the team will initially try to solve the problems that surface during an implementation without asking for outside help. A top-quality, cross-functional team of people who have been trained on the package will be able to solve most of the problems that crop up. They also can look to the vendor's support organization to assist them with many problems.

Soon after it becomes evident that the team members do not have an easy solution to a problem, the problem should hit the issues log. Given the time boxing of individual activities into no more than two-day tasks, the team should know they have a problem within a couple of days of starting work on a task.

As the project manager routinely checks on task status, team members will describe problems they are facing and attempts that have been made to fix the problems. From these discussions, the project manager may get the first indications of problems that may require the assistance of outside specialists. In addition, as a result of monitoring the issues-tracking system daily, the project manager will also see problems that are taking longer than expected to solve.

One of the first responses will be to bring in other, perhaps more experienced, project team members to help with the problem. However, if an issue still is not speedily resolved, then the project manager should consider bringing in outside resources to help the team solve the problem. These resources can come from the package vendor, the consulting organization supporting the implementation, or other third parties.

The project manager should begin with the first two options. These organizations may have competency centers manned by their most experienced personnel (e.g., gurus in specific areas) to address the complex and tricky problems involved in implementing certain package modules or technologies. If resources are not available from such centers, the vendors and consultants may be able to pull more experienced personnel from other projects for a few days to solve a particular problem. Both of these sources should be simultaneously pursued to determine the best resource that is currently available, in the quickest time.

If the right resources cannot be found in the vendor and consultant organizations, or they do not have people available in the required timeframes, then the team should look to other, third-party organizations. Even if forced into this direction, the organization should lean on the vendor and consultant to identify these resources. Both organizations often have contacts and relationships with an entire network of organizations that support a particular vendor's products.

These specialists will be expensive. However, given the alternative of having several team members spend weeks trying to solve a problem, and maybe not ever coming up with a solution, the cost is worth it to the team and the organization. To get the maximum value from the specialists, the project manager should ensure that other team resources are available to describe the problem and the solutions that have already been attempted. Then, the team members should work through a solution, with the specialist taking the lead.

There will be situations where the specialist will determine that some process or function the team is trying to implement is not supported by the package. If this is the case, it is best to learn this quickly, and not after valuable project time is expended to come to the same conclusion. In such instances, the team can look at possible workarounds to achieve the same objective. However, another option is to decide that the desired process or function will just not be included in the scope of this project. In some cases, the function needed may be available in the next version of the vendor's software.

There are several types of specialists that are commonly used in these implementations. They fall into the general categories of package, technical, and organizational specialists.

The *package specialist* knows the detailed capabilities and requirements of specific vendor modules. They know how these modules interact with other modules in the vendor's suite and how to configure the module to support certain approaches to business processes. They are often brought in for the most complex modules available from the vendor, where the learning curve is especially steep—perhaps too steep for the time available in a rapid implementation.

Package specialists are also needed for some new modules where there is not a lot of actual customer experience and parts of the module may not work as depicted in the documentation. Package specialists may also be required when the implementation is using best-of-breed and other third-party packages that are being integrated with and bolted on to the main applications.

Technical specialists are sometimes needed to augment the knowledge and skills of the project's IT support group. They may be specialists in the technical architecture used by the package, as well as in particular operating systems (e.g., NT, UNIX, OS/400, Linux) or databases (e.g., Oracle, SQL Server, Informix). The key is to find people who know operating systems and databases and how these systems are used by the particular package being implemented.

Technical specialists may be used to help resolve bugs in the software, develop data-conversion programs, set up security for the new system, tune the databases to work optimally with the application, design network architectures to reduce data communication bottlenecks, or develop interfaces between different parts of the technical architecture. In many cases these technical specialists will bring to the team experience with new Internet technologies and standards (e.g., XML).

Organizational specialists may be brought in when it is determined that organizational design or change management issues are beyond the capabilities of the project team to quickly resolve. They may provide guidance on organizational structure, employee job design, communication strategies, training techniques, and incentive programs that can support the deployment of the new system.

The project manager must carefully manage the time of specialists. This expensive resource must be focused on the problem that must be solved. This time should also be leveraged as much as possible through the use of other project resources.

The project manager must also quickly determine whether the specialist has the knowledge and experience to solve the identified problem. There will be cases where the specialist does not know as much as was hoped or is knowledgeable in areas that are different from those required to quickly solve the problem. In these situations, other specialists with the right skills and knowledge should be quickly identified.

RAPID IMPLEMENTATION CHANGE

There are a number of changes that result from implementing new packaged applications. The most obvious change is that users will have to learn a new computer system and new screens to process transactions and access information. The most significant change is that business processes—the way the organization does its work—can be done faster, better, and cheaper.

But changes from implementing these applications can impact a number of other areas: organizational culture and structure, workflow, manager and employee job responsibilities, skill and knowledge requirements, worker motivation and incentives, communications pathways, operating policies and procedures, human resource policies, and the use of new technologies.

From a business point of view, these changes are good. If things do not change after go-live, it will not be possible to realize any of the expected benefits from these projects. And, given the rate of change being experienced in all industries, not making changes to the organization and its business processes means not being responsive to the demands of the marketplace.

From the point of view of the organization's managers and employees, these changes may not look as appealing. Change in any form creates doubts and unknowns. And reaction to the unknown is often overt and covert resistance to the changes. As we saw from the CIO survey, this resistance can be a major barrier to successful implementations.

The extent of change varies significantly from implementation to implementation. Every project does not result in all the changes listed earlier. Some projects create minimal change while others result in dramatic changes in the organization. Unfortunately, the projects that usually result in the greatest benefits to the organization are those that create the most changes.

The rate of change also has a significant influence on the amount of resistance that the project team may face and the ability of the organization to absorb change. People can absorb changes better if they come in small chunks, and not all at once. That may be one reason that many large reengineering efforts have failed. They implemented too much change in too short a timeframe. The extent and rate of change was too large for the people in the organization to absorb.

As a result of new technologies and e-business concepts, today there is the potential for greater changes than have ever been experienced in the history of business organizations. New business models are being explored that totally change the relationships among the organizations in an industry or supply chain. Manufacturing companies are creating new marketing channels that eliminate the need for distributors and retailers; they go straight to the end consumer. Colleges are looking at distance learning as a way of changing the way students receive their education. Organizations are creating joint ventures with their competitors. Electronic auctions are being conducted to determine the cheapest sources of materials and services. Exchanges are being created to bring buyers and sellers together in efficient electronic marketplaces.

On top of these massive changes, there are new expectations on how long it should take to implement these changes. Organizations are implementing web-based exchanges, in a matter of months, that totally change the purchasing practices of an entire industry. They are implementing e-retailing applications in eight weeks that bypass a whole marketing channel. New accounts payable and general ledger systems are being selected and implemented, using the hosting services of an application service provider, in four weeks or less.

These changes cannot happen all at once. If they did, they would be too large for any organization to absorb. However, organizations cannot wait for years for these changes to be implemented. Rapid implementations help in both of these areas.

By doing a number of smaller and faster projects, which is a basic tenet of the rapid implementation strategy, the organization is able to reduce the rate of change experienced by its managers and employees. The limited scope of each project results in less change than is typical in a longer project that takes years to complete before go-live. With rapid implementations, changes occur every three or four months, but they are at a manageable level. Small, continuous changes are often easier to absorb than large changes that rock the foundations of an organization.

In addition, a rapid implementation strategy gets changes in place more quickly, so the organization can start receiving benefits earlier. Instead of taking a year to perform a project to implement auction, exchange, and supply chain collaboration capabilities within an organization, a series of rapid implementations will have the auction site up at the end of the first month, the exchange ready three months later, and the supply chain system in place at the end of the year. The total change is spread over three projects and three separate go-lives.

MANAGING CHANGE

The fact that the magnitude of change for any individual project is reduced using a rapid implementation approach does not mean that the team does not have to work hard on changes issues. Change is a relative concept. Any implementation project that meets its goals and objectives will cause changes. And these changes have to be managed to produce a successful project.

There are, however, some indicators to predict when managing change may be a particularly difficult challenge. In general, change management will be more difficult in the following situations:

- There is no visible top management support or commitment to the project.
- A critical business imperative (i.e., burning platform) has not been established for the project.
- The implementation will cross multiple organizational boundaries.
- The implementation will take place in many different locations.
- The organization has a history of failures with similar projects.
- There are a number of other initiatives going on at the same time.
- There is disagreement among top management on the value of the project.
- The financial benefits that will result from implementation are not significant.
- The financial benefits expected from the project are extremely aggressive.
- The project is not a strategic initiative.
- Managers are already positioning to protect their turf, even before the project begins.
- It is difficult to identify an executive sponsor for the project.
- The project manager and sponsor have trouble getting the right people staffed on the project on a full-time basis.
- There are indications that it will be difficult to get significant participation from the key users to support the efforts of the core team.

Hopefully, no project exhibits all of these indicators. However, if the project manager sees even three or four of these symptoms, then there may be a need to take a more formal and extensive approach to managing change on the project.

Change management is a group of activities that the project team does to prepare the organization to accept the changes that result from the implementation. This helps the organization take advantage of the benefits of the new processes and the capabilities of the technologies supported by the packaged application. These activities are critical to the success of most projects. They should be woven into the project workplan and the day-to-day actions of the project team.

During the implementation, the team must continuously assess the readiness of the organization to make changes and identify pockets of resistance to the changes that result from the project. To build support and commitment for the new processes, the team should involve key users and managers in various project activities. Where possible they should be part of the decision-making process. If this is not possible, particularly because of the need to make rapid decisions, then the team should build consensus around the decisions that have been made. The end result is an environment where the users and their managers feel ownership for the system and work to make it successful.

To achieve this end result, it will be necessary for the project team to develop and execute a change management plan. This plan is tailored to the unique challenges of each project. It addresses the activities that the team will carry out to support the four change management levers:

1. Communication
2. Involvement
3. Training
4. Job design

Communication

Good communication is key to the success of any implementation. Communication creates awareness throughout the organization of the objectives, activities, and status of the project. People want to know what is going on. If they are not given accurate and timely information, they will make up and spread their own version.

Frequent communications is also a valuable tool in managing expectations. Success in these projects is relative. It depends not on what is actually achieved, but on how big the gap is between what is achieved and people's expectations. And expectations are in the eye of the beholder. Each user and manager has different expectations. Good communications will help manage these expectations throughout the project so the expectations will move closer to what can actually be delivered.

Managing expectations is especially difficult in rapid implementations. Setting expectations is also difficult. Both facts are the result of the dynamic scope and fixed timetables for these projects.

Since the detailed scope is established as the project progresses, the expectations must change along with the scope. Therefore, it is best to go into these projects with a minimum of detailed expectations. The team will determine what and how much can be accomplished during the project. This occurs only after prototyping and testing various ways to meet the project goals and objectives.

The status of these efforts should be communicated as soon as they are determined. This communication will be done through presentations, newsletters, status reports, system demonstrations, project web sites, and one-on-one meetings—whatever it takes to keep people informed.

Involvement

Getting key users and managers involved in project activities is also a good way to keep them informed. People want to be involved in things that may affect their jobs.

They also expect to be asked to provide information and opinions on areas for which they are responsible or have unique skills and expertise. Therefore, the team should make specific plans to involve key people in requirements definition, design, prototyping, testing, and training activities.

This involvement provides important input and feedback to the core team while creating a sense of ownership in the minds of those who will have a key role in making the new system successful. This involvement should not be superficial; most users will see right through such attempts. The users and managers need to be involved enough to truly understand the issues and options that are available. For the ultimate success of the project, it is important to remember and act on the cliché: no involvement, no commitment.

Training

Training provides another opportunity to manage the impacts of change associated with a new system. People are often fearful of change because they do not understand what, or how much, will be changed. They may also be concerned about their ability to learn a new way of doing their daily tasks. Training helps to ease these fears, doubts, and concerns.

The training in a rapid implementation should be hands-on. The users should perform their normal job tasks using the capabilities of the new system. They should not spend training time reading user manuals or other application documentation. If there are tools to help them do their jobs (e.g., job aids, procedure descriptions, process models), they should be used to support the hands-on training. There should also be sufficient time in the training sessions to answer all the questions that the users may have.

The key users and the core team members from the organization should lead the training. The vendor representatives and consultants may be available (in the back of the room) to answer system and technical questions, but they should not lead the training. This approach helps to promote buy-in by the users. They will see that people like themselves have learned the system and can describe, in terms they understand, how to use the new system to do their jobs.

Job Design

The changes that result from implementing new business processes and applications (especially some of the new e-business applications) may have enormous impacts on people's jobs. As organizations take advantage of the integrated nature of new systems, wider access to information, and the capabilities of new technologies, this creates a requirement to redesign jobs. Job changes can also come from organizations changing their business relationships and organizational structure in response to the rapidly changing business demands of an e-business economy.

People's jobs may expand as a result of having wider access to information and responsibility for performing more steps in a business process. Or their responsibilities may be reduced as the trend toward self-service applications accelerates. The new jobs may also require the use of new technologies such as handheld devices and wireless access through the Internet.

In order to manage these changes, it is important for the implementation team to document changes that must be made to individual jobs and execute plans to help people transition to their new jobs. This transition may require additional training in tools and skills that will be key in performing the new roles. Doing job redesign and transition planning properly requires specific training and experience in the area of organizational design. This a specialty area of expertise that project team members will usually not have. Therefore, it is another situation where specialists should be brought in to augment the skills and capabilities of the core team.

It is easy to see that everyone on the team has some change management responsibilities. All team members are involved in communicating with stakeholders, getting people involved in project activities, training users in their area of the application, and evaluating whether jobs should be expanded or contracted to take advantage of technical capabilities and new business processes.

However, experience shows that if someone on the team is not assigned overall responsibility for change management, many of the activities that should take place will not occur. The time commitment for this project role depends on the magnitude of change that will result from the project. For a project with minimal change impact, this may be a part-time role for one of the core team members. For a project with massive change potential, the role may require a subteam of change management experts.

The key point is that change management is so important that someone should be assigned responsibility to ensure that it is appropriately handled. Doing so will help the team manage the people issues, which can be the most difficult aspect of these projects.

6

MAKING IMPLEMENTATIONS BUSINESS AND PROCESS DRIVEN

One of the key premises of this book is that a rapid implementation—or any implementation for that matter—should be business and process driven. These projects should not be done just to implement new technologies, such as the latest client-server or Internet-based technologies. They are not primarily about implementing a particular vendor's standard applications. Also, these projects provide little value if the new package is implemented in a way that just replicates old business processes and ways of doing business.

Rapid implementations will be successful only if they are done to meet critical or key business needs. And the only way this will happen is if business objectives and interests drive the project.

A number of things can be done to keep the project business oriented:

- Top management can stay involved and show visible support and commitment for the project. Management can also communicate the business imperative to the organization.

- The steering committee, representing the key functions of the organization, can act to ensure that the business objectives of the project are kept in the forefront. They can also designate process owners.

- A business case can be developed and used to define the goals and objectives of the project and guide day-to-day decisions.

- The project manager can be chosen from the business departments, and not from IT.

- Business process specialists can be made key members of the core team.

- Process models can be used as a tool in many of the project tasks.

Process models provide a good example of a key tool that helps keep the implementation focused on business issues. During a rapid implementation process models can be used to:

- Define and communicate project scope.
- Provide a standard process view.
- Graphically define objectives.
- Assign project team tasks by process.
- Document the understanding of the business and its requirements.
- Prioritize processes to be redesigned based on desired benefits and business strategies.
- Define the to-be processes.
- Support package gap analysis.
- Ensure that benefit goals are supported by process changes.
- Document interfaces.
- Support the development of test scenarios.
- Serve as a component of user procedure and training materials.

If properly leveraged, these models provide a way to keep the team focused on the reason for doing rapid implementations: make process changes that take advantage of the capabilities of standard software to address business problems and meet the continuing challenges of a rapidly changing business environment.

At the end of the day, the project will be successful only if improvements have occurred in the way the organization does its work. This requires change. These changes may be in the way processes are performed; the roles and responsibilities of departments, managers, and employees; the way decisions are made with new sources of information; or the way that technology supports all these areas.

This chapter will cover how the capabilities of a package are used to enable the redesign of business processes and how the team approaches the project from a business perspective. It addresses some of the issues connected with making business process changes. It also looks at some of the approaches, tools, and techniques that can be used by the project team to address business issues during a rapid implementation.

A useful model of the degrees of business change that occur in package implementations is shown in Figure 6-1. This diagram shows the continuum of change from paving the cow paths on the left to reengineering on the right. In the middle of this diagram is an approach to implementation that is called *package-enabled process redesign*. This is the recommended approach for rapid implementations.

FIGURE 6-1   Business Process Change Continuum

Paving the Cow Paths   Package-Enabled   Reengineering
                              Process Redesign

Degree of Process Change

NO REENGINEERING ALLOWED

An organization should not attempt to do business process reengineering (BPR) in a rapid implementation project. BPR takes more time than is available for a project with a rapid timetable. It also does not fit well with a strategy of using packaged applications, without modifying the vendor's software, to support business processes. What the organization can do in a rapid implementation is something different, and less ambitious, called package-enabled process redesign.

Pure business process reengineering creates a clean-sheet design for an organization's processes with the goal of making radical, dramatic improvements. The aim of the reengineering team is to design the optimal way of performing a business process, given no constraints. Starting with a blank page and using a great deal of creativity, these teams try to figure out ways to perform a business process in a fraction of the current time and with greatly reduced costs.

An example of this approach may be examining an accounts payable process that takes a lot of resources to match invoices to purchase orders and receiving reports, and deciding not only to eliminate the matching but to pay based on the order, without requiring an invoice from the supplier. Another example might be figuring out how to change a manufacturing process so that the company makes an item only when it has an order (i.e., lean manufacturing), eliminating millions of dollars of finished goods inventory.

When you look at a business process from a no-constraints perspective, there are a number of things that can be ignored. One is the current way the process is performed. In reengineering there is no attempt to build on or improve the existing process. So, the way things have been done in the past is irrelevant, and actually gets in the way of taking an out-of-the-box view of how things could be done. Therefore, a reengineering team does not have to spend a lot of time interviewing the current employees to understand and model the current business process.

Another thing that is ignored is the capabilities of the current legacy systems or potential packages that may be implemented to support the reengineered process. As a result, the implementation of new, radical ways of doing things often requires custom-developed systems or a lot of modification to packaged applications. In many cases the modifications are so large that the resulting system may not resemble the original package. These modifications and custom-development activities take a lot of time and money. And they result in systems that are expensive to maintain and support.

A final constraint often ignored in reengineering projects is the capabilities of the existing personnel to perform the new process. Do they have the skills and experience to be able to do their jobs in the new, improved way? Often the new process design results in job redesign and enlargement, which requires replacing the current personnel, or at least the retooling of their skills and knowledge. Because of this, reengineering projects have often been associated with downsizing and outsourcing activities.

Reengineering *is* appropriate in certain situations. It has been successful in several cases in producing competitive advantages and dramatic improvements that would never have been achieved with other approaches. There are situations where it is the only valid strategy. However, reengineering does not come without its costs. This approach requires a lot of time and money and results in a tremendous amount of change within the organization. In addition, it is an extremely difficult approach to implement successfully. There have been a lot more failures in applying this approach than successes.

One of the reasons for reengineering failures is the difficulty in mixing a reengineering strategy with a standard package implementation approach. After the reengineering team creates the vision and design for the new process, it must be implemented. Often the organization will find that the package that they have chosen to implement the new system (e.g., SAP, Oracle) does not support the way the process has been designed. As a result, the organization is forced to either throw out the package and start a large custom development effort or make extensive modifications to the package. Since these are extremely complex packages, making any modifications to them is a dangerous undertaking. These modifications usually invalidate the vendor's support for the application and make it difficult to implement future versions of the vendor's software.

Another critical problem with a reengineering strategy is that at the end of any two- or three-year project (most of the large-scale reengineering projects take that long), the problem that was originally being addressed has probably changed. Therefore, using this approach may not be as suitable in a rapidly changing business environment.

All this means that reengineered processes cannot be rapidly visioned, designed, programmed, and implemented. Therefore, by definition, the organization cannot do reengineering in a rapid implementation project. Speed is just not a characteristic of projects that take years to complete.

With a rapid implementation strategy, the organization will do many short projects instead of one massive one. The goal will be to make continuous improvements to business processes through a number of successive projects. And the team will design the new or improved processes with a good understanding of the capabilities of the package that is being used to support them.

At the opposite end of the business process change spectrum from reengineering is an approach that is associated with maintaining the status quo. For obvious reasons, this is often an attractive option for managers and users of business systems in an organization. However, like reengineering, it has weaknesses when the organization is attempting a business-driven rapid implementation.

DON'T PAVE THE COW PATHS

There is an inclination when implementing packaged applications to use new technologies to implement the same old ways of doing things. This is not a good approach because it does not take advantage of the capabilities of the package, limits the benefits that will be achieved from the new system, and adds time to the implementation. There are a number of factors that lead the implementation down this path. Some are related to the preferences of the end users and others to the activities of the project team. We begin by looking at the end-user influences.

If team members ask users what the new system should do, the most common answer will be: it should do the *same things* that the old system does today, only easier and better. Hidden in this response is the fact that the end users also want things done in the *same way* as they are done today. They do not want their jobs to change significantly as a result of implementation of a new system.

Sometimes users give this response because they do not know or have not considered other ways of doing their jobs. "We have always done it this way" is the universal response to why things are done a certain way. Most people do not spend a lot of time considering other, better ways of doing things. They may truly believe that the current methods are the best way of doing things. They may not consider it their job to design new ways of performing a process. Or, even if they have ideas about how things could be done better, they may not have the authority or opportunity for getting action on these ideas.

However, there is a more basic reason for preference for the old way of doing things. People do not like change. We know, and feel comfortable with, the current way of doing things. We fear the unknown: How will changes affect my job responsibilities? Will I be able to learn the new ways for doing things? Is it going to take a lot of time and effort to learn the new ways? Will I lose the advantages that come from being the only one who truly knows how things get done around here? Will I lose some of my power and influence as a result of the implementation project?

Everyone acknowledges that change is inevitable and organizations must change to survive. But we all want to minimize the effect of changes on our personal lives.

If the new system mimics the current way of doing things, then changes to an individual or department are minimized.

The end users are also working from a position of disadvantage. They do not understand how the new package works and therefore cannot express their requirements in terms of the capabilities and terminology of the new system. They do not receive the same level of training on the package that is given to the core implementation team. The training the end users receive usually occurs in the last stages of the project, after the scope and design of the system has been finalized.

So, spending a lot of time asking end users about system requirements will tend to produce a design for the new system that mimics the current environment. However, implementation teams are forced to have these discussions with the end users in order to better understand the system requirements and begin to involve the end users in the project. Without this involvement it will be difficult to gain support and commitment for the new system.

Ironic as it may seem, there are advantages in not asking the users what the new system should do or identifying all the things that the legacy system does. Some of the current activities in the departments and legacy system capabilities are not really necessary. They often were created in response to unique situations that may not even exist today. No one knows why things are done that way; that is just the way things have always been done. The result of years of maintenance to legacy systems is a lot of exception processing that creates an unnecessarily complex process.

One of the objectives in process redesign is to simplify things. Simple processes are easier to learn. They are also easier to change in response to business changes. Complex processes are difficult to learn and change.

A guaranteed way for creating an extremely complex process is to implement all the capabilities of the new packaged application. Therefore, a design principle should be to include only capabilities that are absolutely required to get the job done and achieve the benefits established for the project. In determining the scope and requirements for the new system, the project team should resist just asking users what they want from a new system or inventorying the capabilities of the legacy system.

Another approach to be resisted in a rapid implementation is spending a lot of time flowcharting the current processes. This can lead the team down the same path toward duplicating the existing processes in new technology. However, there is a big difference between flowcharting the as-is processes and using process models to define requirements and the to-be processes. Process modeling of future processes does not necessarily contribute to retaining the existing, outdated business processes. Also, as will be seen later, there are a number of benefits from process modeling.

This does not mean to imply that the implementation team would not learn a great deal from developing detailed process diagrams of the current processes. A lot of information would have to be gathered through interviews, document reviews, and observation in order to draw the diagrams. The act of drawing the diagrams would point out gaps in knowledge and raise a lot of questions that could then be investigated. The as-is documents that resulted could be reviewed with the end users to ensure that the team's understanding of the business processes is accurate.

But after this time-consuming activity is completed, the team still has documentation of the cow path. And there will be an expectation or tendency to implement all these process flows using the capabilities of the new package. This is not in the best interest of the organization.

Usually, the packaged application will do things differently from the way they are currently done. Given the integrated nature of the new packages, the use of new technologies, and the fact that they are developed in a highly competitive environment (i.e., there are hundreds of vendors trying to capture market share), the way the package performs business processes will usually be better than the way things can be done with old legacy systems and manual processes. Often, the package will support a process design that is a best practice in the industry.

Given this situation, the organization will generally be better off not spending a lot of time investigating and documenting the current processes. Instead, top management and the implementation team should set expectations early that business processes generally will be changed to conform with those supported by the package rather than configuring the package or modifying the vendor's code to duplicate the way things are currently done.

BUSINESS-DRIVEN PROJECTS

It has been stated that rapid implementations should be business driven in order to get maximum value from the investment in new packaged systems. But what does that mean? Being business driven requires a focus on vision, benefits, integration, processes, performance metrics, and a balanced IT perspective. These aspects are often ignored or handled badly in many implementation projects. As a result, those projects do not deliver on their promise and potential. The teams implement new technologies but do not improve business processes, cost structures, or the competitive position of the organization.

Vision

The way to start is with a vision. What is the organization trying to accomplish? Where do they see themselves in one year? Where do they see themselves in three years? What will they be doing differently at that time? What kinds of things must they be able to do well to survive and prosper in an increasingly competitive world? What are their strategies for meeting the challenges of a rapidly changing business environment?

Visions in the past were often fashioned around market share, size, and stock price. The current vision for many organizations has changed to creating a customer-centric, nimble, and rapidly responsive organization. The capabilities resulting from rapid implementation of ERP or e-business systems are often key factors in achieving that vision. The project team must understand the organization's vision. The project is done to support this vision and decisions must be made throughout the project with the vision in mind.

Benefits

Benefits must also be a major focus for each project team member. The project has been justified because the benefits that will result from it exceed the costs (both financial and other). Some of these benefits are tangible, others intangible. In some projects the benefits are laid out in a formal business case. In others, the benefits are less formally defined.

The only way to achieve either type of benefits is to keep them in mind when the team makes the thousands of decisions during an implementation. The team must focus on achieving benefits with the new system and not just on getting the project completed and going live on the new system on schedule.

In the past, the benefits from these projects primarily have been associated with cutting operational costs within the boundaries of the enterprise. In the future there will be a greater focus on cutting costs across the entire supply chain and increasing customer service and revenues through the intelligent use of technology in the customer-facing processes.

Integration

Integration is another key issue for the implementation. There are several integration areas that must be addressed by the team. The first one is a higher-level issue: the team must understand that getting maximum benefits from the new system requires integrating and aligning people, processes, organizational structures, strategies, compensation practices, policies, and technology. Significant improvements in business results require changes in most, or all, of these areas.

Unfortunately, most implementation teams treat many of these areas as out of scope. As a result they might change technology (through the use of packaged applications) and some business processes, but not organizational structures and policies. In many situations, these limited changes will not achieve the benefits desired from the project. Also, the process changes may not stick. After a period of time, the organization will revert to doing things the same way they used to—not using or taking full advantage of the new system.

Therefore, if the organization is really serious about making changes to take advantage of the capabilities of new software and using the implementation as a catalyst to improve business processes, then they must be open to and support changes that may impact roles, responsibilities, and policies within the organization.

Making substantial changes to business processes, and the associated factors that make process improvements possible, requires a lot of time and effort. On a rapid implementation, the team must be selective in which areas they will invest significant process redesign effort. Given the short timetable of a rapid implementation, there is only time to make this investment in one or two business processes. Therefore, the team must spend their time on areas with the greatest potential paybacks.

Lower-level integration issues center on interfaces with other systems and business processes. Often there are interdependencies across business processes. Many processes share information and processing logic with other processes. The implementation team must be aware of the impact their changes will have on other systems and business processes. Having a cross-functional group on the core team and good communication within the team are helpful in addressing these potential concerns.

Processes

To get the greatest value from the investment in a new system, the team must take a process-centric orientation to project tasks and focus on achieving results through a cross-organizational, end-to-end view of business processes.

Instead of concentrating on system menus, transactions, and computer screens, the team needs to live and breathe business processes. They need to be constantly asking: How can things be done faster, cheaper, and better using the capabilities of the packaged application? They need to look for ways to change processes to eliminate handoffs, delays, and redundant activities. They also need to focus on ways to increase the availability of information to support better coordination across the organization and the entire supply chain.

Most enterprises are not organized by business processes and never will be. Organizations are usually organized by strategic business units, functions, market segments, or geographies. But the team can do a lot to improve the performance of business processes across these organizational entities.

Process specialists are key members of the implementation team. Many enterprises have never developed process models for their organization or designated process owners. Therefore, the concept of a process orientation, or at least the application of this concept, may be new. The process specialists on the team have the experience and skills to support a process orientation for the implementation project.

Performance Metrics

It is difficult to improve anything if you do not measure it. It is also difficult to accurately gauge the results from an implementation project if appropriate success criteria and metrics were not defined and baselined before the project began. Experience has shown that creating metrics around the benefits from a project is one of the best techniques for ensuring that those benefits will be achieved.

Therefore, a business orientation to these projects requires an understanding of the value of performance management using metrics. It also requires some creativity in defining and producing the measurements.

If possible, the new system should report on performance as a natural byproduct of application processing. The metrics should not be calculated manually, outside the system. But either way, measuring and reviewing the right process and system metrics improves the chances of meeting the objectives from these implementation projects.

Balanced IT Perspective

Finally, a business-driven project looks at technology from a proper perspective. Information technology should not be allowed to become the tail that wags the implementation dog. The project is not being done to implement new technologies, no matter how attractive the technologies may be. The project is being done to improve business processes. Fortunately, technologies sometimes create opportunities to perform processes in ways never before possible; and many of the newer packages take advantage of these new technologies.

The project team must decide whether technologies like wireless communication, personal digital assistants (PDAs) and other handheld devices, web portals, and data warehouses make sense from a business perspective. Even if the packages support such technologies, there needs to be a business case for their implementation. Are they needed to make the process changes that produce the greatest benefits for the organization? Does implementing the new technologies add risk to the implementation that exceeds the incremental benefits they provide?

The team must not be afraid of new technologies (a better view is that technology is their friend) but must address the use of technology from a business perspective. Technologies are enablers of unbelievable changes to organizational and industry structures and practices. They should be leveraged as appropriate. But their introduction and use needs to be managed.

PROCESS MODELING

A key objective for most rapid implementations is to improve business processes so the organization can operate cost effectively and be more responsive to the needs of its customers and business partners. The requirement is for faster, better, and cheaper. The e-business revolution and the increasing capabilities of ERP and e-business packages are driving companies to use information and technology to dramatically change the way they perform business processes. One activity that helps keep the implementation team business focused is the use of process models throughout the implementation.

Process modeling is a method for *graphically* representing the *components* of a particular business process and the *relationships* between processes. (The key parts of this definition have been italicized.)

Much of the power of a process model comes from its graphical nature. Business processes can, and often are, described using words. These words are combined in narratives describing the flow of the process and the outputs produced at each step. However, the cliché is true that "a picture is worth a thousand words." A graphical model expresses complex information in a way that can be more easily understood and communicated. In addition, there are insights that arise from a review of a graphical model that would never occur to someone reading a process narrative.

Process models are used to define and communicate project scope, highlight process bottlenecks and changes, describe the interfaces between various processes, and show the parts of a business process that are supported by the package being implemented. When used appropriately they become an indispensable component in the project toolkit.

Variations in process models show what the process does, when and how the various processes interact, what organizational units are involved in performing the process, where costs are consumed, and (through the use of simulation tools) the advantages and disadvantages of various process designs.

Figure 6-2 shows the primary reasons why the implementation team uses process models in a rapid implementation. The use of these models is essential in providing speed, solution effectiveness, consistency, and intellectual asset leverage to these projects. If the project team is not using process models while performing the day-to-day project activities, there is a greater likelihood that the project is merely installing software rather than changing business processes through the use of the package capabilities.

Process models can be used to depict those business processes that are included in the scope of the current project and, equally important, those that are deemed out of

FIGURE 6-2   Why Use Process Models?

Manage Scope and Focus

Organize Our Understanding

Document and Communicate

Ensure Completeness

Leverage Organization's Experience

scope. Refinement of this scope definition occurs throughout the project as the team learns more about the business needs of the organization, the capabilities of the package, and how much will be achievable during the project timeframe.

It is important to note that, in a rapid implementation project, the detailed scope of the project is usually not defined before the project begins. There is a continual refinement of the scope throughout the project. This creates the need for a tool to clearly show the scope, as it is known, at any point in the project. The project process model is a key tool that the entire team and the project stakeholders can turn to in order to answer the critical question: What business processes will be enabled in the current implementation project?

In addition, process models can be used to show those processes that will receive the focus of the team's process redesign efforts. In a rapid implementation, the organization will adapt most of its business processes to the standard way the package performs a process. In many cases there is no need to redesign the processes. The team implements the processes as designed by the software vendor while using configuration capabilities to tailor the design to the specific needs of the organization.

However, the team needs to make a more extensive examination of those processes that are critical to achieving the objectives and benefits of the project. The team analyzes the package alternatives for supporting these processes and various ways to combine process, organizational, policy, and package variables to meet the objectives. These activities take time and require broad knowledge of how the package works and a good dose of creativity. In order to keep the project on schedule, it is necessary to clearly identify and limit the processes for which this additional work will be done.

Models of the to-be processes document how the package will be used to support the business processes in the production environment. The quality and detail of these models is refined throughout the project as the team gains a better understanding of the capabilities of the package and the needs of the organization.

Process models are a great way to document the way the processes will work after the new system is implemented. When properly constructed, they are easy to understand and facilitate communication between team members, project sponsors, and the ultimate users of the system. These models will be key components of the user procedure manuals that are developed by the team. They are also used in the end-user training sessions.

The starting point for creating a project process model is a complete organizational process model. The organizational process model shows all the operational and infrastructure processes. The specific processes included in this model usually vary somewhat from industry to industry. Often the infrastructure processes (e.g., accounting, fixed assets management, payroll) are similar among industries. However, the operational processes (e.g., manufacturing, patient billing, student registration) vary significantly among industries and even segments within an industry.

The processes impacted by any implementation project are a subset of the entire population. However, starting from a view of all the organization's processes and then showing those to be addressed by the current rapid implementation helps define the project scope. The organizational models can be color coded to show processes in scope versus those out of scope. They can also show the subprocesses and activities supported by the packaged application versus those handled manually or by legacy or third-party products.

Finally, the organizational process models that serve as a starting point for the project models are valuable intellectual assets. They contain a great deal of knowledge and information about how things get done in the organization, how closely related activities are grouped, and the relationship between the various business processes. They provide a context into which the activities of current implementation project can be placed. These models also provide a standard organizational structure and terminology for processes within the organization.

Some of the process models will also include a mapping to the capabilities of the package being implemented. These models show clearly which processes are supported by the package and which must be handled by other means.

If the organization does not have its own process model, one should be developed for use by the implementation team. These can be developed from scratch or tailored from those available from other sources.

VENDOR PROCESS MODELS

Many of the software vendors and system integrators have their own process models to support implementations. These models vary significantly in their scope, cost, and potential use. In many cases, they provide a good starting point for many activities in a rapid implementation. With these models, the team does not have to start from scratch to prepare organizational or project-specific process models. These commercially available models can usually be tailored to the unique needs of the organization.

Some of the models are generic and are used in implementations for any industry. Others include processes that are unique to a particular industry. For example, a generic model would not have student registration processes that would be important for a college or university. However, a higher-education model would include these types of processes and subprocesses and others related to educational institutions (e.g., maintaining transcripts, managing student housing).

The generic model would have several processes that apply to most organizations, such as accounting and finance, human resources, payroll, marketing, fixed assets, and accounts payable. Also, the implementation team could tailor the generic model to add missing processes and delete those that may not apply. The processes can also be reorganized and renamed to make them consistent with the way things are viewed in the organization or its industry.

Industry-specific process models tend to be of greater value to an implementation team. They already include those processes that are unique to the industry. They also use terminology and combine processes in a way that makes sense for those who work in that industry. Common industries where there may be industry-specific models include the following: high tech, retail, energy, utilities, telecommunications, manufacturing, public sector, healthcare, higher education, and financial institutions.

Even within an industry there are significant variations depending on the organization's industry segment or vertical. For example, manufacturers are often segmented into automotive, aerospace, process, engineer-to-order, repetitive, consumer goods, and several other manufacturing verticals. Many of the software vendors focus on particular industries or verticals and develop specific functionality in their products to support these market segments. They may have specific process models for each vertical.

The scope of commercially available process models varies significantly. The models from systems integrators and general consulting organizations tend to cover all the business processes of the organization. Often, they do not imply the use of any particular software package. They also do not distinguish between those processes that are manual and those that may be automated.

The process models from many of the software vendors are often application-package specific. They describe the processes supported by that particular package. If the vendor's suite of applications does not include a payroll module, you may not see a payroll process in its model. Also, the models may just show the automated parts of a process and not include those manual steps that often occur in conjunction with automated steps.

There are generally three levels in a process model. At the top level are the high-level processes. The number of high-level processes varies significantly among the various models. Some have five or six high-level processes. Others may have 30 or more processes at this level.

High-level processes include: market and sell products, manage orders, buy goods and services, provide customer support, perform accounting and finance, manage human resources, manage logistics, and control fixed assets. In situations with a smaller number of high-level processes, they may include processes with names like order-to-cash or purchase-to-payment.

At the next level down are the subprocesses. Each high-level process can be broken down into a number of subprocesses. For example, the high-level process, manage human resources, can be broken down into the following subprocesses: plan for employee requirements, manage recruiting, develop and train employees, manage payroll, and manage benefit programs. Obviously, the right number and categories of subprocesses are a matter of judgment.

At the lowest level of most process models are activity diagrams. These are often flowcharts of the steps it takes to perform any of the subprocesses. For example, you may be able to drill down from the subprocess, manage payroll, and see all the steps that are required to process payroll. These might include: add new employees, gather timekeeping data, maintain benefits and deductions, calculate payroll, prepare payroll checks, process direct deposits, and record payroll transactions in the general ledger.

Some process models include a fourth level. This additional level is usually available in models that have been linked to specific vendor products. These models come in two flavors: a user view and an implementation team view.

In the user view, if someone clicks on a step in the activity diagram (this assumes the model is being maintained in a modeling tool), the package screen that handles that transaction appears. This may be just a screen shot (picture of the screen). However, in some model implementations the screen that appears is the actual production screen on which the user can enter data and process the transaction. These models can be used to guide the users through the transaction processing flow.

The second variant provides an implementation team view. In this case, clicking on a step in the activity diagram will take the implementation team member to the screen in the package that is used to configure the product to handle that step. This provides a guide to the configuration components of the package.

There is sometimes organizational resistance to using commercially available models. Many organizations believe that they are so unique that they need to develop their own models from scratch. In addition, managers and employees in all organizations will have different opinions on what the high-level processes and subprocesses should be and how they should be organized.

Most small and midsized organizations have not developed their own process models and are prepared to begin with the ones provided by the vendor or consultants working on the implementation. However, larger organizations tend to want to modify the available models significantly to represent their point of view on how processes should be organized and represented. These modifications (which are often arbitrary) reduce the value of having existing models available and use up valuable time in a rapid implementation.

There are a variety of automated tools used to manage these models. Some are commercially available; others are proprietary tools of the package vendor. These tools usually have capabilities to tailor the process models to the needs of the organization and publish the models on paper and in an online, HTML format. This documentation is valuable in creating procedure manuals and materials for end-user training.

Many of the vendors say their process models reflect industry best practices. Whether this is true, and what that actually means, is subject to a number of different opinions. However, a good test of this claim is the amount of e-business content that has been incorporated into these models. In addition, state-of-the-art process models should reflect the new processes that are supported by best-of-breed packages in particular process areas.

All the vendors are in various stages of e-enabling their process models to take advantage of new process designs made possible by new business models and the use of Internet technologies. Often, these enhancements appear in the activity diagrams of the models. If the models do not include new processes enabled by the Internet, it is a safe bet that they do not reflect best practices in most industries.

Some of the vendors and integrators charge for their models and the tools used to support them; others provide them as part of the cost of the software or consulting services. It is important to determine the costs before committing to any particular tool.

Probably the most widely known vendor model is the *reference model* that comes with SAP R/3 software. This is a complex model that includes all the functions supported by the SAP software. This module contains thousands of subprocesses. Other examples include models used in the Dynamic Enterprise Modeler (DEM) tool that comes with the Baan applications, the models in the Qwizard tool from QAD, and the IndustryPrints and SolutionPrints models from Deloitte & Touche.

Process modeling is an important activity in any package implementation. A key requirement for rapid implementations is a complete process model that the team can use as a starting point. There is usually not enough time to create these from scratch during a rapid implementation project.

BUSINESS CASE DEVELOPMENT

Many people question the return that organizations get from their investments in technology. Included in this category of investments are projects to implement packaged software. On one side of this issue are the technology champions who believe that technology has the potential to play a significant role in solving most problems that organizations face. On the other side are those that believe that organizations are wasting their money with most technology expenditures. Most people fall somewhere between these extremes but wish that there were ways to reduce the business risks associated with these projects and ensure an appropriate return on these investments. This is an important business issue since many companies spend more than half of their capital investments on IT.

At the source of some of these doubts is a perception that many organizations are investing in IT simply because they see other companies, including their competitors and customers, making such investments. There is sometimes a feeling that organizations must make similar investments or else fall behind. Another view is that investments in IT are driven by the IS department and the desire of technologists to stay current with the latest technologies. There is at least anecdotal evidence that both of these perceptions are valid to a certain extent.

Complicating this issue are investments that are considered necessary to position the organization to be responsive to business changes in the future, but may not be justified solely on their current financial returns. In this category may be investments in the technical infrastructure that is required to enable and support a number of the application system and e-business initiatives. It is difficult to justify such investments solely on their own merits. Therefore, organizations need to recognize that there are some investments in IT that have value to the organization but cannot be justified only by tangible benefits and internal rate of return calculations.

Luckily, it is becoming easier to make a business case for application system projects. In the past these projects were focused on back-office applications and applications affecting only people within the four walls of the organization. Advances in communication capabilities, wide acceptance of technical standards, and an increased sophistication in application functionality has changed this picture.

Now, the applications and the process changes they make possible can enhance customer relationships and help generate more revenue. Also, working with customers and suppliers, the new systems enable process changes and information sharing that reduce the costs of the entire supply chain. For example, in many cases the new applications allow organizations to trade information for inventory. If the partners in a supply chain share demand, forecast, and order information then each partner can usually lower its inventory levels.

A key insight in all this must not be missed: Old uses of technology allowed organizations to do things the old way, but faster through automation; new technologies allow organizations to do things differently, in ways that were not possible even a few years ago.

Faster processors, relational databases, sophisticated applications systems, and easy access to communication networks have come together to enable the transformation of organizations, their business models, and the way they do business. The significance of this is amazing.

New technologies allow organizations to be more flexible and quicker to respond to the increasing demands of their customers. These technologies also support new relationships among organizations and their suppliers, customers, and competitors. In addition, they are changing the expectations of customers and employees on how things should operate and the various roles of the participants (e.g., the push toward self-service for customers and employees).

In order to justify investments in new applications and technologies, organizations create business cases. These describe the problems to be solved and the opportunities to be captured. They quantify the costs that will be expended (the easy part) and the benefits or outcomes that will result (the hard part). They usually focus on the tangible or financial benefits and costs. However, some of the key benefits are often intangible (e.g., better information on which to make decisions, flexible systems that will support business changes in the future). There is a growing recognition that intangible benefits are important too.

Experience has shown that if these benefits are not clearly delineated and their achievement not made part of some person's annual goals, there is a good chance that they will not be achieved. Therefore, the business benefits from an implementation must be identified before the project begins. If a formal business case is not required, then the goals and objectives of the project should, at a minimum, be documented in the form of a project charter.

Along with process models, a business case is a key tool to keep the implementation aimed at the right target: business problems and benefits. Surveys have shown a strong correlation between those organizations that have had successful implementations and those that developed a business case before beginning the project.

A business case documents the business imperative for doing the project. It outlines the tangible and intangible benefits that should be delivered by the new system and the associated business processes. It addresses the question of how the project is going to improve the operating performance of the business. As such, it provides a set of criteria to guide project decisions.

The business case is also a living document. As the project scope is adjusted to meet the timetable of a rapid implementation and the implementation team members learn more about the software capabilities and the process requirements of the organization, the business case will need to be updated.

Usually, a rapid implementation will achieve only a subset of all the benefits defined in the business case. Other rapid projects, changing other processes, will meet the other objectives. Therefore, it is important to identify which benefits will be achieved in the current project and designate achievement of other benefits to future rapid implementations.

The project steering committee, executive sponsor, and project manager should all work together to ensure that the project team and the users of the system understand and work hard to achieve the benefits defined for the rapid implementation project.

PACKAGE-ENABLED PROCESS REDESIGN

If an organization is not reengineering processes as part of a rapid implementation, and should not replicate the existing processes, what should they do? The answer is package-enabled process redesign: improving business processes by understanding and taking advantage of an application package's standard capabilities.

This approach should not be thought of as being overly restrictive. It still provides room for creativity and innovation. The current packages are powerful and provide many alternatives and pathways for performing most business processes. The configuration activities in an implementation (i.e., setting system parameters to change how the system works) allow the project team to tailor the software to meet the unique needs of the organization. There is also a great deal of variety in how the detailed transactions and reporting capabilities supported by the package can be combined to create better ways to meet process objectives.

However, there will always be projects that are able to take advantage of the power of the software and others that fall short in delivering on the potential for process improvements. Success depends on how well a lot of very detailed activities are performed. It also depends on how well the implementation team understands how the package works and their ability to design improved business processes using package capabilities.

Consequently, the success of the redesign efforts depends, to a great extent, on the staffing of the core project team. If the cross-functional team is composed of smart, creative, knowledgeable people who understand the vendor's package and are skilled at doing process redesign, there is a high probability that the project will be successful. In this context, success is defined as creating improved processes that provide the benefits defined for the project.

However, success also depends on the willingness of management to consider changes in organizational structures, job responsibilities, and policies. Process improvements often require changes in these areas, as well as changes in the way technology is used to support the processes. Putting unnecessary constraints on the scope of change to be considered in redesigning processes will result in a level of improvement that may not meet the goals established for the project.

The ultimate success of redesign efforts will also depend on how successful the team is in managing change throughout the project. Will the users accept and support new methods for doing their jobs? Will middle management feel threatened by changes in their roles as a result of the enhanced reporting capabilities embedded in the package design? Will users be adequately trained in the new processes before going live with the new system? Has top management made it clear that, to take advantage of standard software, the organization will change its processes to the ways supported by the package? All of these things will affect the success of the redesign irrespective of the conceptual advantages of the to-be processes.

There are a lot of factors to be considered during process redesign activities. How these are handled results in acceptable designs, better designs, or just plain bad designs. The criteria established in the next section provide a standard against which to evaluate the designs that are created.

PROCESS REDESIGN GOALS

Some process improvements will occur as a natural byproduct of implementing state-of-the-art standard applications. There are tremendous advantages just in having integrated systems where information flows in real time across all areas of the organization, one database is used for all applications, and online access is available to information throughout the system. However, the team members should keep some basic design goals in mind as they adapt the organization's processes to the methods supported by the package. In particular, the to-be processes should be designed with the following principles in mind:

- Focus on the benefits.
- Simple is better.
- Leverage the capabilities of the package.
- Speed is king.
- Build on relationships.
- Promote self-service.
- Eliminate non-value-adding steps.
- Design for flexibility.

Focus on the Benefits

The project team must not lose sight of the fact that the implementation is being done to solve a number of distinct problems and take advantage of new opportunities. The desired objectives and benefits are documented in the project business case or charter. Given the aggressive timetable for a rapid implementation, there is a risk that the team will become fanatical about meeting the go-live date and forget the purpose of the project.

This is especially tricky in a rapid implementation where the scope of the project is not nailed down before the project starts. The rapid implementation approach is based on the principle that the organization will be better off in the long run by doing a number of smaller, fixed-timeframe projects rather than one large project. The belief is that smaller projects are easier to manage and more efficient. Because parts of the system will get implemented more quickly (i.e., the organization does not have to wait years for a go-live of all the functions and processes), the flow of benefits should be accelerated.

However, this approach leaves the detailed scope of each miniproject to the discretion of the steering committee and the project team. The team must resist the temptation to implement the easiest processes first. The first processes to be implemented should be those high-priority processes that provide the greatest benefits to the organization. These processes, along with perhaps a few that have low-hanging fruit, should be included in the scope of the first projects. This line of attack results in some initial wins for the rapid implementation strategy and a pleased and supportive group of top managers.

In addition to scope decisions, there are often multiple approaches for performing each process using the new system. One of the criteria for selecting between different design alternatives should be the impact that the selection will have on the flow of benefits to the organization. If the team keeps its eye on benefits in making these, and other, project decisions, then the organization will get greater returns from these implementations.

Simple Is Better

In most process design activities there usually is a choice between a simple approach and one that is more complex. The more complex approach often provides additional benefits, at least on paper. However, in general, the team should err on the side of the simpler solution.

A problem with the more complex solutions is that they are more difficult for people to learn and use. People performing complex processes make a lot of mistakes and the data in the system soon becomes corrupted. After a period of time the users will lose confidence in the existing process and the information maintained in the organization's systems.

As a result, people will bypass this solution and come up with different ways of getting the same job done. This often means using information and processes outside the organization's formal systems. This trend only exacerbates the problems with the formal systems. The end result is the organization never achieves the incremental benefits that were defined for the more complex solution.

Complex processes are also more difficult to change in response to changing business conditions. They are more difficult for new users to learn. And they are more difficult to diagnose when problems occur.

Complexity results from several factors. One is the number of people that have to get involved in handling a process from initiation to completion. Handoffs create complexity, greater chance of errors, and time delays. Another source of complexity is the quantity of exceptions that are handled along with the standard transactions. Some of these exceptions can be eliminated through changes in the organization's policies and procedures. Complexity is also created wherever there are a large number of components (e.g., screens, fields, transactions, reports, forms, and approvals) built into a process.

Designing simple processes means using the smallest number of steps possible. It means having one person do as much of the process as possible, before passing processing on to others. It means eliminating the sources of exceptions. It means hiding fields on screens and menu items that will never be used in the process. It means making the processing as straightforward as possible. Given the alternative, choose the simpler route.

Leverage the Capabilities of the Package

It is a waste of time, money, and effort to try to use application packages in ways for which they were not designed. This often happens when the organization tries to force the package through configuration hoops or code modifications to perform processes the way they currently are done.

If the organization takes a rapid implementation approach and is serious about using software vendors to outsource the development and maintenance of business applications, then the implementation team must use the capabilities designed into the package.

The newer packages are powerful. They have functionality that was never available in custom-developed legacy systems and past versions of standard systems. They take advantage of technologies that were not even feasible five or ten years ago. They also incorporate best practices from leading companies in particular industries. Therefore, using the plain-vanilla package capabilities should provide many advantages not previously available to the organization.

However, all the advantages of standard software do not change the fact that the package probably does things in a way that is different from the way the organization does them today. And there will always be things that the legacy systems can do (because they were customized to the specific requirements of the organization) that none of the packages can do. The organization must be willing to accept changes in the way things are done and work around some missing functions in the package if they are serious about developing a rapid implementation competency and taking full advantage of standard business applications.

Speed Is King

Processes need to be designed with the goal of drastically reducing cycle times. The marketplace has changed its expectations on how long things should take. If people custom-order a car, they expect to pick it up in five days, not three weeks. If they report a problem with their telephone, they expect it to be fixed that day. As customers gain increased power in the e-business economy, those organizations that learn to do things faster, and thereby meet customer performance expectations, will survive and prosper.

Accordingly, as the implementation team designs business processes and looks at processing alternatives, a key criterion should be: Which process design is faster? The team needs to look at bottlenecks and points of delay in the process flow. They need to prototype several different process flows and determine the cycle times for each approach.

Some of the commercial process-modeling tools have simulation capabilities.

These tools allow the process specialist to graphically design various detail process flows, assign resources, costs, and processing times to each step of the process, and then simulate the actual flow of goods or transactions through the process. Using such techniques the team can evaluate the impact of process design changes and base design decisions on facts rather than gut feel or judgments.

One way to improve cycle times is to look at how many people or departments are required to handle the end-to-end process. Handoffs in any process flow usually increase processing time. Therefore, the team should look at alternatives that empower individuals or groups to handle more, or all, of the processing tasks. These types of process redesigns often require changes to organizational structures and the roles and responsibilities of departments and individuals. Therefore, they need top management's blessing and support. They also require access to information throughout the process flow.

Build on Relationships

The e-economy and Internet technologies are driving changes in relationships among enterprises. Organizations are doing things to get closer to their customers and suppliers. They are sharing internal information and giving their business partners access to their computer systems. They are building extranets and virtual private networks (VPN) to facilitate the sharing of this information.

The whole competitive landscape is changing. Instead of simply having organizations compete against other organizations, groups of companies are banding together in a supply chain that competes against other supply chains. Participants share information throughout the supply chain to facilitate performance improvements and take out costs such as unnecessary inventory. These changes work to the benefit of all the organizations, and ultimately to their customers.

At the same time there is an increased interest in business process, information technology, and other forms of outsourcing. Companies are focusing on the parts of their business where they can provide a competitive advantage (and receive high margins) and are leaving other aspects of the business to outside organizations. These new arrangements need to be transparent to the ultimate customer. The customer should not care who is performing the various parts of a business process.

Business processes need to be designed with the new relationships in mind. Organizational relationships, information sharing, and distribution of processing responsibilities must all be factored into the to-be design. The implementation team should also consider including customers and suppliers in requirements identification and design review meetings. Process redesign activities will increasingly have to address cross-enterprise processes, not just those within the four walls of an organization.

Promote Self-Service

There is a fast-moving trend toward providing self-service capabilities within an organization's systems. Customers want to be able to go to an organization's web site and check on the status of their orders or look up technical information on the products they buy. Employees want to be able to access the company's intranet and check on the number of vacation days they have left or the balance in their 401k plans. In general, they just "want to do it themselves."

The nice thing about these new customer and employee requests is that they also can save money for the organization. It is cheaper to let others do their own inquiries and processing. Of course, for self-service to work, the systems must have accurate data and be easy to use. Data integrity requires discipline on the part of those who are entering data and processing transactions on the system, as well as good system edit and validation capabilities. The ease-of-use requirement is facilitated by browser-based interfaces that are more intuitive.

Process design specialists should look for opportunities to provide these self-service functions. At each step in the process flow the question should be asked: Is this something that the customers or employees could do for themselves if we gave them proper access?

Eliminate Non-Value-Adding Steps

There is no room in a business process for steps that do not add value. These steps slow down the process, provide another place for errors to occur, and raise the overall cost of performing the business process. Often, these steps were inserted at some point in the past to address a problem or situation that may not even be present today. People cannot explain why they do the step except by saying "That is the way we have always done it."

The process specialists should consciously challenge each step in the process for the value it adds. Even if there is a valid reason for doing the step, the step can often be eliminated by changing policies or normal practices. There are just too many reports being produced that no one reads, approvals required that are really just rubber stamps, and hoops to be jumped through to handle exceptions. There should be a reason for performing each step in the business process.

Design for Flexibility

Organizations are facing a rapidly changing world. The only thing for sure is that things *will* change. With that fact in mind, the implementation team should try to build flexibility into the design of business processes.

Given an understanding of how things need to be done now and how they might change in the future, can the process be designed to handle both situations? Are there certain design decisions that limit the ability of the organization to handle new products, marketing channels, or organizational structures in the future? Can the to-be process be scaled to handle five or ten times the current volume of transactions?

Some of these analyses require an in-depth knowledge of how the software package works and what configuration and data changes are easy to make. Also, it is important to know which configuration parameters are load-bearing walls that must be chosen correctly the first time and will be difficult or impossible to change once implemented. The requirement for this type of knowledge is one of the reasons that the core team is staffed with experienced package specialists.

Team members that are really good at designing for flexibility have an innate ability to anticipate future changes and come up with process designs that can respond easily to a number of possible business scenarios. These skills are invaluable when designing for a rapidly changing business environment.

There are obviously lots of other good design principles that could be considered. However, a team that takes good care of the ones described in this section usually will handle other areas equally well.

STAYING PROCESS DRIVEN

Looking at package implementation and the organization from a process perspective is a lot different from looking at them from a departmental or functional viewpoint. A process point of view requires assumptions, design principles, and goals that result in implementing a different, and usually improved, solution to business problems.

In the past, application software was implemented module by module. Usually, the modules were selected and implemented for the benefit of one particular department in the organization. In this manner, the accounting function selected and implemented a general ledger module to improve financial reporting and make the financial close process quicker and easier. The manufacturing department implemented a material requirements planning (MRP) system to calculate the material requirements for the production schedule and recommend purchase and production orders to meet this schedule. The personnel department selected and implemented a new payroll and human resources system to facilitate the effective operation of its department.

Often, these modules did not talk to each other except through interfaces that provided periodic batch updates. The output from one of these modules was used to update the information in another module on a daily, weekly, or monthly basis. Access to real-time information to determine status across a process was not available. Each department or function continued to perform its piece of the process with no one responsible for successful completion of the entire process.

These individual, isolated modules often meet the needs of a particular department, but not the needs of the overall organization or its customers. Business transactions flow across departmental boundaries. At each boundary there is a responsibility handoff that introduces a time lag to the total process. Only when one department completes its work on the process is the information forwarded to the next group in line to complete the next step. In these situations the actual time spent working on a business transaction is only a small percentage of the time required to complete the transaction. Most of the transaction's total processing time is spent in queues—waiting to be worked on by the next group in the line.

It takes the coordinated efforts of many functions in an organization to complete most business processes. It also takes an integrated set of software modules to support a process end to end. Unfortunately, in many organizations neither coordinated activities nor integrated systems exist. This creates a situation where business processes take longer and cost more than they should. Even in those cases where integrated software is available, the systems are often implemented in a manner that prevents the organization from taking advantage of the capabilities of the software to support the entire business process.

One common reason organizations failed to realize the desired benefits from package implementation projects in the past was because project teams took a module approach to the implementation. They took the view that they were implementing package modules rather than improved business processes. The package was configured without taking a process point of view. Often this happened because the implementation team was not staffed with cross-functional representatives, did not use process models as a key design tool, and ignored key integration issues.

A lack of process orientation also occurs when the implementation is not guided by a business case or defined business benefits for the system to be implemented. Without having any specific goals and objectives for the project, it is easy to just implement a module to replace one of the existing systems.

A process approach to these projects is motivated by the following goals:

* Focus on process problems and opportunities.
* Evaluate processes end-to-end.
* Standardize processes.
* Continually improve processes.

Focus on process problems and opportunities requires a concerted effort. The implementation team must fight the assumption that people are the real problem. This assumption leads to faulty logic: If a process takes too long to do or costs too much, then it must mean that the employees are lazy, incompetent, or not well managed. By having them work harder, smarter, or longer the problem will go away.

A more productive approach is to assume that the process is the problem and design an improved process that takes advantage of the capabilities of the system and leverages the talents and efforts of the users. The stated benefits for the new process should guide the team in sorting through the various process design alternatives.

In making design decisions, the entire process should be considered, not just the individual steps, in isolation. Making parts of the process fast and effective while ignoring other parts does not result in the best overall solution. As in many things, the business process is only as good as its weakest subprocess. Most of the attention should be focused on the process bottlenecks. As each bottleneck is improved, the team should move to the next bottleneck and focus on it.

Creating business process scenarios that describe the total process flow in business terms is one way to ensure an end-to-end view of business processes. The order-to-cash process begins with someone taking a custom order and is completed only when the goods or services have been delivered and payment is received from the customer. The purchase-to-payment process starts with the creation of a purchase requisition and goes until the goods have been received and the invoice from the vendor is paid.

A key objective from these projects should be to get the organization to standardize on one way to perform a particular business process. In most organizations each unit performs processes differently. And some get better results in certain areas than others.

It is very difficult to improve processes throughout the organization if processes are done differently in each location. This also makes it difficult to take advantage of best practices that occur throughout the enterprise. Therefore, one of the goals of many implementations is to standardize the ways things are done on the best process that can be defined for the organization. Implementing a new system often provides an opportunity to make this happen.

Finally, a process perspective assumes that the organization will be continually improving its processes. Because of this, the current rapid implementation project does not have to solve all the problems of the organization. A rapid implementation will address some of the key problems and opportunities and try to get solutions in place in the quickest times possible. Other problems can be documented and addressed in a future project or implementation phase.

In some cases the best approach for solving a particular business problem will not be obvious. There may also be differences of opinion between the members of the project team and the steering committee on which path to take. Knowing that there will be future opportunities to make changes and that the team does not have to get everything right the first time gives the team the freedom to make decisions and try things without suffering paralysis from analysis.

One of the best ways to find a good solution to a problem is to try a number of alternatives and see which one works best. It will not always be obvious what process designs are easily supported by the package. The only way to find out for sure is to try different solutions. Rapid prototyping and continuous refinement of processes is a key technique used in rapid implementations.

As a final point, the implementation team will need to do a lot of change management work to get buy-in for process changes. This effort will be easier if the project steering committee designates a process owner for the key business processes being addressed by the implementation. This process owner can make timely decisions in order to keep the rapid implementation on schedule and remove organizational barriers to the acceptance of the process changes that result from implementing the new system.

7

TECHNOLOGY SUPPORT ISSUES

There has been a definite emphasis throughout this book on the notion that business issues and priorities should drive package implementations. To be successful these project must solve business problems and allow organizations to take advantage of new opportunities. If all a project accomplishes is a transition to newer technologies without enabling corresponding business process changes, then the investment in newer technologies will be wasted. There are always competing investments and priorities in any organization. Therefore, the organization must find the highest and best use of what are always limited resources. In this arena, technology investments compete with construction of new plants, marketing campaigns, and capital equipment purchases for a share of the capital budget.

There is little return from projects that put in new hardware and software for the sake of keeping up with leading-edge technologies. These projects may be of interest to those in the IS department, but they do not generate the same level of attention with those in the organization's boardroom. In some cases these technology upgrades are justified because of the high costs of maintaining older technologies. Even in these situations, these types of investments are reluctantly made.

While taking these business perspectives on the proper role of technology, we must be careful not to give the impression that technology is not important. The fact is that organizations would not be as excited about implementing new application systems if it were not for the possibilities that have become available because of new technologies. If it were not for the capabilities of new technologies (e.g., distributed relational databases, middleware tools, Internet technologies), many of the business strategies, models, and process changes organizations are seeking would not be possible.

The role of technology is also changing. IT strategy used to be focused on implementing technologies that align with and support the organization's business strategies. Today, the availability of new technologies is driving new business strategies and models. Therefore, the ability to implement new technologies successfully is an important issue for any organization.

Because of the new strategic importance of technology, the technical activities on a package implementation are taking on increased significance. Making all these new technologies work together is a major challenge. As a result, the technical tasks on the implementations are now taking up a higher percentage of the overall project hours. Technical risks are also becoming greater. Therefore, there must be an increased emphasis on managing the technical activities of these projects, so they do not jeopardize the overall success of rapid implementation initiatives.

There are several facets of technical support that have to be addressed as part of a rapid implementation project. They fall into four primary areas:

1. Supporting the project team
2. Preparing the production environment
3. Developing data conversion and interface programs
4. Creating a permanent support function to handle problems and questions after the new system is live

The first challenge is for the technical team members to provide an adequate level of support for the core implementation team. The core team needs a technical environment where they can explore the application's functionality, configure the system to support redesigned business processes, test whether the configured application works as designed, and then use the system to provide hands-on training for end users. This team environment must be continuously available throughout the project. If the development system is down for any significant period of time, it is difficult for all the other team members to make progress on their tasks. Therefore, if the team technical environment is not reliable and stable, it will be difficult for the project to stay on schedule.

While the implementation project is going on, the IS personnel (both those on the core team and those in the IS department) must prepare the technical infrastructure to support the organization when it goes live on the new system. There is a big difference between the technical capacity for a development system that must support 15 to 20 people in one location and a production system that is used by thousands of people to carry out their daily jobs in a large number of locations. Hardware capacity, transactions volumes, system response times, 24/7 availability, and data backup and recovery become critical issues when the organization begins processing real customer transactions on the new system.

Before the new system can go live there are a number of technical tasks that must be completed to make the new system work in the organization's existing technical environment. The new system requires its databases to be populated with accurate and complete data before it can be used to process transactions. This data is often in legacy systems and must be transferred into the databases of the new application. This transfer is often done programmatically through the use of data-conversion programs and utilities.

In addition, there is a need to connect the new system with other systems that the organization uses so the systems can share information and processing logic. The IS personnel create these interfaces between various systems by custom developing interface programs that update the databases of each of the systems or by using standard interface capabilities that have been designed into the newer applications.

The IT representatives on the core team perform most of the technical activities that have been discussed to this point. These people are usually assigned full-time to these projects and may perform similar roles for other projects once the current one is completed. However, some of these IT specialists may become part of the application support function once the new system goes live.

If the project IT team members do not transition to an ongoing support role, there is a requirement to prepare other members of the IS organization to assume that role. A great deal of knowledge transfer must take place during the project if the IS organization is to be positioned to assume this role following go-live.

In some cases, consultants or contract personnel will perform many of the technical support roles during the project. In addition, the ongoing technical support for the system might be outsourced. Therefore, the organization must consider its options before determining how technical support activities will be staffed during and after the implementation project.

IT SUPPORT STRATEGIES

As part of the project-planning process, organizations must decide on strategies for providing technical support for new application systems, both during the implementation project and after the new system is in production. These strategies include options for providing IT support using people from the organization's IS department, augmenting the staff in the IS department with technical consultants and contract personnel, and using an application service provider (ASP) to perform some or all of the technical support activities.

The best strategy, as is always the case, depends on the situation. Factors that influence the decision are the existing capabilities and availability of resources in the IS department, the special requirements of a rapid implementation, the organization's outsourcing strategies, and the costs and benefits associated with each of the alternatives.

One of the first sets of strategies to be developed should address those IT activities that are required to support the implementation team. Someone needs to provide the appropriate technical environment so that the other team members can analyze

the package capabilities, configure the application to meet the needs of the organization, test that the system works as planned, and prepare for going live on the new
system.

This support includes providing a sand box for the team to explore the capabilities
of the package and several development versions of the application that support the
different types of activities that occur during the project (e.g., configuration, integration testing, training). These technical tasks are generally grouped under the package
administrator role on the project. In addition, project team IT support includes developing data conversion programs, interfaces to legacy and other systems, and coding forms and reports.

A second set of strategies focuses on those IT support requirements that are necessary to support the system after it is in a production state. This includes ensuring
that the system has sufficient technical capacity (i.e., processing power, database
size, communication networks capacity) to meet the performance requirements of the
organization after the users begin processing the normal volume of transactions on
the new system. It also includes staffing a help desk to answer user questions about
the package and troubleshoot technical problems.

In addition, these strategies deal with the ongoing requirements for system administration and other maintenance activities such as applying code patches provided
by the software vendor to fix bugs that are found in the system and installing and testing new releases of the software.

The applications that are being implemented today often are more mission-criti-
cal and visible to the external world than were applications implemented in the past.
They are more customer facing and may affect not only the organization but all the
customers and suppliers in the organization's supply chain. Therefore, the need for
outstanding technical support is higher today than it has been in the past.

All of these increased technical demands are taking place at a time when IS organizations are being challenged to stay current with the skills and tools required to support these projects and applications. For all of these reasons, the decision on an IT
support strategy is one that needs to be given careful attention and priority. However,
there are a number of significant challenges that must be overcome.

TECHNICAL SKILL CHALLENGE

Before the IT support strategy can be decided, it is necessary to evaluate the current
skills of the IS organization and the ability of the IS organization to reinvent itself in
order to support e-business and Internet-enabled technologies. There are an incredible number of new technologies and tools being used to develop and implement the
newer applications. Many of them are unfamiliar to those IT personnel supporting
older, legacy systems.

There are many components in the technical architectures of packaged applications. These include hardware (e.g., servers, workstations, printers), applications software (often from a number of package vendors), operating systems (e.g., NT, UNIX, Linux), database management software (e.g., Oracle, SQL Server, Informix), communication network devices and services (e.g., Internet, broadband lines, modems, routers, gateways), local area networks (e.g., NT Server, Windows 2000 Server, Novell), web site software (e.g., Apache, IIS, iPlanet), development tools (e.g., C++, Java, ABAP), and remote devices (e.g., laptop computers, PDAs, and cell phones). Many of these technologies have to be supported during the implementation of new applications and after go-live.

It is difficult, if not impossible, for any organization to keep its IT employees up to speed on all these technologies. Some organizations are addressing this problem through extensive retraining of the IS department. Others adopt a strategy of hiring new IT employees who already have knowledge and experience with the new tools and technologies. Both of these approaches are impacted by the fact that the shelf life of many of the newer technologies is currently one to three years. Therefore, this technical retooling is an ongoing, expensive process.

Those organizations that look to hire new employees who already have the required technical skills face an additional challenge. There is a shortage of people with experience in many of the hot technology areas. And there is a high turnover rate for technical specialists with these skills. Organizations are finding that there are always other, competing organizations that will pay a premium for people with actual experience with technologies that are critical for new development efforts.

Increasingly, organizations, especially small and midsize organizations, must turn to contractors to augment the IS staff or consider outsourcing technical support in some or all of the key areas.

The internal IT skill assessment must evaluate the skills of the IS staff and the level of support for the existing applications. It should assess how effective the IS organization has been in meeting support requirements in the past. How state-of-the-art are the systems that this department has been able to develop and support?

To effectively develop and support business applications, IS personnel need to be more than technically competent. They must also understand business requirements, issues, and strategies. To assess the functional knowledge of the IS staff, it is often useful to talk to people in the user departments. Do the users believe that the IS personnel understand the processes and functions performed by the functional departments? Do IS staff members understand business challenges and priorities? Are there people in IS who have been assigned responsibility to support specific departments and applications?

In evaluating the current IS staff, it should be recognized that the people in the IS organization often are the only ones who understand the technical aspects of the current systems. This knowledge is not something that can easily be outsourced.

Sometimes the people in the IS department were the original developers of these systems. Since most of these systems are not very well documented, it may not be easy for someone to come in cold and determine how to integrate the legacy systems with the new ones that are being implemented. So, even if there is a need to bring in outside resources to support the implementation project, there may still be key roles to be played by the current IS staff.

The approach of hiring IT professionals to support new applications and keeping the existing IS staff to support the legacy applications creates a number of potential problems. The IS staff know that there is little job security in supporting old technologies. Therefore, they want to get on implementation teams so they can learn the newest technologies. Therefore, support strategies should take into account the reaction of the IS organization's staff if they are left out of initiatives to implement new technologies.

In assessing the ability of the current IS staff to perform the technical support roles on a rapid implementation, it is important to have the key requirements in mind. The ideal candidates to support the technical aspects of these projects should have a number of attributes:

- *They should be technically competent.* The team cannot afford big technical mistakes that cause the project to lose momentum or time. Technical problems, like all others on the project, need to be quickly resolved. These people must have experience performing technical support activities.

- *They should be quick learners.* Often new technologies are used on these implementations. Or technologies are used in combinations that have not been tried before. The IT team members must quickly pick up new technologies, understand how to leverage available tools, and analyze and resolve problems with their use.

- *The IT support people should be able to understand business requirements and issues.* The team will look to them to come up with innovative technical solutions to problems that surface. The proposed solutions must make sense as much from a business and project perspective as they do from a technical one.

- *These IT team members must work quickly and with a sense of urgency.* Sometimes it will be difficult for the project manager and others on the team to have a good feel for how long technical tasks should be expected to take. It is important that the team have confidence that the technical members are working as fast as possible and are always looking for ways to speed up the technical activities on the project.

If the current IS staff cannot meet these demanding standards, then other strategies for staffing the technical aspects of these projects must be explored.

LEVERAGING VENDORS' IT INVESTMENTS

Application vendors have done a lot of work to take advantage of new technologies in their applications. They have also done a great deal of research and development to find ways to make these technologies work together to solve business problems in innovative ways. In some cases, much of the technical complexity in the new applications is hidden in the technical architecture of the standard packages and supporting tools that are provided by vendors.

If these vendors' investments in new technologies can be leveraged, their customers do not have to solve these same problems. One of the reasons for buying the new packages is to take advantage of the lessons the vendors have learned in how to apply the new technologies.

Learning how to use the new technologies has been a difficult task for most vendors. As a matter of fact, more than a few of the vendors have lost market share or gone out of business because of a failure to make the transition from old, proprietary technologies to client-server and Internet technologies. And these failures have occurred after spending millions of dollars and much time trying to apply the new technologies. But many vendors now have proven products that use the new technologies. Organizations should side with these winners and take advantage of the technical capabilities that have been baked into these applications.

Vendors offer various levels of support to the organization's IS staff as they try to support these new environments. Most vendors have separate training courses on the technical aspects of their products. These classes cover the technical architectures of these systems and how these products can be installed and supported. Since the training focuses on the subset of technologies that were employed in creating these applications, the IS staff has to learn about only those technologies that were employed.

Vendors often provide procedures and documentation that walks the IS staff through the complex technical tasks on the project. In addition, they provide tools that automate many of these technical tasks. They provide utilities to load the technical components and install them on the organization's server. These tools also are useful in tuning databases and monitoring the performance of the components of the architecture.

The software vendors have also worked with hardware vendors to determine the optimal size of the system components (e.g., processors, disk drives, communication bandwidth) to support the application's processing environment. In many cases algorithms have been developed that use production variables (e.g., number of concurrent users, transaction volumes, data archiving strategies) to appropriately size the technical environment.

To a certain extent the tools provided by the package vendors help the organization jump-start the adoption of newer technologies. It is doubtful whether any organization could develop all these tools and procedures on its own within the times required for rapid implementations.

The vendors (and their consulting partners) also have people who can work with the organization's IS staff to perform the technical aspects of these projects. Sometimes technical specialists from the vendor are assigned to the implementation team as part-time or full-time members. In other cases, vendors support the technical activities of the project through the resources of their help and support functions or by providing access to knowledge in their online technical repositories.

The vendors' user groups also have technical subgroups that present, at periodic user-group meetings, technical topics of interest to those performing these development and support roles. These user groups allow the technical staff to network with technical people in other organizations who are facing the same problems or have solved some of the problems that the organization may face in its implementation.

DEVELOPING A RAPID IMPLEMENTATION SUPPORT CAPABILITY

In order to support the technical aspects of rapid implementation projects, a number of resources, capabilities, and practices need to be in place. One of the first things that should be considered is the current load on the IS organization.

Most IS organizations have their plates full supporting the current applications and technical environment. They spend much of their time fighting fires and keeping fragile technology infrastructures operational. It may be that the IS department does not have the capacity to provide significant resources for a new development effort. One option to address this situation is to bring in contract personnel to perform some of the normal operational and maintenance activities in order to free IS department resources to work on new implementation projects. Another is to hire people with experience with the new technologies to staff the implementation projects and then support these systems once they go live. The third option is to outsource some or all of the processing requirements.

Whether an organization handles support internally or outsources it may depend on how important technology capabilities are to the competitive position of the organization. If technology offers competitive advantages, it may be desirable to keep the support in house. If it has little impact on the competitive position of the organization, it may be better to evaluate contract alternatives.

Many organizations may decide to develop outstanding IT support capabilities in order to support a rapid implementation competency. If making rapid changes to business processes and quickly responding to opportunities is important, the organization may have to invest in developing world-class IT support capabilities within its IS department. This would be a big change for many organizations where IT has traditionally been considered nonstrategic and primarily associated with keeping the back-office systems operating.

The IT team members on a rapid implementation must apply the same management principles and practices to their work as is done in other areas of the project. Their tasks should be broken into small chunks and time boxed. In addition, they should expect to have their work reviewed by the project manager, prepare status reports on the technical activities, contribute issues for the issues log, and do all the other things required to keep these projects on schedule.

The IT team members must also know their limitations. When problems surface that cannot be resolved in a timely manner, they need to be brought to the attention of the project manager. The response may to bring in technical specialists to handle particularly complex tasks, address critical problems, or transfer technical knowledge to the other team members. Bringing in a specialist is an excellent tactic in areas where there is technical knowledge and skills that may be absolutely critical to the success of the implementation but may not be needed on a full-time basis to support other project activities.

In the future, organizations may outsource more of their IS functions. This trend will ultimately provide capabilities and cost savings that are attractive to many organizations. This use of external technical resources should seem especially attractive to small and midsize organizations who cannot afford to develop and maintain in-house world-class IT support capabilities.

Outsourcing is done for financial, technical, and business reasons. The financial justification may be to reduce costs in the IS area or avoid incurring additional costs in the future. (Whether outsourcing is a less expensive way to provide these services remains to be determined.) The technical justification may be to get access to critical skills that are not currently available in the IS organization, are difficult to find and retain, or are needed only on a part-time basis. The business reasons may deal with the organization's goal of focusing only on those areas of the business that are core competencies and bring competitive advantages. In other areas the organization may just as soon have partners or contractors take care of those activities and functions.

Whether or not they realize it, most organizations are already outsourcing part of their IS function. Buying software from a vendor and using consultants to assist on implementation projects are methods of outsourcing. It is all a matter of the extent to which the organization wants to take IT outsourcing and how permanent it wants to make some of the outsourcing relationships.

SETTING UP THE TEAM TECHNICAL ENVIRONMENT

On a rapid implementation, the core team needs to have access to the vendor's software immediately after the project begins. As soon as the core team returns from the initial vendor training, they need to be able to get on the system and start applying what they have learned. Therefore, the IT support team members must install the vendor's software and set up team access to the system prior to the official project kickoff.

The team members need separate versions of the application depending on the nature of the project activities they are doing. In some cases they will need to try a number of things to discover how the application works. This hands-on investigation is necessary to explore the various ways that the system could support a particular business process. In this type of activity, the team members will make errors and corrupt the database in the process of trying different approaches. Technical support personnel should periodically refresh this instance to wipe out the effects of the random tests and experiments.

There is also a need to start building the actual system that will be used to meet the unique needs of the organization. This process will result in incremental development of the new system. The system gets built a little at a time as the team configures each of the processes and subprocesses that have been determined to be in the scope of this phase of rapid implementation. The end result will be configuration of the system to support the to-be processes that will be used after cutover.

The first instance (version of the application) is sometimes called the team's *sand box*. The sand box is a place for the team to play and learn. They should be able to try a number of different approaches and generally explore the various capabilities of the package without worrying about breaking anything or causing additional work for someone to clean up after mistakes are made. This environment can be used to prototype different solutions and approaches, which then are thrown away and created for real in the development instance.

The developmental instances are more serious. Here the team will begin to build the actual system that will be tested and implemented. Therefore, there will be more controls over who has access to these instances, how they are backed up and restored, and when the various versions of the system are transported between the different development instances.

In order to create the project team's sand box and development environments, the IT support team must sometimes purchase and install hardware, systems software, and other technical infrastructure components. This development environment is often a scaled-down version of what will be needed for production processing.

Often a small server can satisfy the needs of the implementation team. In a multiple-tier technical architecture, the IS organization might put both the application server and the database server on the same hardware box for the team's use. Once the implementation project is over, the project team's development system can be used, on an ongoing basis, to test software patches and new versions of the package before they are placed into the production environment.

One quick tactic to get the project team environment underway is to use a hosted solution. Under this scenario, the team will use a system that is already up and running at the application service provider's site. Access is obtained remotely. With this approach there is no need to purchase hardware and install software before the sand box is in place. This approach sometimes can be used irrespective of whether the production environment is being hosted or supported by the IS department.

Another tactic that may be used to quickly get access to a system for use by the project team is to use facilities available from the systems integrator supporting the project. Many of the major consulting organizations have development labs or competency centers where they host the applications they help implement. This may be a short-term solution or may provide the development system the team uses throughout the project.

A major factor in determining the best approach for establishing a project team application environment may be the time it normally takes the organization to select, contract for, and install hardware and software. If the IS organization must go through an extensive technical requirements definition and selection process to procure hardware, this process may take longer than is acceptable for the rapid implementation project.

A warning sign for this situation is the need to issue a formal request for proposal (RFP) to identify potential hardware and software vendors. Since the platform needed for the development environment is often not very expensive (relative to the overall cost of the application software and implementation assistance), red tape and bureaucracy should be avoidable. Since most of the acquisition activities will be done by the IS organization through its normal asset-acquisition process, the timing of the hardware and software procurement and installation must be factored into the project kickoff date.

Whichever approach is used to establish the team application environment, the work to establish the technical infrastructure to support the project team should occur before the project kickoff date. There is no time in a rapid implementation for the team to have to wait, after going to vendor training (or even before if the training is not immediately available), to get on a system and start learning and prototyping various solutions.

Setting up a development system and supporting the project team environment is a good rehearsal for the IT support organization for the role of supporting the same system in a production environment. Interoperability issues among the various components will crop up and have to be addressed. And the IT personnel are often working with technologies that are new to them. Therefore, it is best for them to learn about problems and develop solutions for these problems before preparing the production environment.

Often there will be a significant learning curve for the IT support team with the newer applications. In a rapid implementation, this learning must be accelerated. One way to do this is bring in experienced technical resources to set up the project team technical environment and have the internal IT resources shadow these individuals. Special emphasis should be not only on getting the environment up and running but also on transferring technical knowledge to the project's IT support team.

DEVELOPMENT INSTANCES

Several different versions of the application under development need to be maintained for use by the implementation team. Each version has its own purpose. Sometimes the versions are called *development instances*.

The IT support team transfers the programs, data, and configuration parameters among the various application instances. They also periodically refresh data as normal testing activities corrupt the databases.

The IT support team also controls the installation and testing of various releases of the package and patches (software changes provided by the vendor) that fix software problems. They set up users in the system and establish security and access controls.

Many of these responsibilities may be new to the organization's IS personnel who are assigned these technical roles. Therefore, software vendor and consulting firm IT support personnel often assist in executing these tasks and transfer knowledge to the organization's IT staff who will perform these roles on an ongoing basis. That is one disadvantage of using a hosted environment for the development system: the IS staff will not learn and gain experience putting the team's environment together. They may do these activities for the first time while setting up the production environment.

One of the things that must be tested early is the disaster recovery capability established for the project and production environments. Many organizations have disaster recovery plans; only a few have tested them and know they work.

The project team environment should not be installed on the organization's production server. This rule protects both the team and the organization. The team needs to have fast response times for its transactions and tests. When they change a configuration, they cannot afford to wait days before seeing how things work. On the other hand, the users on the production system should not have to experience performance degradation because someone on the development team kicked off a large database query or database reconstruction job.

There are a number of different technical environments, or instances, that must be supported by the IS organization. They are called sand box, test, quality assurance, training, and production. Some project teams use fewer environments; some use more. They often have different data in their files and different versions of the parameter files that control how the package operates.

Figure 7-1 shows the different instances that can be used by the project team and their relationships. Of course, different projects can combine these environments or add additional ones (e.g., stress testing environment).

FIGURE 7-1 Project Team Development Environments

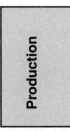

Sand Box

Sample data/configuration periodically refreshed
No access restrictions
Often starts from training course version of system
Try anything to learn and explore

Test

Data periodically refreshed
Access restricted to project team and IS
Starts from preconfigured version
Configuration changes retained
Prototype of to-be processes

Quality Assurance

Data and configuration periodically transported
Access restricted to testers and those doing transports
Starts from test instance configuration
Used to perform integration tests

Training

Training data refreshed before each course
Training IDs and passwords used
Starts from QA instance configuration
Used to conduct training courses

Production

Data created during conversion activities; updated by live transactions
End-user access enabled
Configuration from the QA system
Used to process real customer transactions

As can be seen in Figure 7-1, project teams typically use five different instances of the system during a rapid implementation project. The sand box is used to discover and try out new things with the system. The test instance is used to configure the to-be processes. Parameters are changed as the team discovers what works and what does not. Once the team has the individual transactions correctly configured, this configuration is transferred to the quality assurance (QA) instance. This version of the application is used to perform the integration tests.

If errors are discovered during the integration tests (and they will be), the team goes back to the test instance to work out a solution. Once a solution is found, the parameter changes are transported to the QA instance again and the tests rerun. As the team begins the Prepare activities at the end of the project, the QA version of configuration is transferred to the training and production instances.

Special training data is loaded into the training instance so the training participants can do hands-on exercises. This training data is restored to its original state before each training class so the instructors know that the exercises will work as planned.

The production databases (and sometimes the quality assurance databases) are populated by the data-conversion procedures and programs developed for the project. The access rights are turned on for all the end users and the system is then ready for cutover and processing of actual transactions.

A *transport process* is used to move system changes and data from the test to quality assurance to production instances. The IT support team keeps these systems in synch and reconciles any differences. Periodically, the sand box instance should be refreshed with the configuration in the test system so testing can occur from a baseline configuration.

The IT support team executes load routines to load the test data and live data converted from the legacy systems. In integration testing, it is best to test the data-conversion process along with the business scenarios. Therefore, it may be necessary to run the load routines before beginning the various integration test cycles. If this is not done there are two risks: (1) the team may get to the end of the project and find out that there are still data-conversion problems to be overcome; and (2) the data in fields for the new system may have not been properly mapped from the old system and this will cause errors in transaction processing.

The IT support team maintains access rights to the various functions in each instance. Generally, all team members have access to all functions in the sand box and test instances. However, it is necessary to establish more restricted rights to the quality assurance, training, and production environments.

Finally, the IT support team must establish formal procedures for installing and testing patches to the application software to fix programming errors. The support team should be aware of what patches are available and the problems they are designed to address. In addition, these program changes need to be made in the development or test environments and thoroughly tested before they are implemented in the quality assurance or production instances.

As can be seen from these descriptions, the IT support team plays a key role in supporting the various versions of the application that are used throughout the project. Doing these activities quickly and accurately is a key requirement for a successful rapid implementation.

IMPLEMENTATION TEAM IT SUPPORT ROLES

As was discussed in the previous section, there are several roles that the IT support team must perform to assist the project team. Each IT support specialist may perform one or more of these roles. In complex situations, it may take more than one person to perform each role.

Cross-training should occur within the IT support team so the members can back each other up if someone is out on vacation or at training. Therefore, it is a good practice to designate someone to have primary and secondary responsibility for each of the roles. In addition, some of the roles may be performed by people in the IS department, not on the project team, as they support multiple ongoing projects.

For a rapid implementation, these roles may also be performed by outside specialists with particular expertise in the technologies being used in the application architecture. Often, the organization's IS personnel do not have experience with these technologies. This is especially true with Internet tools and technologies. But this may also be the case for more basic things like new operating systems and database management systems being used by the package.

In these situations, the rapid pace of the project will not provide adequate time for the organization's IT personnel to get up to speed and be able to support the project schedule. So external specialists are sometimes brought in to perform some of the technical roles described in this section. However, even in these situations, it is still a good idea to have the organization's IT personnel assist and shadow the specialists so knowledge can be transferred and the organization's staff can perform these roles on future projects. The internal IS staff will usually have responsibility for supporting the technologies used by the package once the package is in a production mode.

Security Administrator

One of the IT support roles is to maintain application security. This role determines the access rights that the project team members have to the various system resources (e.g., transactions, programs, database tables). Different rights may be assigned to the team members, depending on the activities they are involved with on the project. In general, the process team members need to access the transaction screens and reporting screens on the system. The IT team members need access to update technical infrastructure resources such as databases, printer configurations, application programs, and package administration capabilities. All the team members need access to things like the local area network, e-mail system, and the Internet.

Security controls are often established to prevent team members from making errors and inadvertently doing things that cause system problems. The process team members should not be running transport programs to move data or configuration parameters from development to test. The programmers should not be setting up the configuration tables. There is special training required to perform each of these functions on the project and security restrictions keep people from doing things for which they are not adequately trained.

Later in the project, this application security administrator will be setting up the end-user profiles and authorization rights. However, the process team members will provide a lot of input into these decisions. End users need to be able to do all the application functions required to perform their jobs but do not, necessarily, need full access to all the systems capabilities.

Part of the security administrator's job is to set up new users on the system and to delete users who have left the project. This person will also have to reset passwords for those who have forgotten them.

Transport Administrator

The transport administrator is responsible for maintaining the different project team environments such as sand box, test, and quality assurance. This person also transports data and application configuration parameters across the different instances and is responsible for periodically refreshing the data (i.e., setting it back to an uncorrupted state).

There should be a formal procedure for requesting and approving transport requests. If these actions are not well planned and coordinated they may result in project team work being lost or old data and configurations being applied over newer ones.

Database Administrator

The database administrator (DBA) is charged with making sure that the database is sized and tuned properly to support the development environment. In particular, this person must ensure that the database is up and available to support the team's efforts. To do this requires that certain database activities (backups, restores, archiving, reorganizations) take place during hours when the project team is not working on the system.

The database administrator is also responsible for backup and recovery of the database tables for the various instances. There should be a disaster recovery plan that includes such procedures as periodically storing backup copies offsite and testing the ability to restore the system from the off-site materials. It is a good practice to back up key package files before making significant changes to the system. Then, if these changes turn out to not work as expected, the team can recover to the situation that existed before the changes were made.

The database administrator should also focus on the performance aspects of the database. There are usually a number of things the DBA can do to speed up program access to data once bottlenecks have been identified.

Package Administrator

This person is responsible for using tools that are provided by the package vendor to manage the technical aspects of the package. This person often uses these tools to install the vendor's software on the organization's servers. In addition, there are a number of technical package support tasks that will be required throughout the project.

These tasks include setting up technical parameters so that the application can use the printers that are available, applying code patches when errors are detected, interfacing with the technical support personnel from the package vendor, monitoring system logs and researching technical problems, troubleshooting problems the process and package specialists are experiencing, providing help desk support for the project team, and assisting in testing new releases of the package that may come out during the project.

As a rule, the project team should decide on the package release to be implemented long before the project starts. For a rapid implementation, the general rule would be to install only versions of the product that have been used for a number of months by other organizations similar in size, industry, and modules. However, there may be some situations where it is determined that the package cannot do something that is critical in meeting the key business objectives of the project. Sometimes, this functionality may be available in a release that has just come out (or, even worse, one in beta test status). In these rare situations, the team may decide to look at the new release and the package administrator may get involved in its installation and testing.

Programmers

The final role usually performed by the IT resources assigned to the core project team is that of data conversion, interface, and reports programmer. This role often requires extensive knowledge of both the legacy systems and the technical tools available in the new package.

Data conversion requires mapping data in other systems to that in the new system and loading the data into the new database tables. It requires knowledge of how the data is used in the old systems. It also requires an understanding of the data integrity requirements of the new package, the database schemas, and tools and utilities that are available to facilitate loading data into the new package databases.

Interfaces are required to share data and processes among the new application and custom-developed and third-party applications. Designing, programming, and testing interfaces are time-consuming, difficult tasks. Therefore, the organization will often look at rollout strategies that minimize the amount of this work that is required. The difficulty in developing these interfaces is also one reason for the growing interest in the enterprise application integration (EAI) vendors and products that will be discussed in Chapter 9 on trends.

Even if the project team has taken the position that no custom-developed reports will be used (to make sure users and managers give the standard reports from the system a fair chance), there is still a need to do some report coding in these projects. At a minimum, coding will be necessary so that the system can produce forms (e.g., pay checks, invoices, statements) that meet the organization's requirements. However, there may also be other reports that are required by key customers and regulators that are not available in the package's standard set.

One of the assumptions for a rapid implementation is that the team will customize the package to meet the needs of the organization (through configuration of the package parameters) but will not modify the vendor's code or develop bolt-ons to the vendor's product to provide additional functionality. If there is a need for these activities, and often there are valid reasons for looking at the bolt-on option (including providing competitive advantage capabilities that existed in the legacy systems), then the impact on the rapid implementation approach should be carefully considered. One approach is to develop these bolt-ons as a separate project following the completion of the current project. If the organization waits long enough to kick off the follow-on project, it may find that it can get along without these custom developments.

IS Department Support

There are a number of other technical roles that are performed, not by core team technical members but by the IS department personnel. These roles are normal, ongoing responsibilities for these people, independent of any particular project. Often, these are roles performed in support of all the other applications in production. These roles include staffing a technical help desk, maintaining hardware (e.g., workstations, printers, servers, routers), operating systems (UNIX, Novell, NT), telephone systems, and the data communications network. These people also operate the data center and perform other tasks such as making the backup tapes each night.

PREPARING FOR PRODUCTION

While supporting the project team development activities and the project team technical environment, the technical core team members need to begin planning for and preparing the technical environment that will be used once cutover to production occurs. With many of the ERP and e-business applications there will be significant gaps between the technology resources currently in place in the organization and those that will be required to support the new applications after go-live.

It is never too early to begin identifying issues associated with supporting the production environment and initiating activities so the IS organization will be ready when go-live occurs. It may also be appropriate to consider outsourcing the technical support of the system if there are doubts whether the current IS organization can provide the proper level of support. This may be an attractive alternative if the organization has a strategy to focus on its core competencies and looks for ways to partner with other organizations in other areas.

The technical environments required to support the wide variety of ERP and e-business applications has become very complex. Many organizations have been comfortable with a single set of proprietary technologies from one vendor. They may not be as comfortable with an open environment with hardware and software components from scores of vendors. For many organizations it may not be practical, or even possible, to hire and train their own employees to support all the required components of an increasingly complex technical environment.

To meet production technical requirements, the organization may have to change or upgrade hardware, communication networks, software tools, third-party software products, databases, maintenance agreements, and the skills of the people in the IS department who will have to support these new systems.

So, the technical support team must assess the impact that implementing the package will have on the current production environment. What will be the impact on hardware, databases, network traffic, and the IS support requirements? The team must also assess the impact on the skills required to support the technologies used by the package. What new skills must IS personnel have to provide the necessary level of support?

For some organizations, the question will not be *when* they can have the IT resources in place but *whether* they ever can. Many will come to the realization very quickly that they cannot afford to recruit, pay, train, or retain the key resources required to support their increasingly complex technical environments.

Another key factor to be evaluated is the current IT infrastructure for the organization. This requires looking at hardware, databases, networks, and software. In this area the technical team may need to inventory the organization's computer resources. If the organization will be required to select and purchase additional hardware and software, this is usually a time-consuming task. Given the short timeframe of these projects, the approval and acquisition process may need to be escalated. It may require a decision by and support from the steering committee to make this happen.

In the past, budgeting issues might have actually put a hold on these purchases and the go-live capabilities for the project. In a rapidly changing business environment, the budgeting and capital acquisition process will have to be more flexible and stream-lined. The first rapid implementation project may provide a test of the organization's capability to change in all the areas necessary to support a new way of doing business.

To support a rapid implementation scenario, it may be necessary for the organization to change some of its procurement processes. Long procurement lead times are inconsistent with the desire to respond rapidly to business changes. What is needed is a strategy of making thoughtful purchases but not letting the analysis of all the alternatives get in the way of speed and flexibility. This may be another area where time boxing will have to be applied.

The organization must be willing to live with the possibility that they might purchase some technology components that will have only a one or two-year life. There will be some wasteful purchases with such an approach. However, that is life in a rapidly changing business environment. Spending a lot more time doing the analysis will not necessarily translate into a better purchase decision; but it will definitely put the success of the rapid implementation approach in jeopardy.

The company needs to be continuously experimenting with technologies. However, the best place to do this is not in some abstract, conceptual manner (letting the IS people play with the new technologies and see what ideas bubble up), but rather by using them on actual projects with defined benefits and deadlines. The key is to fail fast, and thereby learn fast.

A technology *gap analysis* will tell the team what technologies must be acquired and implemented to support the production environment. This needs to be done early in the project in order to have time to get things in place. If it becomes clear the organization will not be able to respond that quickly, then it may look to outsource the hosting of the application, at least during the development effort.

The project team environment is easy to size; it may take a lot more work to correctly size the production environment for the system. The production environment depends on two primary things: (1) the volumes of each type of transaction, and (2) how the application package interfaces with the operating system and databases. The volumes can be determined from information in the current systems or other organizational data. How the package interacts with the technical environment is more difficult. This determination often depends on experience and benchmark data. Therefore, the sizing should be done with the assistance of the package and hardware vendor.

One of the areas where there are long lead times is in the purchase of network and communication components. This is an especially difficult problem if the organization does not already have network connections among all the locations with users of the new system.

After looking at how this project fits with the overall IT strategy of the organization, the technical team needs to identify the detailed requirements that must be supported to go into a production state with the processes from the current project. This includes servers, workstations, software, third-party tools, databases, and networks. The key question is: What technology components need to be in place to support the current package implementation?

The technology requirements will be based on the volumes of users, transactions, and stored data in the system. The organization can estimate these factors and then sit down with the software and hardware vendors to determine the number and size of all the components of the IT infrastructure needed to support the system. Some of this capacity may already be available in the organization. Other components may have to be purchased.

There are some predictable areas for surprises. Often, especially for client-server solutions, where part of the processing is done on the workstation, the newer systems will require workstations with faster processors, more main memory, and larger hard drives. Some of the existing workstations can be upgraded; others will have to be replaced. The other area that usually falls short is the bandwidth of the organization's communications network. Online, real-time systems place greater demands on the network and often require significant upgrades to the capacity of the networks. The communication network is often a bottleneck.

As technology infrastructures evolve, some of these issues will go away. As packaged applications go to browser-based access, users can have less-powerful workstations. As organizations leverage the Internet as a communications channel (or a virtual private network using Internet technologies), they often depend on ISPs and telecommunication providers to provide communications capacity. When this happens, the sizing issue becomes the problem of the vendor to which the communications requirement has been outsourced. The organization just specifies a minimum response time and negotiates the costs.

IT SUPPORT AFTER CUTOVER

At some point the responsibility for supporting the new application and its users must be transferred from the project team to a permanent group responsible for providing ongoing support. This could take place at the point of cutover to the production environment. However, in some instances it is better to start involving the ongoing support team even earlier. They could become involved during integration testing and end-user training activities.

Given the fact that rapid implementation projects are not just onetime events—there will usually be a series of projects in any application area—it may be best to identify the support organization early and have them learn the new application while supporting the implementation team. They can participate in project activities and be involved in evaluating project alternatives and decisions from the perspective of ongoing support requirements. To a certain extent, help desk and systems support personnel are like application users. They have requirements, albeit technical ones, that need to be addressed in the technical design of the system and the project training plans.

There are two primary areas that must be addressed by an ongoing application support function. The first deals with the technical aspects of the system. Some of the technical members of the core team will be well positioned to take on some of the technical support responsibilities of the system after the project is completed. As a matter of fact, the use of team members in this role may be a key component of the technical support strategy.

The second requirement is to have people in a support role that can address functional package questions. The people who may best fit this role are on the process teams. In the recruitment and career development activities at the beginning of these projects, it may be best to identify one or more team members who will transition to a support role once the project has been completed. This may or may not be a permanent career change. In most situations it probably will not be. But it must be planned and could be considered a career development position that is filled on a rotational basis by people working on project teams.

If the organization adopts a support strategy using part of the implementation team, then there will usually be a smooth and natural transition to production support. This approach is also easier than having the core team do knowledge transfer to people who were not intimately involved in implementing the new system.

Taking this strategy has the added advantage of providing continuity of knowledge between implementation projects. The people in the support roles will understand why decisions were made and when functions were deferred to later phases. They will also be in a better position to know the things that were not finished because of time boxing and that need to be done in the next projects.

If ongoing application support is outsourced, there is still a need for the IS organization to manage the contracts and monitor the work of ASPs or contract personnel. Outsourced support is sometimes appropriate for individual applications. However, in this environment it is difficult for the organization to have one source to turn to for questions regarding any of the applications or technical components used throughout the organization. This function often is performed by an organization's help desk, which may or may not be outsourced. An effective help desk function is one of the keys to effectively supporting the new applications once they have been put into production.

The scope of the help desk and staffing levels should be determined by user requirements. In the past these requirements have usually been only of a technical nature. In the future, they may also be around supporting the functional use of the systems that have been implemented. The users have to have someplace to go to get answers and solutions to the problems they are experiencing. If they do not go to the help desk, where do they go?

If the help desk personnel are not going to be members of the core team, then it will be critical to identify the people early and have them involved with the implementation; perhaps in a shadowing role. The scope of their interest is wider than for most of the team members. They could potentially get calls on any area of the system. The support organization needs to receive training on the new system and knowledge must be transferred to them before they take over the support responsibilities.

The ability of the organization to staff an effective support function following the cutover to the new system will have a dramatic effect on the success of a rapid implementation project. Good project work can go to naught if there is not adequate support for the end users once the project team has been disbanded. Therefore, it is in the interest of the implementation team and the organization to effectively provide for the ongoing support of the new applications.

8

PROJECT ACCELERATORS

Some of the requisites for doing rapid implementations—support from top management, outstanding project management, experienced cross-functional core team, quick decision-making, strong IT support—have been covered in detail in the previous chapters. Unfortunately, they fall in the *necessary but not sufficient* category of requirements. In addition, a rapid implementation team must have a special toolkit to support an aggressive project timeline.

There is no single tool that will make these projects successful. It takes a combination of tools to support these initiatives. Some teams have completed rapid implementations without all these tools, but having these tools would have made their jobs easier. If the team is missing a significant number of these tools, their ability to complete a rapid implementation on time and budget is put at risk.

These tools are accelerators; they speed up the pace of the implementation. In many cases they provide a framework to jumpstart the time-consuming activities of an implementation. Instead of creating deliverables, the team tailors existing products to meet the unique needs of the project. Their power comes from the fact that it is much quicker to tailor project deliverables than to create them from scratch.

In addition to making things go faster, these accelerators often help the team do things in a better way than they would have been able to on their own. They are intellectual assets that increase the quality of the team's work. They leverage the knowledge, experiences, and best practices from many experienced people doing a number of similar implementations. These tools increase the knowledge base of the team.

These accelerators are available from the software package vendors and from consulting organizations. The accessibility of such accelerators was one of the criteria used to select packaged software that could be implemented using a rapid implementation approach. In evaluating vendors and consultants, the organization should

FIGURE 8-1   Rapid Implementation Accelerators

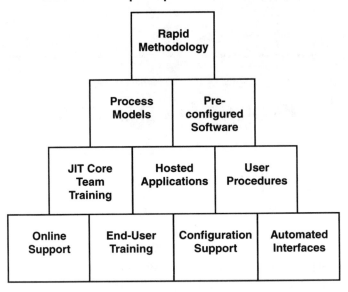

ask to see the accelerators and talk to other organizations that have used these tools in actual implementations. This is an area, like may others associated with software and consulting, where seeing something tangible is the best way to separate hype from fact.

In this chapter we will look at 10 rapid implementation project accelerators. They are not covered in any priority order because they all contribute to the success of these projects. These accelerators are shown in Figure 8-1.

The list of items covered in Figure 8-1 is not meant to be comprehensive. There are, of course, other tools that can speed up particular aspects of an implementation. Standard workplans and estimating guidelines make project planning go quicker. Project management software helps automate many of the computational tasks in planning and monitoring progress on the project. Software that generates test data and automates test transaction processing can make integration testing go more rapidly. However, the items discussed in this chapter will give a good indication of the kinds of tools that the team should be considering to support a rapid implementation approach.

RAPID IMPLEMENTATION METHODOLOGIES

One of the first things the project manager must do is decide on the methodology that will be used during the implementation. Actually, this decision has an impact beyond that of any single project. A consistent methodology should be used on all rapid implementation projects for the organization. Also, it should be continuously enhanced and improved as the organization gains experience in doing these types of projects.

Unfortunately, most organizations do not have a methodology for packaged software implementation, especially one focused on the rapid implementation of these packages. So, in many cases, the first rapid implementation project will do the pioneering work in finding, testing, and adapting a methodology. However, if project experience and lessons learned are captured and embedded in the methodology, future projects will be a step ahead on planning and conducting these projects.

In general terms, a methodology is a standard way of doing certain things: a usual approach to a particular business process. Procedures also document how things are done. The scope of a methodology is bigger than that for procedures. Methodologies include a number of procedures, and a lot more.

Organizations have methodologies and procedures for such things as designing new products, underwriting policies, and registering students for the next term. We are interested in a methodology that documents the process for implementing packaged applications. The general activities involved in this process were covered in Chapter 2. However, the methodology needs to include more than a general approach.

To be of significant benefit to the project team, the methodology should include, at a minimum, a work breakdown structure (WBS), task descriptions, and deliverable examples. In addition, it will be easier to use the methodology if it is available in an online format (not in three-ring binders on someone's shelf) and if methodology training is available for the project team. The best methodologies will also come with a number of the other accelerators discussed in this chapter.

A work breakdown structure is a decomposition of the steps that a team should go through to complete a rapid implementation. It identifies all the detailed steps and organizes them into logical groups. For example, all the steps required in performing these projects could be grouped (as was done in the conceptual model in Chapter 2) into project stages, activities, and tasks. In some commercial methodologies the groupings are phase/module/task or module/task/steps.

Although common in methodologies, these latter terms are intentionally avoided here since they connote a project with many stopping points where major milestones and deliverables are finalized and approved before the team goes on to the next phase or module. This management approach was required for multiyear projects where periodic investment decisions determined whether the project proceeded to the next phase or was canceled. For example, if the company is investing $20 million on the implementation of a new system, top management may want to approve the design of the system before committing to a two-year implementation. In a rapid implementation the projects are shorter, the investments smaller, the project boundaries more fluid, and the process more iterative.

At the highest level, there may be a number of major stages that the project goes through. In the conceptual model for a rapid implementation described in Chapter 2, there were three stages. These stages were referred to as Pre-Project, Project Implementation, and Post-Project.

Each of the stages is broken down into various activities. Each activity is broken down into various tasks. All the items included at each level and the ways they are organized define the work breakdown structure. They tell the team members all the things that will typically be done on these types of projects and their relationships. The actual work breakdown structure of the project is determined by tailoring the generic WBS to the unique needs of the project. It is usually documented in the project workplan.

At the stage, activity, and task level the methodology has descriptions of what is done during the project. Most of the detailed information is available at the task level. At this level the methodology may provide information on:

- The objective for the task
- The key inputs and outputs
- Typical steps to follow in completing the task
- Helpful hints on what to watch out for or how to do the task more efficiently and effectively

All of this is useful information for project team members who are beginning a new project area for the first time and are looking for guidance on what is required and how the work should be approached.

In addition to the task narrative, there should be deliverable examples associated with each of the tasks. Generally, each task produces some sort of document or result that should be documented. These are called the deliverables of the task. If there is no deliverable from a task, then the need to do the task may be suspect.

A deliverable example will help guide a team member in doing the work and documenting its completion. The person does not have to spend a lot of time deciding how to organize the deliverable; the team member just tailors the standard example.

This approach has several benefits. First, there is better consistency between the work efforts of team members doing the same tasks. If they all are working toward producing the same task output, there is a good chance they are doing the same things. Second, the level of detail required in the task is easier to determine. Third, the quality of the work and the status of the task are easier to verify.

In the past, these methodologies were often documented in multiple three-ring binders or bound volumes. In this format the methodology was often seen as intimidating and difficult to use by the team members. Therefore, they stayed on the shelf and were unused. It is much easier to use these materials if they are available online: on the team members' hard drives, on the team LAN, or on CDs. In this format the team members can easily use automated search capabilities and download deliverable examples.

One of the first things on the team's agenda after the kickoff meeting should be training on the methodology that will be used to conduct the project. Each team member needs to understand the overall approach to the project and how his or her role fits into the bigger picture. The team needs to understand where they are going and how they will get there.

Several days of methodology training at the start of the project is important in getting the rapid implementation off to a good start. This training helps building a sense of team and calms some of the fears and concerns of the team members. If the methodology training is enhanced to include information on the business case and objectives of the project, it will often answer many of the team's questions.

It is a good idea to have the project sponsor and some key users attend this training with the team. This allows the sponsor to better understand the approach that will be used on the rapid implementation and to get to know the team members. It also helps the key users understand where their input and involvement with the team will be required.

The better methodologies, from software and consulting vendors, will come with materials to train the team and other interested parties. In addition to deliverable examples, they will also have a number of the other types of accelerators discussed in this chapter. An example of an outstanding rapid implementation methodology is the Accelerated SAP (ASAP) implementation tool provided by SAP. Many vendors are in the process of developing similar online tools.

PROCESS MODELS MAPPED TO THE PACKAGE

The benefits of using process models in a rapid implementation should now be a familiar topic. These models assist in scope management, communication, description of automated versus manual activities in processes, documentation of to-be processes, and many additional process redesign activities. They also have other powerful uses in a rapid implementation.

However, creating process models from scratch is a difficult and time-consuming task. Since most small and midsize organizations (and many large organizations) do not have an organizational process model, there are two options: create the model starting with a blank piece of paper or adapt a process model provided by another organization. The second option is the better approach for rapid implementations.

Creating a process model from scratch takes a lot of time. It can take months to develop and gain consensus for an organizational process model that only goes down two or three levels. This job usually requires gathering a great deal of information through interviews, observation, focus groups, and documentation reviews.

As an example, to understand the order-to-cash process, the analysts may attach themselves to an order and follow the processing of the order from the initial call from a customer, through inventory and credit checking, to the production and shipping of the items on the order, and, finally, to billing and collection. During this activity the team will discuss the process with the people involved, gather examples of all the forms and documents used, and start conceptually grouping the organizational activities into categories of work.

At the end of data collection the real work begins. The team usually produces a draft model of the processes and begins review sessions to gain consensus and approval for an overall model of the organization's processes. Unfortunately, no two people in the organization will agree on what the processes are, what they should be called, how they should be grouped, or the decomposition of activities to carry out the process.

These disagreements result from a lack of understanding of how things are really done, turf and political implications from how the models are drawn, and just basic differences of opinion on priorities, grouping, and terminology. In the best of situations, resolving these differences will take a lot of time. In the worst situations, management will never come to an agreement on an organizational model to be used as a starting point for package implementation projects and other process redesign activities. In either case, this process takes too long for the timetable of a rapid implementation.

For a rapid implementation, the team must not start process modeling with a blank piece of paper. The team should start from either an existing organization model or one provided by the software vendor or systems integrator. These models can be modified much more quickly than creating one from scratch.

Fortunately, many of the software vendors and consulting organizations have process models that can be used as a starting point. However, not all models have equal value to a rapid implementation. The organization should look for models with these key characteristics:

- The model addresses the unique aspects of the organization's industry vertical.
- The model is mapped to the specific package that is being implemented.
- Tools are available so the organization can maintain and adapt these models after the implementation has been completed.

Some of the vendors provide generic process models. Generic process models are meant to apply to all organizations in all industries. However, does it make sense that one model fits all sizes? Are the processes for a bank the same as those for a manufacturer or a university? The answer is: yes and no.

At a high level many of the organizational processes are similar—at least the *infrastructure or support processes* such as accounting and human resources. All organizations process journal entries and produce financial reports. They all manage fixed assets. Everyone recruits, hires, and pays their employees.

They also generally do the same high-level activities in these support areas irrespective of the organization's industry or size. How they do things at the detail level, the terminology used, and the volume of activities varies significantly from one organization to another. But at the process and subprocess levels of a process model these processes are very similar.

However, there are significant differences in *operational processes* across different industries. A bank does not have a "manufacture goods" process. A manufacturer does not "rate policies." A college does not "communicate results from radiology" (unless they also have a medical school and hospital). A local government does not "process stock orders." In these operational areas a rapid implementation team needs, in order to minimize the effort required to change or tailor the preliminary model, a process model that closely reflects the unique characteristics of a particular industry or vertical within the industry.

Even within an industry, there are significant differences among industry verticals. It is difficult for a general financial services industry model to adequately reflect the unique processes of a bank, an insurance company, and a mutual fund organization. And there are significant differences in operational processes between a manufacturer that engineers a product to a customer's specific order and one that repetitively processes oil to produce gasoline and other derivatives. Therefore, the closer the model fits the unique requirements of the industry vertical the organization operates in, the easier it will be for the team to adapt the model for use in a rapid implementation.

To be really useful, the model should also highlight where the packaged application supports the processes. No application will support all the processes and subprocesses in a comprehensive industry process model. Therefore, some of the processes and activities will have to be done manually or be supported by legacy, third-party, or custom-developed applications. It would be nice to know which areas are really covered by the package and which are not.

One way to do this would be to color code the subprocesses and activities to show which ones are supported by the package. If the package has standard interfaces with other products to cover some of the missing functionality, the processes supported by these preintegrated modules could be displayed in different colors.

The team is going to have to figure all this out as part of the project. There is always a requirement to sort out the true package capabilities from the hype, marketing materials, and claims of the vendor. However, this can be a time-consuming process of trial-and-error and calls to package specialists and the vendor's support function. Having a good map as a starting point will speed up this part of the implementation.

In addition to color coding package functionality, some process models tie the models directly to the package. This can be done in a number of ways. The easiest is to add a fourth level to the model (after process, subprocess, and activity diagram) that shows screen shots of the package's transaction screens used to perform each activity. Using this technique the core team and end users can follow the process flow and quickly see the vendor's screens used to support the flow.

The more sophisticated mapped models are linked directly to the vendor's package so that clicking on an activity actually brings up the live production screen to process the transaction or a screen with fields to configure that activity. There have even been attempts to create functionality so that changing the business process model will cause the system to automatically configure parts of the package to enable that form of the process (this was one of the concepts of Baan's Dynamic Enterprise Modeler). This is a great idea, conceptually, but it has not been realized to a great extent in practice. Nevertheless, all these advanced functions in process models can support a more rapid implementation of the packages.

When looking at standard models to jump-start these project activities, the organization should also consider what tools are available to manipulate the models. Some vendors' models can be changed only with proprietary or expensive modeling tools. In other situations, the consultants may provide their own tools to manipulate the models during the project.

However, after the project is completed, the organization needs a way to maintain the models as business requirements and processes change or the vendor comes out with new releases of its software (hopefully, with increased functionality). Therefore, the organization should select a process model and a modeling tool that can be used with a number of different software packages and can be used to maintain the process models as changes occur.

PRECONFIGURED VERSIONS OF THE PACKAGE

Configuration is the way the project team tailors the packaged application to meet the unique needs of the organization without having to modify the vendor's code. Most packages support several different methods for performing many of the business processes. By selecting among parameter options (i.e., keying in values or selecting codes), the team sets up the system to work in a certain way.

Some project teams begin package configuration from scratch. They set up all the configuration parameters one at a time in order to tailor the package to support, as much as possible, the way the organization wants to perform its business processes. However, this is frequently a difficult and time-consuming activity.

Setting configuration parameters is difficult for several reasons. First, there are a tremendous number of parameters to track. For integrated application suites, the number of parameters to be configured can run into the thousands. It is impossible for any one person to understand all these parameters, what they do, and the various options they support. Therefore, team members must work together to keep track of which fields have been configured, what options were selected, and which parameters remain to be set up.

Second, there are a lot of interdependencies between the parameters for the different modules. Decisions made in one module may have surprising and unpredictable impacts on the processes supported by other modules. Sometimes a number of parameters in different parts of the package must be set in concert to achieve the desired result. In other situations, the parameters must be set up in a particular order with some settings being prerequisites for others.

Finally, there are some parameter settings that the team must get right the first time because once they are set, they are difficult to change. These settings often model the organization's structure and drive the file structures supported in the package's databases. Decisions for these parameters must be carefully researched and often will constrain reporting and processing options in the future. As was noted in Chapter 3 on software selection, it is best to choose software that does not have a lot of these load-bearing walls. A large number of these unchangeable fields will make the system less flexible in meeting continuously changing business requirements.

Because these configuration rules, dependencies, and requirements are often not well documented, the project team will make many mistakes during configuration. To a great extent this work becomes a trial-and-error effort. The team tries certain parameter combinations. Sometime they will work. However, in many situations the right combinations are discovered as a result of finding out that things did not work as planned and then researching the reasons and potential solutions.

Having people on the project team who have configured these modules before provides a jump-start for this activity. However, each implementation is different. Therefore, the team members cannot always rely on how they configured a particular module on the last implementation project for the answer to the current requirements. For complex configuration situations, specialists may be required to figure out how to make the packaged application perform in a certain manner.

Design books and automated configuration support software help in these activities. The design book, often in the form of an Excel spreadsheet, lists all the parameter options and provides guidelines on how they are used. In addition, some packages, such as SAP R/3, provide software that guides the developer through the configuration process and documents the status of configuration and the rationale for the selections that are made.

As can be expected, configuration can take a lot of time. There are a large number of things to research, analyze, decide, and test. There are decisions that need to be coordinated between the various process teams. Some of the configuration attempts lead down blind alleys; the package cannot be made to support the desired process design. Others result in errors or problems that are resolved only with a lot of investigation and creativity. Starting from scratch, it may take several weeks of configuration before the team can even handle simple processes like taking a customer order.

A rapid implementation cannot afford to start configuration from scratch. In order to complete these projects on time, the team needs to start from a functional version of the package with most of the parameters already set up to handle normal processes. The project team can then spend its time optimizing the configuration for key processes and handling the tricky configuration challenges that result when the team must figure out how to make the system do things that it may not have been designed to do.

Therefore, the availability of a preconfigured version of the software is a key success factor for rapid implementations. Also, since the software is often configured differently to meet the needs of various industries, it is best to start with a preconfigured version supporting an industry similar to that of the implementing organization.

Many software vendors and consulting organizations offer such versions of their software. They sometimes charge extra for these prebuilt versions, but the team will usually find this to be a good investment. Starting from something that works and changing it to meet unique requirements takes a lot less time than starting the configuration activity from scratch. It is also an approach that minimizes some of the project risks.

Working from a preconfigured version of the software will allow the team to quickly build a sand box environment so they can start learning how the package works. It also makes it easier to isolate the effect of specific changes to parameters. Depending on the fit of the preconfigured version to the requirements of the organization, this accelerator can reduce the amount of time spent in configuration activities by 60 to 80 percent.

JUST-IN-TIME TRAINING FOR THE PROJECT TEAM

One of the things that is often underestimated is the amount of time it takes to train the core project team members on the packaged application being implemented. This training is important because the team members cannot do package-enabled process redesign without understanding the capabilities and limitations of the package. For a rapid implementation to be successful, the team members must quickly get up to speed on basic package functionality, design concepts, data architecture, integration points, and navigation.

The core team should receive formal training at three levels. First, all team members need to have an overview of the entire package and how all the modules fit together to support an organization's business processes. At the next level down, team members need to know a great deal more about the functionality of the package in the areas that will be the focus in the project. Finally, some of the team members need to have detailed module knowledge on things like configuration, reporting, and the most complex functional areas of a module. In addition, there is an entirely separate set of training that the IS team members need on installing the software, administering the applications, and tuning the technical aspects of the system.

The package vendors usually provide these training courses. The amount of training available in each module area depends to a great extent on the complexity of the package. For example, training in the sales and distribution modules of QAD's

MFG/PRO application may take one week. Training on the same modules for J. D. Edwards' OneWorld and SAP's R/3 applications may take three weeks and five weeks, respectively.

This formal vendor training is supplemented by on-the-job training as the team members learn by experimenting with the application in the sand box and development environments and as team members with prior experience implementing the particular package transfer their knowledge to other team members.

A challenge to a rapid implementation is scheduling this training. The ideal situation would be for the team members to complete their training right before they attend the project kickoff. Unfortunately, the required classes may not be available when the team members need to receive the training. Some of the vendor's courses are offered only monthly or even less frequently. In addition, training classes for popular products like Siebel and Ariba often fill up fast. It may take several months to get the team members trained in all the necessary areas. By this time the rapid implementation project may be half over.

An additional problem is the scope of the vendor training. Given the fact that participants in a vendor course usually come from a number of different organizations (representing a number of different industries and unique problems to be solved), the standard training that is provided by the vendor has to be broad. The downside to this is that a team member taking training on the financial applications may have to sit through several days on the consolidation capabilities of the package, even if the scope of the rapid implementation project will not include financial consolidations. As a result of the generic nature of the training, the vendors' standard training usually covers some areas of little interest to the upcoming implementation and does not go into enough detail on the areas that are of particular importance.

On the positive side, the vendor's training is usually hands-on, with a minimum of lectures and slides. Therefore, the team members will get actual experience using the software. There is no substitute for actually processing transactions on the system in order to learn how it works. The training is especially beneficial if led by an instructor with actual implementation experience with the product.

In addition, it is important that the training be correctly timed so that team members do not receive their training months before they get to the task of designing and configuring the system. Since retention of knowledge that is not used quickly is low, those receiving training too early will have to relearn some of the package processes and functions at the time they begin to apply that knowledge.

To summarize, the traditional approach to package training has a number of potential problems. It provides training that is inefficient because it is not tailored to the unique needs of team members working on a specific rapid implementation project. Often, this training cannot be scheduled when the team members need the training. It is expensive (including registration fees and travel expenses), so only a core group of people usually gets to attend the training. The team members do not necessarily get to put this training into practice soon after they receive the training, so retention is low. And there is no way to get access to training (other than looking at the three-ring binder from the course) as the person is doing the project tasks.

What the project team members really need is just-in-time training: training they can get soon before doing a task that requires specific knowledge. On a rapid implementation, this training can be provided through on-site, computer-based, and focused spot training.

Some of the training can be provided at the organization's site, rather than at the vendor's regional training locations. Since this training is provided only to one organization, it can be tailored to the specific needs of the implementation project: modules not in scope can be left out, more time and discussion can be spent on those in scope, and specific project needs and issues can be discussed in the class setting. The application vendor, the consulting organization, or a third-party organization that provides training on the package being implemented can provide the instructor for this training. This training should be hands-on, so it may require installing the vendor's training database on the system (this often comes as part of the standard software installation) and requires terminals with access to this database for all the participants.

Since the cost of this on-site training is often a fixed amount per training day, plus expenses, this training may be also offered to those outside the core team—for example, to the power users. The organization will receive a number of benefits from inclu-ding as many people in this training as possible.

The project sponsor and even a few of the steering committee members should be encouraged to attend the two- or three-day overview training. This will give them a better understanding of the system being implemented. In addition, having the power users participate in the training will help create enthusiasm and interest in the new system. This provides good change management benefits.

After the overview training, specific module training can be planned to support the project schedule. As the team begins designing and configuring processes in certain areas, on-site training can be scheduled on the business processes to be addressed. This training should generally be in areas where a number of the organization's people need to receive the same training. This is usually appropriate for the second level of training, which focuses on modules or high-level business processes.

If only a few people need training in a particular area, they can attend the vendor's regional training classes. It is usually not cost effective to deliver formal on-site training courses for only a small number of people.

Many of the vendors are now offering computer-based training (CBT) versions of their courses. These training modules may be offered on CD ROMs or on a web-hosted basis. Some of this training provides only general and conceptual knowledge of the packaged application. However, training modules are becoming increasingly available that guide the participant through transactions processing on the actual screens used in the package. This self-paced training offers a number of advantages, especially for rapid implementations.

This training can be taken right before the knowledge or skill is needed. It can be taken *just in time*. This creates the highest level of knowledge retention and value to team members as they complete their tasks. This training can also be taken at the pace appropriate for the team member. Areas that are difficult can be taken more slowly or can be repeated. This is not possible in the normal class environment.

Computer-based training can be offered to a larger audience. Since this training can be done during slack time or evenings, it can be offered to all users who want to learn more about the system that they will use to perform their jobs after go-live. Finally, just-in-time, self-paced training modules make scheduling training a much easier task. Specific training does not have to be scheduled months in advance just in case the team will need it.

Focused, spot training is training that is given to team members in response to particular needs of the project. Sometimes this training is given to the entire team as they start a new set of activities in the project. For example, the entire team may get three or four hours on developing test plans, creating test data, and running tests before beginning integration testing activities. In other situations, this training may be given to a small group of team members on a particular area of package capabilities.

Often team members with prior package and implementation experience give this spot training. It is a little more structured than the normal on-the-job training that occurs throughout the project. Since this training helps team members rapidly become productive in new package or project areas, it often is valuable in supporting a rapid implementation approach.

Rapid implementations are shorter-duration, iterative-development projects. Since the scope and direction of these projects is less specific at their beginning (although the goals and objectives may be clearly defined), the implementation team must be flexible as the project progresses. The training support for these projects, therefore, should also be flexible. That requirement makes the availability of just-in-time training very important to these projects.

HOSTED APPLICATIONS

A bottleneck for a rapid implementation can be the inability of the IS organization to get a sand box and development system up and running in time to meet the requirements of an aggressive implementation schedule. Even in the best of situations, setting up the project team technical environment is on the critical path for these projects. In the worst, the IS organization may be unable to support the technologies used in the new applications. There are a number of reasons for these problems, many of which are outside the control of IS.

First, as was covered in Chapter 7, there are a large number of new technologies employed in these applications. Some of these are relatively recent technologies, particularly those associated with the pure-play Internet and e-business applications. However, even the ERP applications use technologies that are not used in many IS organizations. This is especially true for small and midsize organizations that have IS staffs of 20 people or less. Unfortunately, the learning curve for these new technologies is both steep and long.

Second, many of the technologies used in new applications, and especially their combinations, are not mature. These are not plug-and-play situations. It takes a lot of work to make these technologies perform well together.

Rather than coming from one vendor who ensures that all the components work well together, these technologies come from a number of vendors. No one vendor can provide all the pieces to the puzzle. They all have holes and weaknesses in their offerings. Some of the components lack essential functionality. Others do not scale well. As a result, the IS organization must support a multivendor, multitechnology environment with a lot of challenges and surprises. This is always a difficult task.

The third problem is that it is hard to find and retain the technical specialists required to support these environments. These people are in high demand. They command premium salaries and often want to work on the bleeding edge of technology. In many cases, they prefer custom development to implementing packaged solutions or being responsible for ongoing support for these systems. Many of these technology stars want to work for Internet startup companies that provide stock options. (However, some of the recent stock market adjustments have to some degree tempered this talent migration.)

So what is an organization to do if it needs this technology support but cannot climb the technology curve as fast as is required by a rapid implementation? One approach may be to not start the rapid implementation projects until the IS organization is prepared to support the technical infrastructure. This approach does not help solve business problems or take full advantage of opportunities. A second approach would be to add a lot of technical specialists to the core implementation team to perform these tasks while the IS organization is learning to support the new technologies. A third and increasingly attractive approach is to have the technology hosted by a third-party organization.

There are organizations that will host various e-business and ERP applications for others. They will purchase (or may already have) the hardware needed for the applications, hire the IT professionals, load and administer the packaged software, provide help desk support, do backups daily and maintain disaster recovery sites, and act (at least for a certain set of applications) as the IS department for other organizations. This approach can take a lot of the challenges and headaches away from an organization trying to use new technologies for the first time. And these capabilities can be made available in short timeframes. In some cases these organizations can provide the project team with a sand box application environment in a matter of days.

The idea of having third-party organizations host business applications is not new. The banking industry has used this approach for over 25 years—with the larger banks and independent organizations doing the processing of loan, demand deposit, and credit card applications for other entities. And other industries have long used the applications and networks of third-party providers to process electronic data interchange (EDI) transactions. What is new is the wide scope of applications that are becoming available through this method and the advantages that this approach provides.

Most of the newer e-business applications are available through application hosting. If a company wants a web-based retail presence (with personalization, shopping cart, credit authorization, payment processing, and other standard e-tailing capabilities), there are vendors who will provide this facility on their own systems. In a similar manner, there are vendors who will host e-procurement, CRM, and exchange applications.

In most of these situations, these providers supply a relatively quick and easy way for an organization to take advantage of the newer breed of applications that leverage the capabilities of the Internet. However, the cost of the services varies significantly as the vendors experiment with various pricing models.

These same hosting capabilities are also becoming available for most of the leading ERP application suites and are being provided by a number of large third-party organizations, as well as the package vendors themselves. They are not available for all the packages that may be implemented by organizations but they are currently available for those that want to implement the major applications, such as those from SAP, J. D. Edwards, PeopleSoft, or Oracle.

Although this hosted capability for e-business and major ERP applications is relatively new (and in many cases unproven), it does offer a lot of promise as a means to quickly get an application development environment up and running for use by the project team. In many cases access to these systems is browser-based, so the time required to get access for the team is minimal. These applications are already installed on the vendor's systems, so all the vendor has to do is create a new instance for use by the project team. This approach also eliminates the long lead times associated with having the IS organization hire people with new IT skill sets or develop these new capabilities in-house.

In some instances, these hosted capabilities enable an organization to have limited application functionality available in a matter of days or weeks. When you hear claims that an application can be implemented in five days or less, it is safe to assume the vendor is providing a hosted application. Whether this is a good way to support the ongoing processing for an organization's applications is a different question. This issue will be covered in more detail in the next chapter. However, there is no doubt that using application-hosting capabilities can accelerate the implementation of some of the key business applications.

USER PROCEDURE MANUALS

In order to accelerate the implementation of application systems, it is necessary to significantly reduce the effort on those activities that traditionally take a lot of time to do during the implementation. One of the time-consuming activities is developing the user procedures.

These are important deliverables for a project. They document the way things are to be done using the new system, provide an aid to those who are learning to do their jobs differently, and are a prime source of reference materials for end-user training courses. If the team can develop these materials more quickly, they can accelerate the implementation timetable.

There are a number of reasons why it takes a long time to develop these materials on most implementations. First, there are usually a large number of procedures to be written. It is not uncommon for a team implementing an integrated suite of applications to have to write up to a hundred user procedures.

Sometimes the procedures represent the various business processes being implemented. In other cases, they are written to represent the major subprocesses. Given that some of the more complex integrated suites support thousands of processes and subprocesses, it is easy to see how writing these procedures can take a lot of time. This is an area that is usually vastly underestimated for most projects.

The second reason that this activity takes so long is that most implementation team members dread doing this task. It is one they will put off as long as possible. Most team members dislike writing assignments. Since most implementation teams are not staffed with technical writers and business and technical documentation specialists, we have a situation where people who do not like to write are required to develop hundreds of pages of written documentation.

Typically, the team members spend a lot of time staring at blank pages while trying to decide what to say about how to use the new system. Putting what they know on paper becomes a painful task. And spending hours and hours revising this material to make it useful is an even more distasteful task.

Finally, this task takes a long time because this is difficult work when properly done. These procedures need to be clearly written. They will be used not only by an organization's current employees but also by those that join the organization in the future. They need to describe the business processes and objectives, industry practices, organizational policies, roles and responsibilities, and the way the new system can be used to support all of these areas. They need to be easy to understand. Writing these procedures requires an in-depth understanding of the business processes and how complex business software works—and of how to communicate these concepts on paper.

For all these reasons, user procedures usually take a lot of time to develop and often are poorly written. Poorly written procedures will contribute to errors in transaction processing. They will also not be maintained and updated as processes, and the way the system is used, change. As a result, people will use the system inconsistently and develop their own job aids and cheat sheets to help remember how to use the system to get their job done.

This whole activity can be made a lot easier, and the ultimate procedures will be of better quality, if the package vendor or the systems integrator can provide procedure templates for use by the project team. For example, the CD ROM for SAP's ASAP rapid implementation methodology includes hundreds of prewritten user procedures in the form of Microsoft Word documents. These procedures not only describe the steps that a user goes through to perform a task using SAP, but also include pictures (screen shots) of the actual screens in R/3 that will be used to perform each task. And SAP continuously adds to the quantity of procedure templates that are available to support its product.

Another example of accelerators in this area comes from J. D. Edwards. For its OneWorld product, J. D. Edwards provides software that specifically supports the procedure-development process. This software allows the project team members to pick and choose, from a complete set of user documentation, the parts that will be included in a tailored procedure manual for each user role. Using this software, the team can relatively quickly combine all the procedures that are performed by an accounts payable clerk into a procedure manual for this position. A similar procedure manual, showing the relevant procedures for each role, can be quickly generated for general accountants, production supervisors, and human resource specialists in the organization.

The key point with both of these tools is to provide the team with a starting point for the development of user procedures. Although it is usually not possible to adopt the standard or template procedures directly as the user procedures for the implementation, it is much quicker to tailor these procedures to how the organization will use the system rather than starting from scratch to write the procedures.

It can take days to develop a procedure for a relatively complex process from scratch. Tailoring a preexisting procedure can sometimes be done in a matter of hours. And most teams will find that the overall quality of the procedures is much higher when the team starts from a sample procedure and not a blank page. There will also be much greater consistency in the quality of the documentation developed by the various process groups on the team.

A new benefit from the procedure development tools is that they support the generation of online system documentation. Instead of having only paper versions of the procedures, these products can generate documentation that is available online from any workstation. These tools develop HTML versions of the procedures that can be read with any browser.

Using this format, links can be embedded throughout the documentation to quickly take the user to different, related information. Also, this approach ensures that everyone is always working off the current version of the documentation. Since the online documentation is stored in a single location on the system, once it is changed all users have access to updated system documentation.

ONLINE VENDOR SUPPORT

Packaged software never works exactly as expected during an implementation. In spite of all the best efforts of the vendor's developers and the implementation team members, problems will arise. That is why the team does a great deal of testing throughout an implementation project. The goal is to find and fix these problems before the system goes live and the problems impact the organization's customers. Fortunately, there are usually fewer bugs in packaged solutions than would be present if an organization custom develops its new business applications.

Some of the problems are caused by errors that the team members make. Often these problems are detected and corrected by the team members themselves. If the team cannot quickly solve a problem, they may turn to the vendor's support function in order to find a solution.

Support from packaged software vendors has traditionally been provided through an 800 number and a call center. If the implementation team has a problem, it calls the vendor's support number, describes the problem to someone manning a support desk, and then usually waits hours or days for the vendor to get back with an explanation and potential solution.

Sometimes the answer that comes back is that there is a bug in the version of the software that has been installed. If it is a known bug, there may be a code fix that can be applied to solve the problem. If it is a newly discovered software bug, the vendor may require several days, or even weeks, to come up with a solution.

In some instances, the solution provided by the vendor may not fix the problem. This can occur in situations where it is difficult for the vendor to replicate the problem on its systems. This is sometimes the case when certain test data combinations on the implementation team's development instance have exposed the problem. If the fix does not work, then the team has to continue the resolution process with the vendor.

In other cases, the problem may not be a bug in the software but, instead, a misunderstanding about how various parts of the application system work. In some situations the implementation team may have chosen parameter settings that are incompatible. Or a parameter that has been selected may not produce the result anticipated by the team. Some of these problems can be easily handled by changing the parameters. In other cases, the team may learn that the system does not support a certain function or method to perform a process, and a workaround must be found or the process changed.

Behind the scenes, the vendor's support personnel are performing a triage drill to determine whether there is a documented solution to the problem or more experienced developers need to get involved in problem analysis and solution development. In addition, they are balancing priorities among the various customer and partner requests for help. In many situations the support group does not have the capacity to handle all these requests in a timely manner.

This problem analysis and resolution approach often does not meet the needs of a rapid implementation. It may take days before the problem reaches a person in the vendor organization with the knowledge and experience to come up with a solution. In the meantime, the team may have to work through several vendor support people who know less about the system and the way it works than members of the implementation team. In addition, there may be a lot of telephone tag between the team members that can describe the problem in detail and the person working the problem from the vendor's side.

While the vendor is taking days and weeks to fix a problem, the implementation schedule is usually being impacted. The team may not be able to finish testing cycles until the system is fixed. They may also have to wait before finalizing user procedures and end-user training materials and continuing data-conversion activities. The team may also be losing credibility and support from users and managers who will start to worry that the system may not provide functions that address critical business problems or produce the benefits desired from the project.

One of the tools to accelerate problem resolution is online support from the vendor. With online support the implementation team can directly interact with the vendor's support systems and, through these systems, its support personnel. Although the use of these tools varies by vendor, in general these interactions can occur in a number of ways.

First, the team can log its problems directly into the vendor's support system and track the progress that is being made toward its resolution. They can see the actions that have been taken to resolve the problem and the problem's priority and status. They may be able to exchange e-mails or interact in a chat mode with support personnel working the problem. Using this information, the team is in a better position to estimate how long it may take to get a solution. Also, they will know when to push the vendor or the service provider to escalate the priority for problem resolution.

Second, online access often goes both ways. In addition to getting into the vendor's support system, the vendor often can get access to the implementation team's development system. The support personnel can look directly at system settings, file sizes, and databases. They can see for themselves the problem that the team is experiencing. They can try solutions on the team's systems that could take a lot of time to set up on the vendor's systems. For some systems they can also look at the history of upgrades and patches that have already been applied to the system. Obviously, this direct access to the team's systems must be controlled (e.g., backing up the system before changes are attempted, restricting access to production data), but use of this approach may speed up the resolution process.

Finally, the e-business revolution has brought attention to the benefits of self-service, both to customers and suppliers. This self-service approach applies nicely to the support needs of an implementation team. Many of the online support systems now give customers direct access to information in the vendor's support systems that in the past was available only to vendor personnel.

Using search tools and problem categories, the implementation team can look at the history of reported problems with a vendor's software and the solutions that have been implemented. They may be able to identify and contact other customers that have experienced the same problem and found solutions. They can see documentation on the system that may not be normally available to customers. They can download bug fixes through the online connections. They may also be able to add their solutions to the databases so the developers and other users can benefit from their work.

These online support capabilities will not provide immediate solutions to all the problems that the implementation team faces, but they should at least speed up the process of analyzing and resolving problems. In some cases, problems that may in the past have taken days and weeks to resolve can be handled in a matter of hours given increased access to information for the team and the vendor support personnel. Quick resolution of these problems is very important to the success of a rapid implementation.

END-USER TRAINING MATERIALS

The development of end-user training materials is a time-consuming task on most implementations. Ironically, the only projects where this does not take significant time are those that do not adequately train the end users before going live with the new system. However, experience has shown that inadequate end-user training is one of the reasons many implementations fail. Therefore, this task must be quickly and properly done for a successful rapid implementation. As is the case for most of the items covered in this chapter, if the team can find ways to accelerate this activity, the project can be more quickly completed.

The materials used to train the end users are different from those used to train the core project team members at the beginning of the project. Core project team training often covers the generic capabilities of the software. It is wider in scope than end-user training and is usually presented by the software vendor or third-party trainers. This material is typically part of a vendor's standard training curriculum, which includes one- to three-week courses on each of the module areas. The vendor training uses a combination of slides, discussions, and hands-on case exercises. Normally, there is a standard training scenario (e.g., our training company manufactures bicycles or pens) and database used throughout the training.

End-user training focuses on the processes in the scope of the current project and how, at a detail level, the organization will use the new system to support these processes. Although the team may need to provide some training on business or systems concepts as background information (e.g., discuss some general inventory management concepts before jumping into how to record inventory movements on the computer), most end-user training is hands-on training on the tasks that users will do on a day-to-day basis.

End-user training can occur through the same three modes as the training for the core team: classroom, computer-based, and on-the-job. There are tools available from the package vendor and consultants to support each of these modes of training.

The organization's core team members and key users, rather than vendor and consulting personnel, normally conduct the classroom training for end users. Having the organization's own people lead the training helps build buy-in for the new system. This training is usually done on-site or at a location close to the organization's facilities. Often, 8 to 10 workstations are set up in a classroom to conduct this training. It is normally structured in four-hour modules covering related processes and subprocesses. This training covers how the business processes and transactions will get done using the new system.

The classroom training incorporates the user procedures that have been developed by the implementation team. Normally, the instructors will discuss a business process, demonstrate how to perform the process using the new system, and then have the participants do the process, with the help of the user procedures.

There are several tools that help develop and deliver this end-user classroom training. First, the vendors and consultants often provide sample end-user training courses and training templates to speed up the development of each training module. In addition, many of the vendors provide good system administration tools to facilitate refreshing of the training databases before the start of each session. As can be expected, these databases are corrupted as a result of the transactions processed by prior training sessions. Finally, there are some standard training courses, on things like navigation on the system, from the vendor that can be delivered without a great deal of modification.

Some of the vendors provide CBT or web-based training on various aspects of their packaged applications. This training can be used as prerequisite or companion training to the materials covered in the classroom. The availability and quality of these training materials should be factored into the overall training strategy for the project.

These e-learning training materials offer several advantages. They can be used just in time—right before the participant needs the training. Each learner can take this training at a pace that is comfortable and at a time that is convenient. Many of the courses allow the participant to take an online test to provide feedback on which areas the learner already knows and which ones provide new knowledge. With this approach, the person does not have to spend time on training that provides little value. Finally, these materials are available for refresher training and for training new employees, or those that have changed jobs, after the organization has gone live on the new system.

On-the-job training will always be the primary way that most users learn the new system. Retention of knowledge and skills from any sort of training that is not followed by timely application in the work environment is low. People tend to remember and focus on things that directly tie into their day-to-day activities. So, the time a user spends working with the application, figuring out the capabilities and limitations of the new system and how it differs from the old ways of doing things, is invaluable.

Training that occurs on the job can also be done one-on-one with key users and core team members. This is common during the first weeks after go-live when the users may experience situations not addressed in the training. It is also common as the end users have problems and questions as they post their first real customer transactions. However, this is also an area where there are tools to accelerate learning.

The primary tool provided to accelerate learning in this area is good online help. Some vendors provide excellent context-sensitive help information. If the user does not understand what a field means or how it is used, there is often a key that can be pressed to bring up a detailed description. Also, most vendors have online documentation of the various components of the system that can be used to research more general questions. In some cases, the user documentation (describing step by step how to perform each process or subprocess) is also available online, only a click away.

Since preparing and delivering the various forms of training is a time-consuming task, it is easy to see how the availability of sample training materials, CBT modules, and online help can speed up the training process. Like the other accelerators, these types of tools speed up the implementation process.

CONFIGURATION SUPPORT

Different companies and industries have adopted diverse ways of doing some of the same basic processes. Significant variations occur in the way organizations perform processes like product pricing, performance reporting, and salary and benefits administration. In these and other areas, companies have convinced themselves that the way they do things is the best, or the only way, that things should be done. In many cases there are legitimate reasons for these differences. In other cases, the differences are more a matter of personal preference or tradition.

Regardless of the cause, software vendors have to include a number of ways for doing each business process in order to make standard applications marketable to a wider audience. To pull this off they have designed switches, or parameter settings, into their software to select which parts of the software will be turned on and off. This allows the system to support different methods of processing and allows the software to be tailored to the unique needs of the organization.

We have seen in the description of the implementation process that one of the main activities in the analyze-configure-test cycle is to configure the software. Configuration is the process of changing system settings in order to modify the way the application works. This allows standard software to meet the needs of a large number of organizations.

Configuration is one of the most important activities during the implementation of a packaged solution. It is also one of the most challenging ones. When properly done, the system that results can meet the processing requirements of the organization with a minimum of problems and errors. If poorly done, the system that goes live will not meet business needs—it may not even work.

One of the reasons that configuration is a challenging task is that there are an extremely large number of parameters and options for large, integrated software suites. Not only are there thousands (tens of thousands for the most complex software) of parameters, but also each parameter often has several codes or alternatives that can be selected. Just identifying all the parameters and figuring out what the alternatives mean can be a daunting task.

A second challenge is the fact that these parameters are interrelated. Choosing a parameter setting in one module may have an impact on the settings for other modules. In other words, to accomplish some process designs requires the coordinated setting of parameters across the application. They may have to be set in combinations that are not always obvious in the vendor's documentation.

A final challenge is that some of the parameters are difficult to change after they have been set. Therefore, the team must get them right the first time. Most of the parameters can be changed on the fly without major repercussions. This capability is extremely important for software that must be able to adapt to support changing business requirements. However, a small subset of the parameters requires a great deal of effort to change. If not carefully done, these changes may create major problems with the way the system works.

Given the volume and complexity of parameter decisions, it is easy to see how configuration can take a lot of time. Fortunately, there are some tools that can support and accelerate the configuration tasks. One of these tools has already been mentioned: preconfigured versions of the software. Two others that are available to accelerate configuration are *design books* and *automated configuration software.*

Preconfigured versions of the software come with all the necessary parameters already set to have a working system that meets the major needs of a particular industry. As described earlier, this provides a great jump-start for a rapid implementation project. However, since no two organizations are the same, some of the preconfigured settings will have to be changed. That is where the other tools can be helpful.

Design books identify, describe, and document the parameter settings. Many of the software vendors and consulting organizations provide this tool to support the implementations in which they participate. The books often come in the form of Excel spreadsheets or Word documents. Therefore, they can be changed and maintained as living documents throughout the life of the application.

Conceptually, you can think of a design book as having three columns. In the first column is a listing of all the parameters that need to be set by the team. These often are organized by software module and the application screen on which the parameter appears. A better organization would be by business process, since that would allow the team to better identify all the parameters that have to be set to enable each business process. In either case, the field name that appears on the parameter screen is used to identify the parameter. With an automated design book, the parameter names would be links to the development software. Clicking on parameter name would take the user to the screen where the selected parameter option could be entered.

In the second column are all the alternatives that can be selected and codes to identify each alternative. For example, a particular parameter could have valid values of 1, 2, or 3. Each of these numbers would represent a different way of using the application to support a business process. Beside each code would appear a description of the alternative and the impact of selecting this option. A well-developed design book also documents any integration issues between the options selected for this parameter and those chosen in other parts of the system.

The final column documents design decisions: Which parameter option was selected and what was the rationale? This information is important for quality assurance reviews on the current project. However, it is also of value to those members of future implementation projects who are changing parameters to implement new functionality and process designs. In some situations, knowing why a certain option was selected in a prior project or during ongoing maintenance of an application will prevent the future team from making changes that impact the processing for current transactions.

Some of the vendors provide configuration support software as part of their delivered product. A key example of this type of tool is the Implementation Management Guide (IMG) software that comes with SAP's R/3 system. This software automates many of the things that are manually done with a design book.

The IMG lists all the parameters and options. It records who made the parameter selection and the reason for the option that was selected. It identifies the screen that is used to implement the selection. It also produces a number of reports that can be used to identify all the parameters that remain to be addressed.

Any of these tools are useful in speeding up configuration tasks and ensuring that the correct options are selected. However, we must not forget that there are other resources available to the team. A key resource is the core team members who have implemented this application system before. In spite of all the tools and documentation, there is still great value in having people on the team who have configured these modules before. There are a lot of confusing aspects and surprising effects from these software applications that are only learned by trial and error when implementing these packages. Therefore, knowledgeable team members and good vendor support personnel are essential to the success of these projects.

AUTOMATED INTERFACES

In the last chapter, we covered a number of tasks that take up a lot of the time of the IS team members during implementation. Writing data-conversion and interface programs were two especially time-consuming activities. Without special tools to support these tasks, these activities quickly become part of the project's critical path and can jeopardize the viability of the rapid implementation approach.

The data-conversion task that requires a lot of time from the team's technical members is writing, testing, and running programs that take the data out of the old systems (or some intermediate file that has been created to store this information) and load that information into the new system. This is sometimes an extremely difficult task for IS personnel to do without vendor-supplied tools.

There are several reasons that this can be difficult. First, although the IS team members may understand a lot about the data in the legacy systems, they often know little about how the new application's databases are structured. And this information is essential for properly loading the new system with historical and current master file and transaction data.

It is difficult to know all the interrelationships between the data in the vendor's databases or files. When the vendor's software processes a single transaction, it may update information in several different databases. The application logic controls these database updates and ensures the *referential integrity* of the data. This term means that all the right places are updated as a result of the transaction, and if the system is unable to post the transaction in all the required locations the partial updates will be backed out of the other files. Referential integrity is corrupted if a programmer directly updates the databases, without going through the application logic, and does not get all the locations properly updated.

A second difficulty may be a lack of experience with the type of databases that are used in the new applications. Most of the current applications use relational databases such as those provided by Oracle or Microsoft. However, many of the legacy systems use flat files and older forms of databases. Therefore, the programmer may be uncomfortable coding the database calls that will be used to update the databases.

In some cases, these data-conversion technical challenges lead the team to choose a data conversion strategy where most of the data is entered into the new system manually, using the normal transaction-processing and master file update screens. This approach may work for a startup organization with no historical data. But for an existing organization of even moderate size this approach would mean that most of the historical data, and even some of the current master file items, would not be converted to the new system as of the go-live date.

Fortunately, most software vendors now provide tools to support the data-conversion process. This should be expected since this is a standard requirement on most implementations. These tools provide conversion programs that read files prepared by the programmer and automatically update the system in all the right locations.

Usually, there is good documentation on the format of the files to be read by the vendor's conversion utilities. Therefore, the challenge for the programmer changes from trying to understand the vendor's database structure to finding the source for the information that the conversion programs need. This is often a more manageable task given the timetable of a rapid implementation.

The other area that takes a lot of time for the IS team is writing programs to interface the legacy systems with the new applications. Similar to the data-conversion situation, this has traditionally been hard and takes a great deal of time because of the difficulty in understanding the processing logic and the database structure for the new applications. The new applications are often extremely complex. Without good documentation this is an impossible task. With good documentation it is still a very difficult one.

Once the IS team understands the technical architecture of the new application (or at least believe that they do), there is still the problem of figuring how to update the new databases to properly reflect processing in the legacy systems, and vice versa. The normal approach is to directly update the databases of the new application. This, once again, creates referential integrity risks. Also, if these updates occur in real time, there is a chance that these interface database postings will adversely impact the processing that is going on in the new applications.

As can be seen from these discussions, there are a great deal of risks and challenges involved in developing interfaces between legacy systems and the new applications. Basically, this is a difficult task because the integrated suite vendors did not originally design their applications to be interfaced with those from other vendors or an organization's custom-developed legacy systems. The recommended solution was to implement the other modules in the vendor's suite of applications. However, that situation is changing.

Many vendors have now created standard application programming interfaces (APIs) for their applications. These interfaces define, similar to the data-conversion situation, how the programmer can invoke transaction processing from outside the application. Under this approach the new application processes the interface data through its normal processing logic. This provides assurance that the data will be properly processed (which may not happen if the programmer directly updates the databases), and brings to bear the tools (e.g., roll-forward, roll-back) that ensure the referential integrity of the databases.

There are a number of additional lines of attack that are being pursued by vendors to make it easier for them to interface each other's applications. It is in the best interest of the application vendors to have predefined interfaces with all the major packaged applications. Two of these approaches, using enterprise application interface (EAI) middleware and the XML Internet standard, are covered in Chapter 9 on trends affecting rapid implementations. Both of these technologies will support the effective and efficient interfacing of a number of applications within and across organizations.

As a result of all these changes, the task of integrating various applications should become easier in the future as vendors and third-party software providers create additional interface capabilities. As standard interfaces become available, it will make this area of a rapid implementation less problematic.

9

TRENDS AND IMPLICATIONS

Things are changing fast in almost every area connected with the implementation of packaged applications: staffing, processes, technology, vendors, packages, expectations, and capabilities. A lot of these changes are the result of the rapid growth and development of e-business applications and technologies. Many are in response to the changing business dynamics and strategies. There have always been continuous changes in the capabilities of these packages and approaches for implementing them. The only difference is that these changes are happening much faster than they have in the past.

A few words of warning should precede the discussions that follow. For some of these trends the trajectory and potential impacts on the implementation landscape are easy to see. For others, there is no way of knowing for sure how important they will become. However, all of these areas should be considered by those organizations implementing package applications. They will be especially important for those that are pursuing a rapid implementation strategy. The major changes and trends that will be discussed include:

- Consolidation of e-business and enterprise resource planning (ERP) vendors
- Moving back to best-of-breed applications
- Increased availability and interest in outsourcing
- Connecting applications across enterprises
- Wireless technologies and applications
- Challenge of Internet technologies
- Consultant capability challenges
- Increased importance of computer security

The only thing that can be said with certainty is that many aspects of how we implement packaged applications three years from now will be different. However, most of the principles and approaches presented in this book will remain relevant. We will just have to adapt them in response to these trends and the potential impacts they have on successful rapid implementations.

CONSOLIDATION OF E-BUSINESS AND ERP VENDORS

As should be obvious to anyone who has been paying attention for the last couple of years, all organizations will be dramatically impacted by e-business. This is true for manufacturers, hospitals, banks, schools, government institutions, and the corner Mom-and-Pop business. This is not a trend that will be here for a few years and then will fade away; it is truly a revolution.

Despite all the hype to date, we are just beginning the e-business journey. For most organizations, that journey will be closer to the path taken by the Dells and the Ciscos of the world and less like that of the Amazons. Business-to-consumer applications received most of the initial attention but most people realize that business-to-business applications offer the real potential for e-business.

E-business represents a deep and fundamental change in how things will get done in the world we live. At the most basic levels it changes the relationships between a company and its suppliers and customers. It affects how we get information as organizations and individuals and what information we share with others—even our competitors.

In spite of all the attention given to Internet technologies, it is a mistake to think of e-business as primarily a technology phenomenon. It is true that e-business has been made possible by the timely confluence of new hardware, software, and communication capabilities. And the importance of widely accepted technology standards cannot be minimized. But the real impact of e-business is the effect it has on new business processes, models, and relationships. These changes are important because they alter how organizations and individuals communicate and relate with one another.

These process and organizational changes have also created changes in the type of business applications that are being implemented, the strategies and activities of the software vendors, the participants in implementation projects, and the expectations of all involved.

A key change is the development and implementation of standard packages with an external rather than internal focus. The ERP systems were inward focused. They were mainly about making an organization's internal processes more efficient and reducing costs as a result of these efficiencies. As such, they were primarily focused on the back-office functions: accounting, human resources, production scheduling, and logistics. They helped reduce an organization's costs but had little impact on revenue and growth. As a result, many organizations were disappointed in the results they achieved from these implementations.

Contrary to popular opinion, ERP is not dead. There was a large dropoff in ERP activity after the Y2K work was completed and e-business applications starting getting investment attention. However, there are a large number of organizations that still need to improve their back-office processes and systems. Some of them had unsuccessful first implementations of ERP systems and need to reimplement these in order to get the original benefits defined for these projects. Newer organizations need to implement these systems for the first time. However, it is true that ERP has definitely fallen out of favor.

None of the software vendors want to be considered ERP vendors anymore. They are all calling themselves e-business vendors, even if their products have not substantially changed. And most of their development budgets are going into e-business applications and integrating their existing products with those of alliance partners who already have e-business applications. All the software vendors seem to have alliances with all the other package vendors and all the major system integrators. However, the number of these alliances that have products that work together in any meaningful way is very small.

We should also expect an increase in the acquisition of smaller e-business software vendors by the larger, traditional software organizations. In most cases it is much quicker to purchase a company with working products and integrate these products into the application suite than to develop new functionality from scratch. Unfortunately, the difficulty in truly integrating these products will mean that, for many customers, the option of purchasing totally integrated, full-function e-business and ERP applications is still not a viable one. In the short term, enterprise application integration (EAI) middleware products and custom-developed interfaces will be needed to effect the integrations.

The consulting organizations and other IT professionals who prided themselves on their ERP integration capabilities are also retooling themselves to be e-business, customer relationship management (CRM), and collaborative supply chain management (CSCM) system integrators. These are the hot areas in the industry.

E-business applications are externally focused. Some are targeted toward getting better coordination and collaboration among the organizations in a supply chain. Others are focused on creating better relationships with an organization's customers. The newest applications are designed to bring buyers and sellers together in efficient electronic marketplaces.

Implementing these new systems often requires cross-enterprise projects. Because of the external focus, organizations are finding that they have to involve their customers and suppliers in these implementation projects. Many of these projects will be successful only to the extent that business partners change their systems and processes. Making such changes is usually in the interest of all the parties, but that does not mean that there will not be difficulties in selling and implementing these solutions.

Finally, organizations expect to implement these e-business applications in a matter of weeks and months, not years. Fortunately, using the approaches and tools described in this book, this is often possible. These are usually limited-scope applications. Organizations are not trying to replace all the major systems with one integrated solution. They are usually implementing point solutions to respond to specific problems and opportunities.

In these projects, organizations may not be implementing all the functions in Siebel—just the part that supports marketing campaigns. Instead of all the functions in Ariba, they may be implementing just the auctioning capabilities. As we have seen, the time it takes to implement a new business application is directly related to the number of processes included in the scope. If we limit the number of processes to one or two, these packages can be implemented in much less time.

MOVING BACK TO BEST-OF-BREED APPLICATIONS

In the 1990s, there was a shift toward implementing multiple applications from a single vendor's integrated suite. Prior to that time there was a preference for point solutions—selecting and implementing the best package in each functional area regardless of the vendor or the other systems the organization had in place.

Two things fueled this trend: (1) the benefits of preintegrated systems and (2) the availability of good software modules from the major package vendors. Both of these trends worked to the advantage of the organization and offered great improvements over a custom-development approach.

Integrated systems offer a number of advantages over multiple point systems. Each point system usually has its own database, often with some of the same information that is incorporated in the databases of other applications. The architecture for integrated systems usually includes a single database (location) where each item of information is stored. This results in less redundant data entry; the same information does not have to be entered into multiple systems.

Integrated systems also reduce synchronization and integrity problems that inevitably occur when an organization enters the same information in multiple locations, at multiple times. There are fewer situations where the information needed to serve customers and run the business is different depending on which department's system you got it from. In addition, the information in integrated systems is usually available in real time across all modules.

It is easier for a vendor to make available interfaces between applications in its product suite. When buying applications from several vendors, the organization has to develop interfaces so information can be shared across the applications. These interfaces are often difficult and time consuming to develop and test. They do not always work as well as expected. Since they usually provide periodic, batch updates to databases, the shared information is not available in real time.

The technologies used by a particular vendor generally are consistent across the applications in its suite. The only time this may not be the case is when a vendor purchases applications from other vendors to fill out the suite. In the past, an organization looking for best-of-breed applications might find that the best-in-class products all ran on different database management systems or that there was no one operating system that could support all the various modules. This was especially the case when some of the applications were provided by computer hardware manufacturers that used proprietary operating systems.

Integrated systems also have the same look and feel throughout the application suite. This makes them easier to use than trying to work with a number of packages with different design philosophies and user interfaces. It also makes them easier to learn; the user does not have to learn different navigation techniques for each application.

The second primary factor that favored integrated suites is that the key vendors all had relatively good solutions to offer in common functional areas. By the 1990s, the standard application industry had matured to the point where an organization that wanted relatively full-function financial, inventory management, or payroll systems could find these systems from a number of vendors with integrated suites.

The true situation back then, as it is today, is that most organizations really only used a small fraction of the capabilities in these systems anyway. Therefore, for bread-and-butter transaction processing, an organization could usually find what they wanted from any of the major software vendors. And most organizations needed to get these backbone applications in place before they could even think about other, more advanced applications.

E-business changed this whole environment. Suddenly, new types of applications were being developed that coordinated the actions of customers and suppliers. For the first time, these applications offered functions to truly support revenue enhancement, competitive advantages, and new business models. These were advanced applications in specific functional areas: advanced planning and scheduling, customer relationship management, e-procurement, and web-based sales and support. These applications were designed without the technology limitations from investments in older technologies. These new applications took advantage of the capabilities of the Internet and used development tools designed for these technologies.

The new applications produced by a large number of niche players (some of which are becoming very large) are often better than similar ones offered by the ERP vendors. Much of this state of affairs is a result of the benefits of focus. Siebel produces a better CRM tool because for almost a decade they have focused on sales force automation, call center, and service functionality. Ariba produces better e-procurement products because they do not have to spend part of their R&D budget developing CRM systems. BroadVision has better personalization capabilities because its organization began with a web culture and orientation. None of these vendors has to worry about deve-loping and maintaining financial and HR products while, at the same time, enhancing their specialty applications.

The ERP vendors have been slow to catch up in these new application areas. For some of them, their prior success and size work against them. It is difficult to turn a large organization around quickly, especially without changes in top management. This puts the traditional package vendors at a competitive disadvantage when the competition is generally smaller and nimbler organizations. In addition, the ERP vendors have a large customer base, paying hefty maintenance fees each year, that expects the vendors to continually enhance and refine the traditional applications.

The ERP vendors have taken a number of steps to turn themselves into e-business and best-of-breed players. As previously noted, their first response was to change their web sites to say that they were now e-business, and not ERP, vendors. As can be expected, this was not a difficult task to accomplish—talk is cheap. However, behind this change in representation was a genuine attempt to make their organizations and products responsive to the changing needs of their customers.

The next step was to provide Internet and browser-based interfaces for their existing modules. This has generally been accomplished. For most of the products, access to most, if not all, of the functions is available through browsers. This provides a common and familiar look and feel to these applications. Many of the vendors started working on these interfaces four or five years ago.

The third step was to get out an e-business and Internet version of their software. Oracle did this with version 11i, and SAP with mySAP.com. A requirement of these new versions was to add enough functionality to be able to say that the vendor has modules in the new application areas. However, filling out the functionality of these modules and making them competitive with best-of-breed applications is a longer-term challenge.

The fourth step was to develop alliances with best-of-breed providers so that an integrated suite vendor will have a viable solution for someone who wants to go to one vendor for traditional and best-of-breed combinations. Many ERP vendors are resellers of products like Siebel and Ariba in certain market channels. In addition, they are developing standard interfaces between their products and these best-of-breed solutions.

The fifth step was to repackage some of the modules from the vendor's integrated suite as best-of-breed modules. This is certainly the case for the financial systems from SAP, J. D. Edwards, and Oracle. It is also the case with human resource systems from PeopleSoft and Lawson. Part of this effort is to provide interfaces between these modules and those of other vendors.

For example, it is in the interest of both SAP and PeopleSoft to have an interface between SAP financials and the PeopleSoft human resource modules. With this combination, both vendors can be part of a viable solution to customers looking for best-of-breed functionality in a number of areas. The development of EAI products will make these best-of-breed package integrations even easier.

Oracle seems to be the only vendor that still is taking an all-products-from-one-vendor strategy. Even SAP has started to acknowledge that they cannot support all the complex functional areas with internally developed applications. Therefore, they have started to develop alliances with a small number of other vendors to fill gaps in their product offerings.

It will be interesting to see how all this plays out in the next few years. If Oracle can come up with relatively good functionality in all the major application areas, will the benefits of buying all the software from one vendor and having it totally integrated in architecture win out over a best-of-breed preintegrated solution? I believe that the jury is still out on this proposition. However, there is a lot at stake.

INCREASED AVAILABILITY AND INTEREST IN OUTSOURCING

As previously discussed, one way to accelerate the implementation of new applications is to outsource the processing and technical support for the application to a third-party provider. Although this may be an option that should be considered in many implementation situations, it is especially attractive for a rapid implementation project. This approach mitigates several of the risks associated with implementing new technologies. It also supports a business strategy of focusing on those things that provide competitive advantages and outsourcing as much of the other things as possible.

Companies have been outsourcing their data centers for decades; there are a number of organizations that have major service lines and extremely large, multiyear contracts in this area. But even in these situations, the application development function is often kept in-house and not included as part of the outsourcing arrangement. At the current time, hosting major packaged applications for a large number of organizations is generally a new and unproven business proposition. So, organizations should be careful while pursuing this option. For some, it may be a good approach for providing these services; for others, it may not meet their needs.

The main reason this approach is unproven is that it is relatively new. Although all the major ERP and e-business vendors advertise hosting capabilities, these are relatively recent offerings. There are a lot more organizations with plans to provide outsourcing services than there are those with actual experiences providing these services. These outsourcing organizations include the vendors themselves, most of the major consulting and integration firms, and large IT organizations (e.g., IBM, EDS).

There are a number of open questions that must be answered before it will be obvious that using hosted applications is a viable option for most organizations. These include:

- What is the organization trying to accomplish with a hosted application approach?
- Are the capabilities of the hosting organizations real?
- What model for hosting is actually being implemented?
- Does this model give the organization the flexibility to respond to changing business needs?
- Considering both the short and long term, is it in the best interest of the organization to pursue this alternative?

To evaluate the business case for outsourcing it is necessary to clarify the reasons an organization would consider this option. What are the goals and objectives for these arrangements? What benefits is the organization looking for? What risks is the organization trying to mitigate?

There are a number of reasons why an organization might pursue having its applications hosted by a third party. One of the primary reasons is that most organizations, especially small and midsize ones, do not have IS personnel with the skills and experience to support the new technical environments. The learning curve for developing these skills is often very steep. In addition, the existing IS staff may still need to spend the majority of their time supporting and maintaining legacy applications that run on older technologies.

Organizations may not be able to recruit and retain people with critical skills in their local market. They may also not be in a position to effectively use people with the right skills because sometimes these skills are needed only on a periodic basis. The professionals with these skills generally want to work on the bleeding edge of technology and may be unhappy in a situation where they do not get a lot of opportunity to work with the newer technologies.

People with these hot skills are also in high demand. So, an additional concern is the high salaries that would have to be paid to these individuals and how that would impact the overall compensation schemes in the organization. The organization would also have to spend a lot of money on the continuing education of these individuals to keep their skills current.

A second reason for looking at outsourcing is that the lead time for purchasing and installing new hardware and software may not meet the schedule requirements of a rapid implementation. With hosting, some applications can be implemented in a matter of weeks. For most organizations, it takes longer than that to fill out a purchase order for new equipment.

A third reason for considering hosting may be because the existing IS staff may have to spend all of their time maintaining the old applications and therefore have no time to participate on and support new development projects. Rather than hiring more people for the department, the increased load can be contracted out through a hosting arrangement.

So, in many situations the objectives for outsourcing are to overcome problems with skill shortages, excessive lead-times, and staffing issues. Outsourcing organizations may already have the right staff and equipment in place to mitigate these kinds of risks. They have people with the right technical and application skills. They also have other risk-mitigating means such as backup and recovery capabilities. They usually have enough critical mass in the key technical areas so that losing one person should not have a devastating impact on their ability to support the newer technologies.

The organization may also be looking for a way to make IT costs more predictable. Many of the outsourcers will charge monthly rates based on the number of users, or on a transaction basis. This may reduce some of the uncertainty associated with implementing new technologies.

Hosting organizations will often do the testing on upgrades for the applications hosted, so the effort required to implement new versions and bug patches from the vendor will be minimal for customer organizations. It will be much more efficient for the hosting organization to upgrade the applications at one site than to have all its customers do the same project on each of their own computer systems.

Once an organization knows what it is looking for from an outsourcer, it is in a better position to evaluate the different providers. To what extent does the hosting vendor's organization, staffing, and capabilities meet the objectives? Does it have people with the right skills and experience? Does it already have data centers with the applications running and is there adequate capacity to handle the transaction load of their existing and new customers? How responsive can the vendor be in getting the organization up and running on these systems? How good are its help desk and support functions? Does the vendor process the current releases of the software?

Remember, these organizations face the same personnel challenges that an organization would face in developing and supporting this environment. For many of the companies getting into the outsourcing business, this is a new service offering. It often requires a different staffing and pricing model than they may be familiar with. So, an organization should not assume that all these things have been addressed; it should check that this is so.

There are several delivery models being practiced by the outsourcers. The organization must be sure that the one being provided meets its needs. The three primary models are: (1) standard configuration, (2) custom configuration, and (3) data center. Each has various advantages and disadvantages, both to the organization and the outsourcer.

The standard configuration model may be the one that is in the best interest of the outsourcer. Under this approach, the application to be hosted is preconfigured to the most general requirements and any organization using the hosting service will use this version of the application. This tactic is the easiest for the hosting organization to support.

With this model all the customers use the same configuration and the same version of the application. When changes are made to the application, they can be tested and implemented once. Under this scenario, the application is like a utility that provides a standard service. There may be a little flexibility for the organization to tailor the application through the use of code tables and the way they use the system, but basically the system comes in only one flavor: vanilla. However, there is a high likelihood that this flavor works and costs less than some of the other hosted options.

Under the custom configuration model each customer has the option to determine its own configuration settings. In effect, an organization can have its own version of the software. Usually, there will be a standard configuration initially available as a starting point. However, since configuration can be done remotely, the implementation team can tailor the application during their project. After go-live, the configuration can be changed as required by the organization.

This option will probably cost more than the software utility approach, but it will give the organization more flexibility in how the application is set up. However, this option is not as attractive to the hosting organization since it will have to support processing on many differently configured versions of the application. If there are errors in processing, who is at fault: the hosting vendor or the organization that determined its own configuration settings?

Under the first and second models, the applications that are available to be hosted are still determined by the outsourcer. If the outsourcer supports Ariba as the e-procurement software that runs with J. D. Edwards' OneWorld and you want to use Commerce One, you are out of luck. And what does the organization do if it wants some of its legacy applications to also be hosted? That brings us to the third model.

Under the data center model, the outsourcing organization basically runs the processing for the organization on a data center dedicated to the organization. The organization or the outsourcer may own the equipment. The organization decides what applications will be loaded on the data center and the outsourcer supports the processing of these applications. The outsourcer provides the specialists in operating systems, databases, networking, hardware, and in some cases, applications, and is in charge of hiring, training, and retaining these key resources.

As can be seen, even with these brief descriptions, there are significant differences in these three approaches and what they offer an organization. Therefore, the organization needs to clearly define its needs and understand which option the vendor is supporting. Making assumptions in this area will often lead to disappointment.

The option that is best for the organization will depend on its business and technical requirements. Some of these requirements will depend on the amount of change the organization is experiencing or expecting in the future. If these changes could be extensive, the organization may require more control over the version of the application that is being hosted. If the organization's environment is relatively stable and predictable, then some of the more utility-like functionality could be acceptable.

The time horizon under consideration may also be important. The decisions made in these hosted arrangements do not have to be final (although the outsourcer will try to get long-term contracts with expensive escape clauses). For example, the organization may want to use a hosted application for development purposes and then after a few years consider bringing the processing back in-house. Or, at a later time, the standard solutions provided by the hosting organization may be more acceptable. The key point is that hosting offers many benefits, but the organization must be careful and go into these arrangements with eyes wide open.

CONNECTING APPLICATIONS ACROSS ENTERPRISES

A lot of effort is being expended to connect application systems and share information across enterprises. This trend supports some of the e-business strategies leading to greater collaboration between organizations and their customers and suppliers. It also is required to get many of the benefits from the externally focused applications. There are a number of advantages to this line of attack; there are also a number of challenges.

Organizations have to work closely together to meet increasingly demanding customer requirements. In order for a manufacturer to be able to produce goods in response to specific customer orders (rather than manufacturing to a forecast or inventory stocking level), its suppliers must have raw materials and components on the production line at the right time and place. For this to occur, the manufacturer must share its production schedule and orders with its suppliers on a daily, and sometimes hourly, basis. Information must go up and down the supply chain in a continuous, fluid, and real-time manner.

There are tremendous advantages to all the participants from pulling this off. Customers can get exactly what they want in a relatively short period of time. An order can be taken and the product the customer wants, with all the right colors and options, can be manufactured and delivered in a matter of days. The manufacturer and suppliers benefit because these techniques can take a significant amount of inventory out of the supply chain: information can be substituted for inventory. This lowers carrying, warehousing, obsolescence, and materials handling costs. Lean manufacturing and just-in-time techniques become practical if the right systems are in place and everyone has good, timely information.

In the past, this type of information moved by telephone or fax. Those modes cannot keep up with the current pace of business changes. There are too many handoffs, time delays, and errors with these manual processes. If organizations want to be able to react to customer requirements and the related changes in real time, they will have to take people out of the direct communications process. The computers in the supply chain need to talk to each other, and have the applications determine appropriate actions, to make a higher level of responsiveness possible. Companies like Dell have already proven that this manufacture-to-order, continuous sharing of information with suppliers and customers is possible. But that does not mean that it will be easy to do.

We have already discussed the challenges of interfacing new systems with the legacy systems within the four walls of an organization. Now we are talking about interfacing computer systems throughout the supply chain. This seems like an impossible task.

The only way that it seems possible is for all the members of the supply chain to have the same application systems. If everyone had OneWorld (or any one of the other major application systems), organizations would have no problem connecting all these systems and sharing information up and down the supply chain. Of course, there would be problems and challenges even in this scenario, but it would make the solution a lot easier.

The fact that everyone does not have the same systems, and never will, is perhaps the main reason why supply chain collaboration has never been effectively implemented in the past. An additional contributor to this problem has been the high cost of creating and maintaining communication networks to connect the various participants. Those high costs were one of the reasons that electronic data interchange (EDI), for most organizations, never proved to be the solution to this problem. Other problems with EDI included the limited transaction sets that were supported and the slowness with which additional message standards were developed and approved.

However, there is hope for achieving this vision of a connected supply chain through the emergence of two technologies: enterprise application integration (EAI) and eXtensible Markup Language (XML). Organizations may get to a point in a few years where interfacing disparate computer systems between enterprises is not the great challenge that it is today.

Enterprise application integration is an emerging class of applications, often included in the category called *middleware,* which takes a different approach to the problem of interfacing application systems. This approach seems to offer a number of advantages in performing a difficult and demanding task. Interfacing these systems is also a time-consuming task, which makes improvements in this area of particular relevance to rapid implementation projects.

In the past, the interfaces between applications were direct and one-to-one. The interfaces between different systems were usually custom developed by each implementation team. If an organization wanted to integrate its application, say OneWorld from J. D. Edwards (JDE), with suppliers that had Oracle, PeopleSoft, and Lawson applications, then the IS personnel supporting the project would have to build three interfaces: JDE to Oracle, JDE to PeopleSoft, and JDE to Lawson. If one of the suppliers had customers with ten other systems, then ten new interfaces would have to be developed in order for that supplier to share electronic information (other than that provided through EDI) with its customers.

This proves to be an impossible task for most implementations. Given that all these systems are complex and the technical architecture and data dependencies are often not well documented, most organizations do not have the time and resources to figure out all these interfaces. And the interfaces would probably have to be continually updated and retested as each trading partner changed versions of their software.

Several third-party software providers have developed interfaces for a few of these common one-to-one connections. There has been similar activity by some of the application vendors to develop interfaces to the top packages in other areas to support their attempts to reposition certain of their modules as best-of-breed solutions. For example, it would be relatively easy to buy tools that interface SAP financials with the HR modules from PeopleSoft. However, a different model is needed to provide a better overall solution to this interfacing problem.

The EAI vendors have come up with such a model. What if interfaces were developed to map the major packages to a single conceptual framework for what all these packages do and the kinds of information they normally need to share? This conceptual framework could be used to translate the data and processes from each vendor's package to a common language. This would create a one-to-many interface. If all these systems spoke this common language then they could communicate with each other without needing to know the details on how the other systems worked (their special languages).

Using this concept, EAI vendors do all the detailed analysis to determine how a system like SAP works and how SAP data and processes map to the common framework. If they do this same analysis and translation for a number of other vendors' products, then they have an interface that can connect the computer systems of all the trading partners that have products supported by the EAI application. If one of the trading partners has a unique, unsupported application (for example, a custom-developed legacy system), then only one interface needs to be developed: the one that maps the legacy system to the EAI framework.

In this manner, EAI provides a solution to the complex technical challenge of creating a number of interfaces between the disparate applications. The EAI products are often expensive but many organizations will find them to be cost-effective ways, and some times the only way, to implement collaborative supply chain sharing of information.

eXtensible Markup Language is an Internet standard that can be used to create systems that pass data between partner systems. It is the technology that is being used by many of the EAI vendors in their cross-enterprise applications development. Many people have heard of XML's cousin, HTML. The HTML is the standard used to describe how our browsers will read static pages on a web site. The XML can be thought of as a way for providing variable format messages that can be shared between any two computer systems, as long as they both understand the format (tags) that is being used. And, like HTML, these messages use Internet technologies and can be sent over the Internet or on virtual private networks (VPN) that use Internet protocols.

Another way of thinking about XML is in relation to EDI, which defined a standard format for the messages that would be exchanged between trading partners. A standard-setting body had to decide when a new transaction would be added to the approved EDI set, and what each field of the message would be; XML allows any group of organizations to create their own language and common standards for exchanging information.

Some organizations got together to decide on the format of XML pages that will meet their needs. An example of this is RossettaNet, which has created XML standards for the high-tech industry. Any one organization can go to the RossettaNet web site and see how these standards have been defined and exchange information formatted using this standard.

So the combination of EAI products and XML standards offers new ways to solve the computer system connection problem. Hopefully, these advances will help organizations share data to meet the increasing demands of an e-economy.

WIRELESS TECHNOLOGIES AND APPLICATIONS

A fast-growing technology for ERP and e-business applications is wireless. In particular, the characteristic getting most of the attention is providing wireless access to information through the Internet. This is a technology that is being touted, and demonstrated to a limited degree, by most of the major software vendors. It is also being heavily covered in the business press. Therefore, it is coming to the attention of managers and employees throughout most organizations.

From one perspective, wireless is just another form of interface to ERP and e-business applications. However, its advantage comes from the fact that it is a mobile interface. Using wireless technologies, people can get access to the information stored in these applications when they are not at their desks and workstations. Using Internet-enabled cell phones, personal digital assistants (PDAs), and laptop computers, employees can do many of the inquiries and transactions that can be done in the office. Having this remote access can provide significant advantages to sales employees, service personnel, and managers working away from the office.

Wireless can impact rapid implementations in a number of ways. The potential effects of the wireless phenomenon seem to be greatest in the areas of project scope, process design, technology support, and end-user training.

The scope of an implementation can be impacted in two main ways. First, there is a good chance that the requirement to provide wireless access will be added to the scope of many implementations. In certain cases, having this capability will have been factored into the business case for the project. Some of the defined benefits may be possible only if sales and service personnel have remote access to information. In other cases, there may be an expectation that this feature will be available even if it is not needed to achieve the objectives of the project. These expectations may have been set earlier as the new system was demonstrated to management during the software selection process.

In both of these situations, the project manager and sponsor need to be sure that adequate time and resources have been allocated to deliver this functionality along with the other things that will be expected from the project. The option of deferring these capabilities to a future phase using process prioritization or time boxing should be explored. The project leaders need to understand what options are available.

A second scenario may occur when providing remote capabilities *is* the scope of the project. This level of scope fits well with many of the strategies for rapid implementations. In such a situation, a team may be pulled together for a short time (maybe three to six weeks) to implement new processes that take advantage of wireless capabilities. These limited-scope projects still have to go through the same implementation process—but faster.

If wireless is included in the project scope, the availability of these remote capabilities needs to be factored into the process designs. People can do their jobs differently if they have this access. That may require that two process variants be designed: one for activities when the process is done in the office and a second for when the task is done remotely.

A salesperson at the customer site without remote access to supporting applications may have to phone someone at the office to check on inventory availability. Or the salesperson may have to go back to the office to prepare a quote for a customer because this processing is done on the system. In this traditional field environment, the standard answer to many customer questions has to be: "I don't know the answer to that question, but I will find out and get back to you."

With remote access, orders can be entered on PDA devices and transmitted over the Internet to the organization's application systems, and real-time information can be sent over the Internet back to the PDA device. Much of the same information that is available in the office is available remotely.

It is important to realize that currently not all the same information will be available through remote access. When pressed, some of the vendors will admit that, of the hundreds of transactions that can be done on the system from the office, only a handful are currently available through the use of remote Internet capabilities. However, that percentage will grow quickly over the next few years. The point is that the implementation team must determine what is available before deciding what processes can be redesigned.

In many customer-facing situations, sales will be made with wireless that were not possible before. Getting back to the customer with information at a later time allows the customer to defer a decision and, perhaps, bring in a competitor for a second quote. Having the information available in a timely manner will result in better information being provided to the customer (which creates its own benefits) and often will help the salesperson close the sale on the spot. The new processes should be designed with some of these objectives in mind.

Wireless is a new technology for most IS organizations. Therefore, there will be a learning curve that needs to be climbed before the IS members of the team can provide the needed technical support for these projects. Programming a PDA device is different from programming a normal application. There are different languages and tools used as well as different technology constraints that need to be addressed. Therefore, if the current IS organization does not have experience with these technologies, then IT specialists should be added to the team as core team members or advisors to ensure that the technical aspects of the project will be adequately covered.

There will usually be lead times associated with selecting and purchasing the remote devices. If the organization does not currently have standards around which cell phones and PDA models will be used and supported, the team may have to include selection activities in the early weeks of the project. The key here is to use only hardware and technologies that are proven. The application vendors should be willing to demonstrate these capabilities and specify the acceptable products that can be used to interface to their applications.

Wireless also requires a communication link. Therefore, contracts with Internet service providers (ISPs) and communication companies will also have to be negotiated. Since Internet access is needed for the development system, as well as for the production system, the time required to get this access should be factored into the project plans. The best approach is to start these activities early.

The final area affected by the wireless capabilities is end-user training. Doing a transaction on a PDA device is different from doing it on a workstation. The screen on a PDA can display only a limited number of fields. Therefore, the flow of data will be different. This should not take long to learn, but it is still something that people often need to be taught. In addition, there needs to be training on the techniques for entering data on the device. The PDA information can be entered using character-recognition software. If the data is entered using a cell phone, there are various ways of entering the numeric and alphabetic data.

There will be problems with these applications if the Internet connection is bad or is not available. The end users must learn how to test the access before whipping out a PDA in front of the client. This access test is a good thing to do in the car before going into the customer's site.

Wireless capabilities will become increasingly popular. But they are the first of a number of technologies that will become available to support applications in the future. Organizations need to learn how to address these capabilities, and the associated challenges of any new technologies, in their rapid implementation projects.

CHALLENGE OF INTERNET TECHNOLOGIES

The technologies used to develop and support business applications in the future will be dramatically different from those used in the past. Also, the ways the technologies are used will be different. Most organizations are ill prepared to take advantage of these technologies. They are not even ready to support the technical infrastructures that will be employed with the new packaged applications. This creates both business and technology issues. It also explains part of the growth of the packaged application industry and the increased interest in application hosting.

The reason for this grim situation is pretty clear. Organizations have gone through three generations of technology for their application systems during the last 10 years. The IS departments have not been able to keep up with this pace of change. Most of these IS organizations spend 40 to 60 percent of their time maintaining legacy systems, so there has not been enough time and resources for their staff to experiment and learn how to use the new technologies.

Before too much blame is placed on the IS organizations for failing to climb these new technology mountains, it should be recognized that the standard package vendors, with their millions and tens of millions of dollars in R&D budgets, struggled tremendously with these same technology transformations. Several ERP vendors, who were at one time leaders in the industry, have lost their market position because they were not able to adapt their packages to the new technologies.

In the early 1990s, most applications were still being developed for proprietary operating systems, using development tools that had been around for years. In the mainframe world, application packages were primarily developed to run on IBM mainframes often using COBOL (programming language), IMS (nonrelational database management system), and CICS (transaction processing tool). If an organization had a different type of mainframe, some of the vendors provided versions of their software that ran on other hardware. However, new releases of modules for these other environments were often not available until months after the IBM versions were released.

Vendors, developing packages for small and midsize organizations, designed them to run on HP 3000, DEC Vax, or IBM AS/400 minicomputers. The PC had been around for 10 years but was still being used to run personal productivity applications like word processors, spreadsheets, and graphics programs. At this time, military and university techies were the only ones using the Internet.

During this time, the systems were designed so that the three components of an application—user interface, processing logic, and data storage—ran on the same machine. Graphical user interfaces were not available yet, so the interfaces were character based. To a great extent, developing in this environment was easier since most of the components (e.g., operating system, languages, databases) came from the same vendor and generally worked well together.

Around 1992 or 1993, people started developing computer systems using a new paradigm: *client-server*. PCs had become cheap and powerful by this time and were widely available. Some models of PCs had become so powerful that they could be used as workstations (to run high-powered graphics and computer-aided design programs) and servers on networks. There was a lot of pressure to get a return on the investment in these devices.

Given the large amount of money being spent on personal computers, organizations started to question whether they were getting an appropriate return on these PC investments. There was increasing concern about putting on each worker's desk a computer that was more powerful than the mainframes of a few decades before and that was being used only a couple of hours a day to read e-mail and draft memos.

With this mindset, a client-server architecture seemed to make a lot of sense. Why not separate the design for an application into its three main parts—user interface, application logic, and database—and put components of this design on two or three separate machines? That way, the rationale went, the developers could take advantage of the power of the PCs (the client) on desktops to do the presentation (user interface) processing and the dedicated high-powered minicomputers and workstations (the servers) to do application logic and database processing.

With this approach, the applications could have easier-to-use graphical interfaces and look more Windows-like. The different variants of client-server placed the three components on the machines in different proportions. *Fat clients* did a lot more of the processing (perhaps presentation and some of the application logic) on the PC while *thin clients* basically did just presentation processing on the PC. The servers could do both application logic and database processing on one machine; or separate machines could be used for each function.

The logic and conceptual clarity of the client-server architecture made a lot of sense. Software developers had been talking about *cooperative processing* since the 1980s and it seemed like client-server was finally going to make this possible. Unfortunately, two things stood in the way of client-server nirvana: the difficulty of the technical migration and the Internet.

Although conceptually easy to understand, implementing client-server technologies turned out to be a difficult challenge. It was a lot more difficult, as some IS organizations found out, than just sending programmers to Visual Basic or PowerBuilder training and then having them develop new applications using these tools. Many IS departments that tried to develop new client-server applications failed to ever get anything that worked. Those systems that did work often did not scale well and could not handle production volumes.

Vendors that had developed packages for mainframe or minicomputer (e.g., AS/400) environments underestimated the challenge of retooling their staffs with the new technologies and approaches (object-oriented development was part of this new concept) and porting their applications to these new technologies. Some announced that new client-server versions would be available in six months to a year. Two or three years later they were still trying to get software out the door that actually worked.

To a certain extent, the success of SAP's R/3 product is the result of SAP being one of the first vendors to get a working client-server system to market. However, the investment that SAP had to make to do this was in the hundreds of millions of dollars. That investment was larger than the revenues of most of its competitors. Ironically, while making these investments, SAP, like all the other application software vendors, failed to understand the impact that the Internet would have on their businesses.

Client-server was an attractive technology architecture but it did not substantially enable different ways of performing business processes. In many cases, it required organizations to upgrade their PCs (even more powerful PCs were required on each desktop) to handle the client-side processing. Around the middle of the 1990s, the World Wide Web was created and people learned that if they had access to the Internet through an ISP and a browser (which was free), they could run almost any application that was on a web site. And they did not need a very powerful PC to run these applications.

So, during the late 1990s the software vendors started incorporating Internet technologies into their applications. They started by Internet-enabling the applications so they could be accessed over the Internet with a browser. Then they started rewriting their applications using Java and other Internet tools. The final step was to start developing new application modules that supported e-business initiatives (e.g., e-retail, exchanges, e-procurement) and some of the externally focused applications (e.g., CRM, SCM).

Some of the progress in these new areas was slowed down and masked by the large number of ERP sales and implementations done to replace applications to mitigate Y2K concerns. However, most of the vendors announced in 2000 new versions of their applications and new modules that were developed with and take advantage of Internet technologies. These new modules are not necessarily full-function modules, but at least they are directionally correct and provide a migration path for those organizations that have implemented other products from these vendors in the past.

While the ERP vendors were migrating from client-server to Internet technologies, there were a number of new application vendors (e.g., Siebel, Ariba, Commerce One, BroadVision) who started business in the 1990s and developed their initial applications using the new technologies and Internet capabilities. These organizations did not have to port products from older technologies and support customers in both environments. So, in general, they were able to move faster than their large ERP competitors. Although they have been very successful to this point, it will be interesting to watch how they perform as the traditional application software vendors try to move into their space.

For all these vendors the trend is clear. Internet technologies must be used to develop these applications and they must be designed to take advantage of the business process changes that are enabled by these new technologies (e.g., wireless access). As should be clear at this time, these new technologies and the processes they enable will dramatically change the world of business. The successful vendors and organizations will be those who can develop, support, and rapidly change these applications in response to business problems and opportunities.

Given the problems and large investments that the vendors had to make to learn how to use and support these new technologies, it is clear that supporting these technologies will create tremendous challenges for the organization's IS staff. However, organizations must find ways to support the technology aspects of these projects (e.g., through application hosting or IS staff retooling) if they are to take advantage of the new capabilities these technologies enable.

CONSULTANT CAPABILITY CHALLENGES

The bigger systems integrators and other consulting organizations generally have a good track record supporting traditional ERP implementations. Most of these organizations have a large number of people with prior experience implementing the major packages. Often they can staff implementation teams with people who have implemented a particular vendor's module three or four times and are specialists in the processes supported by the module. The consulting organizations also have tailored methodologies and tools to support these implementations. All of these factors reduce the risks associated with these projects.

At the same time, it must be acknowledged that involving consultants has not always resulted in successful projects. There were a lot of ERP failures in the 1990s. Many of these were the result of organizations trying to implement these complex packages themselves, without the assistance of vendor personnel and consultants familiar with the packages and their implementation. However, there were an equally large number of failures where good consultants were involved. The reasons for these failures, in spite of the fact that the organization included consultants in the team, have been covered elsewhere in this book.

Overall, most organizations would agree that having the right consultants involved in their ERP implementations improves the probability of having a successful project. Most would say, "The consultants were expensive, but well worth the money." That may not be the case with projects to implement the newer e-business applications.

The e-business applications being implemented today provide a number of challenges:

- They use Internet technologies that are unfamiliar to most implementation teams.
- They address external and customer-facing processes that are different from the back-office processes that most consultants have focused on in the past.

- They use products that may be more like toolkits than packaged applications.
- There are a larger number of competencies required to successfully implement these packages.
- Most of these implementations must be done in a rapid manner.
- There are not many experienced implementers available to staff these projects.

Most of the consulting organizations now say that they have capabilities to address all these issues. They are all full-service *e-consultancies.* These claims are being made by both the new e-business consulting startups established during the last five years, as well as all the traditional consulting organizations. It is important for organizations to understand these issues and be careful in evaluating the capabilities of the consultants to deliver on their promises. A good starting point is to look at the first issue associated with the challenges associated with Internet technologies.

As mentioned earlier, the newer applications are being built using Internet technologies and tools. In implementations of these packages, the technology component of the implementations will be more important and challenging. With ERP the technology components of the project were easier. The software vendors handled the difficult part: making all the technology components work together. To a certain extent, a lot of the technical complexities were hidden from the implementation team. With e-business applications the technology issues are right out in front.

With ERP you could send a business process specialist to training to learn how to configure the package. With e-business applications the person you send to the training might have to know how to code in C++ or Java. This difference represents the change in technical maturity of the new packages. Someday, the technical complexities of the e-business applications will also become background issues. But we are not there now.

There is a shortage of people who understand and have experience with these technologies. Most of them are younger—people who grew up on the Internet. Using these technologies requires a different way of thinking about how technologies can and should be employed. It is not a matter of just sending existing IS personnel to several weeks of training on the new tools. There may be a large number of existing IT specialists who will *never* get it—who are not retrainable in the new technologies.

Because of this shortage, the people who *do* get it are in high demand. There is a lot of turnover as these specialists get lured from their current employers to positions with significant salary increases. Special compensation and development approaches need to be employed to keep these employees happy.

In addition, many of these people would rather work for Internet startups and pure-play e-business consultancies than for the Big 5 and other traditional consulting organizations. They want access to equity. They do not want to work in stuffy environments. (The fact remains that, in spite of increasingly common casual-day policies, most large consultancies are formal and stuffy.)

Therefore, the traditional consultancies are faced with the problem of recruiting technical employees who do not fit the normal career profile, are asking for compensation options that do not exist, cost a great deal, and may not like the formal policies and practices that make up the traditions of these organizations.

Some consulting organizations are trying to come up with ways to meet these requirements within the bounds of the organization. Some of these bounds are being stretched as a result (e.g., many consultancies are working on ways to give their employees equity positions). In other situations, the consulting organizations are looking for ways to outsource these technical activities on projects or partner with organizations who can attract and retain people with these strong technical skills.

The second issue is that the people in the consulting organizations with implementation experience normally do not have experience in the processes covered by the new applications. They have a lot of experience with financial, distribution, manufacturing, and human resource processes. However, they have little experience with things like sales force automation, call centers, field service, e-retailing, exchanges, and advanced planning and scheduling. They will get this experience by working on projects in these areas for their clients, but they will be learning on the customer's dollar.

This situation should not necessarily create any sense of alarm. This is the way that consulting organizations have always gained experience and moved into new areas. The point is that organizations implementing these new systems should not expect to have these projects staffed with people with a great deal of experience in the new areas. If the consultants have people with these skills, it usually means that they have been hired in the last year or so.

Given that there are not a large number of people with the specific experience needed for these projects, there are still advantages of using consultants on these projects. They usually are bright, high-energy, motivated people who are quick learners. And they do bring generic process design and implementation experience to these projects. So, in the short term, they may be the best option.

The third issue is subtle but important. The term *packaged application* has been used throughout this book for both ERP and e-business applications. The general implication is that the vendor has created software that can be tailored to meet the needs of the organization by changing fields in parameter tables. This is not always the case with the newer e-business applications. For these modules "some installation may be required."

Some of these applications work more like toolkits rather than prepackaged products, and lie somewhere in the finished spectrum between a standard package and custom development. They are closer to the standard-package end of the spectrum but implementing them requires more hands-on technical support than is usual for packaged implementations.

Some of the causes of this situation are the relative immaturity of these products. It takes a lot of time and effort to design something that can be modified by selecting parameters than by putting together a number of components. Another explanation is that these are not complete packages; they require a number of components from several vendors, interfaced and working together to offer the complete solution. Putting all these components together requires more technical tasks. Either way, the organization should expect to have to do more technical tasks on these implementations.

The consulting organizations are trying to address the need for greater technical knowledge on implementation teams. As stated earlier, they are trying to recruit and hire people with Internet technology and programming experience. In evaluating different consultants, the organization needs to be aware of the requirement for more technical components in the implementation and evaluate how well the consultants have addressed these issues with their proposed project staffing.

There have always been a number of core competencies required in any implementation project. With traditional implementations the primary competencies have been project management, process design, technology support, and package configuration. Most consulting organizations have always provided these competencies. With the newer systems, however, the implementations require a number of other competencies. And there are few consulting organizations that truly have competencies in all the areas that are required.

E-business has upped the ante. Several new competencies are required to support these e-business projects, besides the technical ones that have already been covered. A key one is e-business strategy knowledge and experience. It is difficult, if not impossible, to separate strategy and business model issues from some of the new implementations. The new e-business systems are being implemented to enable new business models or at least provide an opportunity to reevaluate these models.

In many of the e-business projects it is important to have people on the team with graphical design capabilities. This is another result of the toolkit nature of some of these products. It is also increasingly necessary to have people on the project (usually on a part-time basis) with tax, computer security, compensation and benefits, industry, and organizational design expertise. Many of the new e-consultancies (e.g., Viant, Scient, Razorfish) have excellent graphical design and technical skills. However, they are short in many of the other areas. The Big 5 and other large consultancies have the others areas covered but are missing some of the technical competencies. The buyer of consulting services should understand all the skills needed and evaluate how the various consultancies are meeting all these needs.

Another issue associated with these newer applications, and the reason for this book, is that the newer applications need to be implemented in a rapid manner. As hopefully has been made clear, this often requires a different mindset, approach, and set of tools. Many of the consulting organizations know just one way to implement business solutions. And this way normally creates a lot of formal reports, tries to lock down scope and design before implementation, and takes a long time. These characteristics do not meet the needs of current business situations.

Therefore, the consulting organizations need to develop methods and tools to more rapidly implement the new applications. Some have started to develop these; others have not. The organization should check the flexibility of the consultant to adapt its approaches to the needs of a rapidly changing business environment.

The final issue is the fact that most of the consulting organizations do not have a lot of experience implementing newer CRM, e-procurement, exchange, self-service, and personalization applications. They are rapidly retooling their ERP practitioners to implement these applications, but the fact remains that they will not be able to staff these projects with people as experienced as those they have in ERP. This should not be a surprise, given the newness of these applications. However, this should be of concern to their customers. The consultant's and the organization's implementation team members may be learning the new package together in the initial projects.

The point of this section is not to put down consultants. The use of consultants on these projects is, and always will be, one of the key success factors for complex, rapid implementations. They bring a lot of knowledge, experience, and resources to the table that the organization would not be able to provide on its own. The organization should be aware that implementing e-business applications is new to everyone. So, do not expect the same level of support on these projects as maybe was the case in the past. And fill in the gaps in expertise as part of the normal project planning and risk management activities of the project.

INCREASED IMPORTANCE OF COMPUTER SECURITY

In the past, computer security consultants have had a relatively difficult time selling their services. Systems were usually contained within the walls of the organization, with perhaps a few dialup connections to provide access from the outside. In these situations, computer security was often sold with two approaches. First, having adequate security would get your financial auditors off your back. Second, computer security was often seen in the nature of an insurance policy: the probability of ever experiencing the risk for which it was designed was low, but you sure were happy that you had it in case it was ever needed. All that has changed with the Internet and e-business. Now, adequate computer security has become an important requirement for these new systems.

Connections with the outside world are what make e-business and the Internet attractive. An organization wants to make it easy for its customers, suppliers, and employees to have access to its systems information at any time, from any place. If they are doing commerce on the web, they also want to handle financial transactions—including credit card transactions—in an easy, convenient manner. The Internet allows all these things to happen; however, it also opens up entirely new risk areas for the organization.

The reason for this enhanced concern is that everyone in the world with Internet access suddenly has access to your web site, and through that site to the organization's information. Most of this access is fine; this was especially the case when all a web site contained was general information about the organization—brochureware. This is a much bigger deal when, through an organization's web site, customers can check on order status, suppliers can look at production schedules and forecasts, and employees can look at electronic copies of their pay stubs. Now, companies have information that they must protect from outside access.

In addition, there is an increased area of risk of viruses spreading throughout an organization's systems given the widespread use of e-mail systems, with the e-mails going over the Internet. These viruses traditionally cause files to be corrupted or erased. Recently, a new variant of attack uses valid access rights and creates such volumes of false transactions that the real customers and transactions cannot get through. These denial-of-access viruses have caused organizations to implement new techniques to control these risks.

There are a number of tools and techniques that can be used to reduce these risks. They include firewalls, passwords, encryption, tokens, and virtual private networks. Each of these techniques has its place; however, there are costs associated with overprotection as well as underprotection.

Firewalls are security software that stands between the organization's resources and the Internet. This software can control access by requiring user IDs and passwords before someone can get from the Internet to the organization's systems and information. The firewalls also have other functions to limit access to the resources.

Passwords have been the traditional approach for protecting access to ERP, e-mail, and most other systems. However, passwords have never been a particularly good security mechanism. Many people choose easy-to-guess passwords. In addition, there are computer programs that can *automate* the guessing of passwords. Many people do not change their passwords very often and use the same passwords for multiple systems. (No one blames them because if we are not supposed to write our passwords down, how can we be expected to remember four or five passwords to get into different systems?) What most people do not realize is that often the passwords we enter go over the Internet where they can be intercepted and stored for future use. One way around this problem is encryption.

Encryption takes the messages sent over the Internet (and things like our credit card numbers and passwords) and scrambles them so that only the receiver, with appropriate de-encryption tools, can convert the messages back into something readable. There are several encryption tools and techniques. In general, the best encryption techniques are procedurally and systemwise more complicated and expensive.

These encryption tools have become even more important as laws are changed to recognize electronic signatures for documents and therefore open up the path to electronic processes that in the past had to be performed face-to-face with manual signatures.

Tokens are small devices, perhaps the size of a credit card, that generate unique passwords on a continuous basis. Rather than my having to create my own password and worry about changing it frequently, the token generates a unique, one-time password that can be scanned or keyed into the system. The receiving end processor also generates this same password. Therefore, the password that someone intercepts becomes invalid for future transactions, even minutes later. Tokens are expensive since they require each user to be issued a physical device.

For organizations that cannot live with the risks from an open communications network like the Internet, there are other, more expensive options. One is a virtual private network. This network can be used to connect an organization with its trading partners on proprietary lines not open to nonauthorized personnel or organizations. These are more expensive than using the Internet but may have other advantages. For example, there is more reliability on communication networks where access has been restricted and where the proper capacities can be adjusted to support increasing volumes of transactions.

All of these options are available, along with a lot more. But the question is: Which one is appropriate to the particular situation that an organization is facing? The answer depends on the objectives of the system, the risks that are present, the probability of the risk actually occurring, and the ability to leverage other security mechanisms already in place. The risks are business risks in the sense of loss of sales if the system goes down or loss of assets through fraudulent access and transactions. But there is an equally important risk: that a customer's information will inadvertently or fraudulently be made public. These risks need to be taken into consideration in deciding the appropriate level of security in a particular situation.

To do risk assessment, security architecture design, and security mechanism implementation requires the knowledge and experience of experts in this area. This is not something that the normal business or IT type is capable of doing. Therefore, on rapid implementations there needs to be appropriate involvement from information security specialists. These people may get involved with setting up application security (who gets access to what information and transactions within the organization and its partners). But increasingly, the expertise that is needed is in the area of Internet and e-business security. These are not areas for organizations to try on their own. These specialists can also be used in tiger teams to evaluate the current security by trying to break into the organization's systems under controlled circumstances.

10

CONCLUSIONS AND FINAL THOUGHTS

It is safe to assume that anyone who gets this far is still open to the idea that organizations should change the way they approach e-business and ERP projects. Most people can also see the business benefits of a rapid implementation approach. For those still sitting on the fence, it is time to make one final push to get you to the rapid implementation side.

REASONS FOR A RAPID APPROACH

We have covered many reasons why organizations should consider a rapid implementation approach to these types of projects. The primary reasons for changing from the traditional approach to these projects are:

- Other approaches have not been successful.
- An e-business economy requires quicker solutions to problems.
- The 80/20 rule supports smaller, focused projects.
- Rapid implementations deliver business benefits more quickly.

Large project teams, long-duration projects, and broad project scope characterize the traditional approach to standard software implementation. If projects using this approach were generally successful, then there would be no need to develop other implementation strategies. However, this is not the case. Most application implementation projects have been unsuccessful. In general, these projects go over budget, are not completed on time, do not produce the desired results, and are bad experiences for those involved.

A fundamental problem is that it is difficult, and sometimes impossible, to successfully manage these large projects. There are just too many people doing too many things at the same time. It is difficult to coordinate the activities of all these groups and effectively communicate the actions, issues, and decisions that are being made in a large number of pockets throughout the project.

A whole layer of management must be placed on top of several project subteams to try to plan, coordinate, and control these initiatives. Teams, not individuals, do all the activities. Therefore, individual accountability is difficult to establish. Decision making, on even small matters, becomes a formal process. Decisions are made by committee, which has never been a timely or effective way to evaluate alternatives and quickly decide on a good solution.

Everything must be put into formal documents that can be reviewed by a large number of participants. Because of the inherent bureaucracy of these projects, they take a long time to complete and the goals and objectives are often lost somewhere in the overall process. There have been a few successful large projects (e.g., putting a man on the moon) but most of the projects that were deemed successful also had large cost overruns and took extremely long periods of time to complete.

Most people know that large implementation projects have generally been failures in the past—either from personal experience or from hearing or reading the stories of people who have gone through these projects. However, for some strange reason, business leaders and project managers continue to act as if taking the same approach on future implementation projects will somehow change the outcome. If organizations want different results, they must change their approach.

Rapid implementations are a better approach to these projects because they address many of the reasons that other projects have been unsuccessful. It is easier to manage a number of smaller projects (with smaller teams and limited scope) than it is to manage one large, complex project. Therefore, rapid implementations help the organization better manage the risks that have caused these large projects to fail in the past.

Managing these risks is increasingly important in an e-business economy. In the current business environment things are changing at a faster and faster rate. Business models, organizational structures, relationships, processes, and systems change at a rate that most people find incredible. Organizations need to be able to respond to these changes in a rapid manner—to solve business problems and take advantage of opportunities. In this new e-business economy, organizations must get an acceptable solution implemented quickly, in a matter of weeks and months, not months and years.

This rapidly changing business environment is not compatible with long-term projects. Given the current rate of change, if an organization takes a long time to develop a solution, you can almost guarantee that the original problem will have changed by the time the solution is implemented. Getting a good solution implemented quickly is better than getting the perfect solution implemented late. Fortunately, the 80/20 rule applies in these situations.

In the context of an implementation project, the 80/20 rule says that an organization will generally get 80 percent of the benefits from only 20 percent of a package's functions. Therefore, why not just put in the 20 percent in a rapid project and leave other functions and processes to later projects? The 20 percent that gets put in first should be those functions that support redesigned business processes that produce the benefits and achieve the objectives established for the project.

This has not been the traditional approach to implementation. Traditionally, the projects have started with an effort to figure out how long it will take to implement all the functions of a particular module. Often, the parts of the new system that provide little or no incremental value to the organization receive the same attention and use the same amount of resources as those that provide real business benefits. Most organizations do not take the time to really understand what they are trying to accomplish with the new system and what parts of the system need to be implemented to achieve those results.

A rapid implementation is driven by the business case that defines the benefits to be achieved. It first implements those parts of the new system that are needed to achieve the benefits. Other parts can be deferred until later projects. In many cases, the requirements will change and the deferred parts may *never* be required.

Given the importance of the business changes that should result from these projects there should be a sense of urgency surrounding them. Things need to be accomplished in the fastest time possible and the implementation teams must be kept under constant pressure to produce the best results in the time available for the solution. However, they should have a deadline and not take any more time. They should also not be worried about gold-plating the solution. Workable solutions need to be implemented quickly.

This is where time boxing comes in. The entire project should be time boxed to ensure that something of value will be delivered during the weeks or months dedicated to these projects. The project stages and activities should be time boxed so people feel a sense of urgency to finish major aspects of the project by frequent milestones. Individual tasks should be time boxed to create a daily sense of urgency and to quickly identify items on the critical path that are falling behind schedule.

Given its limited scope and shorter timeframes, a rapid implementation approach delivers benefits sooner than can occur with a traditional implementation approach. With full-scope projects the organization has to wait till the end of the project, when there is a big go-live, before receiving any benefits. If the full project produces benefits A, B, C, and D, the organization may have to wait for a year to get any of these benefits; they all come with the big go-live in the future.

With a rapid implementation approach the one-year project can be broken into four miniprojects. The first project can deliver the A benefits after three months. The second project delivers the B benefits after six months and the third project the C benefits after nine months. And the final project delivers the last benefits at the end of the year. By the time the traditional project would go live, the rapid-implementing organization would have already been receiving many of the benefits for six to nine months.

Besides phasing in benefits earlier, it is much easier to manage smaller projects than larger ones. The project team that produces the A benefits will be much smaller than a team that has to produce all the benefits. The smaller team will have less communication and integration challenges and will be easier to manage.

OTHER ADVANTAGES

There are a number of other advantages resulting from a rapid implementation approach. These include easier change management, increased staffing with top performers, and higher visibility with management.

Most people understand that the users are very important to the success of any of these implementation efforts. If the users cannot understand and support the new system and its associated processes, it is not very likely that the desired changes will stick. If the changes do not stick, the organization will not receive the desired benefits.

It is easier to absorb change in smaller chunks. The project that produces benefits A, B, C, and D will have changes in a number of areas occurring simultaneously. The smaller projects will allow the organization to get used to some of the changes before the next wave of change takes place.

Some people say that it is better to make all the changes at one time and get it over with once and for all. But that approach tends to overwhelm the organization and its employees and is a much higher-risk approach. People must realize that the level of business stability experienced during the last 20 or 30 years is gone forever. Things will have to continuously change in the future. In spite of this, organizations still need to be sensitive to the fact that they should do what they can to ensure that changes occur at a rate that managers and employees can absorb.

Another benefit from the rapid approach is that it is easier to get people assigned to shorter projects than longer ones. A department may be willing to give up a star performer for a two- or three-month project but not for a one- or two-year project.

On longer projects these people are often permanently gone from their departments. Replacements are found for the positions the team members used to have. Therefore, at the end of the project, project team members are often assigned to new positions. These positions may not even be in the departments the people came from. On shorter projects, the departments may be able to come up with temporary measures to make up for the loss of the person without hiring a permanent replacement.

Department managers often are more receptive to this idea of giving up key employees to the team if the system being implemented will have a major impact on their departments and people. Having people who are good representatives of their areas on these projects is important. So giving up these employees is more palatable if it is just for a short period of time and allows a department to have someone represent its interests on the team.

Finally, it is easier to keep the attention and support of top management on shorter projects. If managers go a long time before seeing benefits from their investments, they tend to lose interest in the projects. This is natural, given the large number of things on the typical manager's plate. On shorter projects that create quick benefits for the organization or solve an immediate problem, it is easier to generate some enthusiasm and involvement from top managers.

TRADE-OFFS

Obviously, there are trade-offs associated with taking a rapid implementation approach. Many of these trade-offs are a byproduct of having a large number of smaller projects. Others result from some of the basic assumptions dictated by this approach.

Although managing a small project is easier than managing a very large project, there are significant management challenges associated with coordinating the work on a number of separate small projects. In many cases, each of the projects is focused on achieving a subset of the benefits of a larger business case, and someone needs to manage the achievement of the total set of benefits across a series of projects. In addition, methods need to be established to achieve continuity and knowledge transfer across the projects implementing various components of the same vendor's products. Lessons learned and information important to rapid implementation of a vendor's product should be captured and shared among the teams.

There are several approaches to minimizing these coordination and continuity problems. One of the approaches is to create a *program manager* position to coordinate the planning and execution of a number of related projects. The program manager can sit on the steering committee of all the projects to ensure that the work is coordinated. This involvement allows the program manager to minimize the amount of redundant work among projects and identify gaps not addressed in the various project plans. The program manager can also periodically meet with the managers of the various projects to understand the status and issues for each project and provide information to integrate the activities of the various projects.

Another approach for handling these coordination issues is to use the same project manager—and perhaps some of the same core team members—on a related series of projects. Use of resources in this manner will help coordinate activities on subsequent projects since there will be people on later project teams who understand why certain decisions were made in prior projects. This approach also allows the organization to substitute its own people for some of the resources that were provided by the vendor or consulting organizations on earlier projects.

A second trade-off with a strategy that uses several smaller projects to achieve the organization's goals is that it requires the teams to create of a number of temporary interfaces between systems. Each time a new vendor's module is implemented there is usually a requirement to create an interface with other legacy or standard software modules. If all the modules of a vendor's suite are implemented at one time, many of the intermodule interfaces will already be available from the vendor. In that situation the main interfaces that will be needed are between the packaged software and legacy systems.

For example, if the project team is implementing the financial, distribution, and human resource modules from one vendor in a single project, the interfaces between these modules are already designed into the vendor's technical architecture. However, if the first project implements only the financial module, the team will have to create custom interfaces to the existing legacy distribution and HR modules. These interfaces take time to develop and test. They will also be thrown away as the organization implements the other package modules in future projects.

So, there is some inefficiency associated with getting parts of a system up quickly rather than doing all the parts at one time. Temporary interfaces will have to be developed. Even if manual interfaces are used in the short term as an alternative to custom-developing throwaway interfaces, there will be additional work for the users to maintain these interfaces. Obviously, this overhead must be considered against the advantages of getting benefits sooner and having a higher possibility of success with the shorter, limited-scope projects.

A number of assumptions were inherent in using a rapid implementation approach. These can limit some of the activities and results that can come from these projects. Therefore, they should be balanced against the advantages of this approach before deciding whether a rapid approach is best for a specific situation.

One of the principles of rapid implementation is that the project team will not modify the vendor's source code. In effect, the organization is outsourcing to the package vendor the ongoing development and maintenance of business applications. Modifying the vendor's source code will often invalidate the vendor's support agreement and pass responsibility for maintenance of the applications back to the organization. Developing custom modifications also takes a lot of time. The activities needed to define requirements and design, code, and test the changes may significantly extend the timetable for the project.

In many situations an organization will be able to live with the functions provided by the vendor. After all, configuration options provide a lot of flexibility in how the software will work to meet the organization's needs. However, there are some situations where this constraint must be lifted.

There are some industries that have unique requirements that are not met at this time by the major application packages. There are also situations where modifying the vendor's code allows the organization to execute innovative practices that provide true competitive advantages. Other situations exist in which the vendor's code and data structures must be changed in order to provide interfaces that take advantage of unique, value-adding capabilities in custom-developed legacy systems and best-of-breed applications from other vendors.

Not all code development has to modify the vendor's source code and therefore invalidate the vendor's support agreements. A corollary condition for rapid implementation is that there will not be a great deal of custom development even outside the boundaries of the vendor's code. It is possible to invest in custom development for bolt-on functionality. This code uses the vendor's standard application program interfaces (APIs), and therefore does not change the vendor's source code. But again, this approach mitigates many of the benefits of a rapid implementation approach.

Modifying vendor code or creating bolt-on functionality takes a lot of time and effort and introduces additional risks associated with any custom-development activity. Therefore, it should be discouraged when using a rapid implementation strategy. However, if this is the only way to provide functionality not supported by the package, whether because of unique industry requirements or to implement newly redesigned processes as a result of reengineering efforts, then it may have to be considered. The best way to handle this situation may be to initiate a separate project, with its own team, to develop this new functionality. Obviously, there needs to be close coordination between this team and the team rapidly implementing the vendor's product.

PRECONDITIONS

It should be obvious by this point that not all organizations, or projects, will be good candidates for a rapid implementation approach. The following is a checklist of the 10 enablers required to make these projects successful:

1. A strong business imperative to solve a problem or take advantage of a unique opportunity in a short period of time.

2. A business case that clearly defines the benefits to be achieved from the project and is used to guide project plans and decisions.

3. The desire to try a different approach to implementing business applications in order to overcome some of the things that have made these projects unsuccessful in the past. This approach leaves the detailed scope of the project flexible and time boxes the rapid implementation project. It also supports a general philosophy that the organization will change its processes to those supported by the software package and that there will be no modifications to the vendor source code.

4. The willingness of top management to support the project team (e.g., remove organizational barriers) and stay close to these initiatives so that the organization can develop a core competency in doing these projects faster and accelerating the benefits stream.

5. The selection of a standard package that generally fits the needs of the organization and has been designed to have flexibility so that it can be changed frequently to meet continuous changes in business requirements.

6. The selection of a software vendor and systems integrator who have a rapid implementation methodology and tools (e.g., preconfigured versions, configuration aids, procedure and training templates, sample project deliverables) available to accelerate the implementation of the selected package. The organizations should also have specialists that can be brought in to quickly handle the most complex and difficult parts of these projects.

7. An outstanding project manager from the functional side of the organization and an excellent management coach from the vendor or systems integrator.

8. Technical support capabilities to get a development environment available before kickoff, complete the technical support project activities in a timely and professional manner, and support the ongoing production environment and other technical support requirements.

9. An experienced cross-functional core team from the organization that works full time on the project and are empowered to make significant decisions as representatives of their functional and technical groups. The team should be staffed with people who have gone through these projects before and are specialists in particular business processes or package modules.

10. Heavy involvement from end users throughout the project, especially in the iterative development and testing activities.

There are no hard and fast rules on how many of these conditions should be met before an organization is ready to use a rapid implementation approach. However, if two or three of these conditions are missing, using this approach will be a much riskier proposition. Even in these cases, the organization will be better off in the long run if it starts some of these projects as pilots and works through overcoming these limitations. Doing so will position the organization to better meet the continuously changing challenges that all organizations will face in the future.

FINAL THOUGHTS

Most organizations have not had a lot of experience doing rapid implementation projects. There is a lot of interest in this area in organizations trying to figure out better ways for increasing returns on their technology investments and more rapidly responding to business problems and opportunities. In addition, software vendors and consulting organizations are making significant strides in developing tools and software capabilities to make this approach to implementation less difficult. The project accelerators and support capabilities that are being developed should make these projects easier to perform. This is an area that should see increased activity in most organizations over the next two or three years.

However, there are many success factors for these projects that have to come from within the organization implementing systems using this approach. Many of these changes have to do with organizational culture and people issues.

Top management has not historically had adequate involvement in these projects, perhaps because they have not had strategic implications in the past. Staffing these projects with the best candidates in the organization and empowering these people to make significant decisions is not something that has been common practice. The business cases for these projects have been deficient and not effectively used during the projects. There has not been enough involvement and participation by the key users who can help make the final designs better and more palatable to the organization. These cultural and organizational issues will have to be overcome for these projects to be successful.

The key premise of this book is that things have to change. The traditional approach to implementing standard business applications with big teams and long projects has not been successful and will not meet the needs of a rapidly changing business environment. This approach also does not fit well with how the new e-business applications should be implemented using iterative development and hosted processing. Organizations need to learn how to do a lot of smaller, targeted projects in order to keep up with the demands of the e-economy.

This book has not provided all the answers for how an organization can take advantage of this new, better approach for implementing application systems in response to continuously changing business requirements. The special challenges and capabilities for doing these projects will continue to evolve. The specifics will also vary with the particular package that is being implemented or the process being improved. However, the overall philosophy, principles, approach, and prerequisites for successfully completing rapid implementation projects will endure.

If your understanding of the issues involved with a rapid implementation approach and the keys to its success is a little clearer at this point—and piloting such an approach seems like something that most organizations should be at least considering—then this book has accomplished its purpose. Together, we can figure out how to do these projects better in the future—for the benefit of all our organizations. The journey should be challenging and rewarding—what more could we ask?

INDEX